£17.99

management
series

cms

a Quality
Service

Linda Nazarko

www.heinemann.co.uk

✓ Free online support
✓ Useful weblinks
✓ 24 hour online ordering

01865 888058

Heinemann
Inspiring generations

Heinemann Educational Publishers
Halley Court, Jordan Hill, Oxford OX2 8EJ
Part of Harcourt Education

Heinemann is the registered trademark of
Harcourt Education Limited

First published 2004

09 08 07 06 05 04
10 9 8 7 6 5 4 3 2 1

British Library Cataloguing in Publication Data is available
from the British Library on request.

ISBN 0 435 40127 0

Designed by Lorraine Inglis
Typeset by TechType, Abingdon, Oxon

Original illustrations © Harcourt Education Limited, 2004

Cover design by Wooden Ark Studio

Printed in the UK by Bath Press Ltd

Cover photo: © Alamy
All other photographs by Gareth Boden

Acknowledgements
Every effort has been made to contact copyright holders of material reproduced in this book.
Any omissions will be rectified in subsequent printings if notice is given to the publishers.

Websites
Please note that the examples of websites suggested in this book were up to date at the time
of writing. It is essential for tutors to preview each site before using it to ensure that the URL
is still accurate and the content is appropriate. We suggest that tutors bookmark useful sites
and consider enabling students to access them through the school or college intranet.

Contents

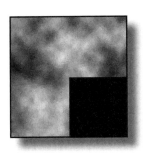

Foreword

There are lots of books for nurses about management, but this is the first book about management which focuses specifically on managing services for older people. Moreover, it is equally relevant to managers of these services both in the NHS and in the independent sector. As such it is especially welcome, because services for older people have historically been the "Cinderella" of healthcare, and have not enjoyed the kind of investment in management or management training that other parts of the health services have enjoyed. Although the National Service Framework (NSF) for Older People has "rooting out age discrimination" as the first of its eight standards which all healthcare organisations are now required to meet, ageism is as rife in management as it has been shown to be in clinical care. This book is as big a step forward in changing such attitudes as it will be in helping nurses and other managers bring about the necessary changes.

It is no accident that the title of the book includes the word *Quality*. Everyone, from government policy makers to the individual care assistant who is trying to care for older people, often with inadequate resources in an inappropriate environment, recognises that quality must be the provider's aim because it is the user's entitlement. That does not make it easy to achieve.

This book will help because it is intensely practical. Linda Nazarko brings not only a lifetime of commitment, experience, and expertise in the care of older people – it was for this that she was elected Fellow of the Royal College of Nursing, and it shines through every page. Every chapter is filled with sound practical advice, always underpinned by the relevant theory and the best available evidence, enriched by case studies, useful tools, and a wealth of references for further reading. This book also demonstrates a rare creativity and imagination – which makes it fun to read!

I hope that you will enjoy reading it as much as I have!

Professor Dame June Clark PhD, RN, RHV, FRCN
Professor Emeritus, University of Wales Swansea
August 2004

Introduction: How could I possibly make a difference?

When you first register as a nurse you may feel unprepared but you've had the benefit of three years' preparation. As you become more experienced things click. You learn to apply theory to practice and to combine the art and science of nursing.

If you are good at your job and wish to progress you apply for promotion. A more senior role gives you the opportunity to change things and to improve quality of care. In order to gain promotion you may have to do a short presentation on how to introduce policy changes in your workplace. Employers usually offer staff ongoing education and development but this frequently concentrates on clinical skills. You may find it difficult to work out how national policies have the potential to improve care for the older person you care for.

If you are promoted you may find that there is little preparation for your new role. The challenges you face are how to work what can be improved and how to change things for the better. Older people are particularly vulnerable to the effects of poor-quality care. Older people who do not benefit from high-quality care are at risk of loosing ability and of becoming depressed and despairing. Sadly the lessons from research and reports of investigations into poor-quality care tell us that all older people do not yet benefit from high-quality care.

The difference between high-quality care that makes us proud and the type of care that makes us want to hang our heads in shame can be summed up in one word – leadership. Leaders work out what needs to be done to improve things and work with staff to improve care while retaining all that is good about the past.

One of the great myths about leadership is that great leaders are born not made. The truth is that anyone can be a great leader if they understand how to listen to the people they care for and support and develop staff to give of their best.

The care of older people has for decades been dogged by negative images of death, disability and poor-quality care. If we are to do things better and to provide older people with the kind of care and support that we would wish for ourselves then we must jettison the old ways. We need to do things differently. The time is right to do things differently. We have for the first time in clinical governance a coherent framework that supports us in our efforts to move forward.

Managing a Quality Service aims to explain how you can use the quality framework to do things differently and to make a real difference. It aims to enable you to understand and implement national policy at local level. It explains how to work out what you are currently doing well and what you need to improve. The real world is a muddled and messy place full of shades of grey and people often resist change because of fear. *Managing a Quality Service* explains the theory of change management and uses real-life examples to show what to do and what not to do.

These are exciting times to be alive and to care for older people. We stand on the brink of a revolution. Our knowledge of the diseases that older people suffer from and how to provide effective treatment is increasing.. We are beginning to understand why some people develop chronic diseases. We know that lifestyle changes can prevent or delay the onset of diseases such as diabetes. Our knowledge of healthcare interventions is growing and will enable us to manage chronic diseases more effectively and to prevent or delay the onset of complications that mar quality of life. We are increasingly aware of the importance of working in partnership with older people to enable them to have the best possible experience of healthcare and to live life to the full. This book aims to help you find out what really matters to older people and to work with them as partners

Older people move through a continuum of care. The older person may require care from district nurses at home, care in community hospitals, acute hospitals, care homes or intermediate care units. The care that the older person receives at each stage of the care journey impacts on other stages and on that person's recovery. This book aims to enable nurses leading and managing care in care settings to communicate effectively as the person moves from service to service.

Leading teams and enabling staff to provide excellent care requires knowledge, thought and effort. I have done my best to provide you with some of the information that will help you on your journey. The rest is up to you.

I would appreciate your comments and suggestions on this book.

Linda Nazarko
August 2004

Doing things differently

Introduction

This chapter aims to enable you to understand what ageism is, how it affects day-to-day practice and how it affects the older person's ability to access high-quality care. It explores quality issues in the care of older people and how these themes have persisted for almost sixty years. It then goes on to explain the government's quality strategy and how quality of care is inspected and regulated in the NHS and in the independent sector. The National Service Framework for Older People is explained and the implications for practice are outlined. The chapter explains how you can use clinical governance as a tool to enable you to involve patients in the planning and delivery of care so that you can provide high-quality care consistently in your work.

Those of you who care for older people will be well aware that there is a hierarchy within nursing and other care professions. In this hierarchy staff who provide care to other client groups are regarded as more skilled than those who care for older people. Older people are considered only to require 'basic' care, and the implication is that all nurses have the skills required to meet the needs of older people. This is a mistaken view and research spanning decades demonstrates that older people have complex needs. Older people are the major consumers of healthcare and are most vulnerable to poor-quality care. If you are to deliver a quality service you need to have the skills and knowledge to offer services that are effective and meet the needs and aspirations of older people. Government policy now recognises the importance of ending age-related discrimination and encourages staff working with older people to develop the specialist skills and knowledge required to care for them.

Aims

1.1　Ageism

1.2　Quality issues in the care of older people

1.3　The importance of doing things differently

1.4　The government's quality strategy

1.5　The Commission for Health Improvement

1.6　The Commission for Healthcare Audit and Inspection

1.7　The National Institute of Clinical Excellence

1.8　Care homes

1.9　The Commission for Social Care Inspection

1.10　A regulatory muddle

1.11　National Service Frameworks

1.12　The National Service Framework for Older People

1.13　NSF Standards

1.14　The challenges of clinical governance

1.15　Conclusion

1.1 Ageism

Robert Butler (1969) invented the term *ageism* to describe stereotyping and discrimination based on age. He commented: 'Ageist attitudes may do tangible disservice to older people. Nowhere is this more apparent than in healthcare.'

Ageism is not simply the negative attitudes of some individual towards older people. Ageism is reflective of a society where prejudice and discrimination based solely on age pervade the social climate. In our society it is still acceptable to discriminate against people on grounds of age. People may find it difficult to obtain certain jobs because of their age. People are forced to retire at a certain age; government posts are only open to people below a certain age. There are plans to introduce legislation to outlaw such discrimination in 2005 but it will take much longer to change attitudes.

People who work in healthcare may be particularly vulnerable to developing ageist attitudes because the people cared for are infirm and ill. It's very easy for clinicians to develop a skewed view of reality. Years ago I worked on a neurosurgical ward and considered that brain tumours were fairly common. When I went to work on a surgical ward I thought that it was strange that the patients did not have bandages around their heads. Those of you who care for frail older people or people with dementia can easily begin to think that all older people are frail and infirm and unable to manage independently. You may forget that most older people live independently and are as capable of making decisions about their lives as you and I. You may also forget that people who are ill are less able than those who are well, and that it is illness not ageing that is causing the problems you see.

There are terrible dangers in stereotyping people. If you consider that all older people are the same then you may begin to treat all older people in the same way. You may fail to listen to the older person or to give the person's concerns the same consideration as those of a younger person, simply because of irrational prejudices that we have all developed.

All of us are at risk of developing stereotypical views about older people and of going down the path of seeing older people as a group and not as individuals with distinctive needs and desires. Education can enable people to avoid developing stereotypical views and unfavourable attitudes towards older people. All prejudice is born out of ignorance, and ongoing education can enable people to retain a perspective and to realise that all older people are not the same. Older people differ as much as the general population.

CASE STUDY — Stereotyping

Veronica Gibbs is a ward manager on a general medical ward that cares for older people. Mrs Violet James was admitted following a stroke. Her recovery was slow. Veronica suggested referring Mrs James to intermediate care for further rehabilitation. Annie Edmondson, the ward physiotherapist, disagreed: 'I think Mrs James would do really well in the specialist neuro-rehabilitation centre. She was well before her stroke and has huge potential but she needs specialist rehabilitation.' Veronica arranged to have the referral documentation completed and waited for a place for Mrs James. Time passed and staff at the centre assured Veronica that Mrs James was on the waiting list.

Veronica met a colleague in the staff coffee room and discovered that one of her patients (who was twenty years younger that Mrs James) was admitted to the rehabilitation centre with minimal delay.

Reflect on practice

Why do you think that Mrs James' rehabilitation needs were considered less important than those of a younger patient? Can you think of similar instances in your day-to-day practice? What can be done to overcome such problems?

1.2 Quality issues in the care of older people

Older people are vulnerable to poor-quality care. They may be cared for in healthcare environments that are less well resourced than other healthcare settings. Although older people have complex needs they may be cared for by practitioners who do not have specialist expertise in caring for older people. Practitioners who do not have specialist skills may consider that common problems (such as incontinence and immobility) are untreatable and so older people are not enabled to function to capacity.

There have been concerns about the quality of care older people receive since Marjorie Warren wrote of the care of the chronic aged sick in the 1940s. Marjorie Warren (who is now acknowledged as the mother of geriatric medicine) found that many people who were considered untreatable had a great deal of potential and could lead meaningful lives if they received specialist care. In 1969 a series of scandals led to the (then) Secretary of State for Health setting up the Health Advisory Service. In 1980 Thelma Wells wrote of how geriatric nurses were very busy and worked very hard but, unfortunately, that hard work did not always benefit patients because nurses often lacked the education and skills required to enable older people to function to capacity.

In 1998 the *Observer* ran a campaign entitled 'Dignity on the ward'. The campaign exposed many instances of substandard care, including neglect, lack of assistance in bathing and eating and lack of respect towards older people. It attracted many letters from older people and their relatives, who expressed concern about standards of care. Frank Dobson, the Secretary of State for Health at that time, commissioned the Health Advisory Service to investigate and publish a report. This report exploded many myths about older people and their care. For example, professionals often considered that older people are less demanding and more satisfied with their care than younger people. The report found that this was not true. Older people had real concerns about the quality of care they received and were less satisfied with their care than younger people. The report identified eight major issues. These are summarised in Figure 1.1.

1 Admission delays.

2 Poor physical environment.

3 Shortage of medical, nursing and therapy staff.

4 Lack of expertise and education in care of older people.

5 Lack of fundamental care, dignity, respect, assistance with eating and bathing.

6 Low expectations of recovery, lack of awareness of rehabilitation.

7 Poor communication with older people and families.

8 Poor discharge planning.

Figure 1.1 Findings of the Health Advisory Service (1998)

The HAS report stressed that many wards provided older people with high-quality care but there were serious concerns regarding a significant proportion of wards. These issues are not new. In 1990 Denham and Lubel analysed Health Advisory Service reports issued between 1985 and 1989 and found that they highlighted similar issues.

The problems that were first identified at the end of the Second World War are still with us in the twenty-first century. A policy statement from Help the Aged (2000) outlines problems experienced by older people and their families (see Figure 1.2).

Research by advocacy groups can appear disheartening to nurses who may feel that older people and their relatives do not understand the pressures they face in their efforts to provide quality care. It's important to take a step back from day-to-day practice and to consider how your services appear to the people who receive them. When you're busy it's so very easy to forget what older people and their relatives think of your services. The patient perspective is vital because professionals cannot determine what is and what is not a quality service without consulting and working

- Dirty, run-down wards.
- Poor standards of care.
- Insufficient food and drink.
- Negative attitudes ranging from rude and abrupt behaviour to neglect.
- Too little understanding of the needs of vulnerable older people.
- Not involved in decisions about treatment.
- Poorly planned discharge.

Figure 1.2 Problems experienced by older people and their families during hospital stays

with the people who use that service. Mrs Khan's case illustrates how professional and patient perspectives can differ.

CASE STUDY – How professional and patient perspectives differ

The nurses who cared for Mrs Jamila Khan felt that she was a sweetly confused lady who had a devoted family. They felt Mrs Khan had received high-quality care in their ward.

Mrs Khan's family were quietly appalled by the lack of skill and understanding shown by the nursing staff. Mrs Khan, a retired university lecturer, had lost the ability to speak English (her second language) when she developed dementia. Mrs Khan's daughter explained carefully that her mother had dementia and would need someone to order a soft diet for her after her throat surgery. She also explained that her mother needed someone to pour drinks into a glass and encourage her to drink. She also asked staff to remind her mother to go to the toilet before meals, mid-afternoon and last thing at night.

Staff did not assist Mrs Khan to choose suitable meals. Her family tried to explain this to nursing staff without success, and her daughter felt obliged to visit daily to order meals. No one offered Mrs Khan drinks and the family felt that they had to visit four times a day to give Mrs Khan fluids. Mrs Khan became incontinent and was supplied with incontinence pads.

Mrs Khan's daughter commented: 'The care was dreadful. My mother has lived with us for four years now. Normally she manages well and we knew that she'd have a difficult time in a strange environment. What shocked me was that no one seemed to listen or to provide the care that I knew would avoid problems.'

Technically, Mrs Khan's hospital stay was successful. She required an operation, the operation was carried out, there were no complications and she was successfully discharged home. During her stay Mrs Khan was upset; she cried frequently and wandered around the ward looking for her daughter. She was unable to choose appropriate food and could have become malnourished if her daughter had not intervened. She was also at risk of dehydration. Mrs Khan was continent on admission to the hospital but became incontinent because of her increased disorientation and because she was not reminded to use the toilet at suitable times.

Reflect on practice

Can you think of an occasion where you considered that the patient and family were happy with care received and then you were stunned to receive a letter of complaint? Why do you think that you were unaware of the patient and family dissatisfaction? Have you made any changes to the way you work with patients and families as a result of such complaints?

Health services exist to deliver care to patients. If you are to deliver quality services you must take into account the patient's perspective of services: 'Only when we can see through patient eyes can we be confident that we are building into organisations and systems deliverables that are meaningful for the patients at their centre' (Nicholls et al., 2000).

A research project by Help the Aged (2002) examined older people's priorities in relation to healthcare. The researchers found that older people did not want to be treated differently because of their age. They wanted the same range of services as younger people had. Older people did not necessarily want to have interventions that might be unsuccessful because they had other conditions and felt that quality of life was of great importance. Older people wanted to be involved in their own care and to make their own decisions about treatment. Older people felt that it was important that healthcare providers recognised that they were adults and could make their own decisions even when unwell. Figure 1.3 outlines older people's priorities in healthcare.

- Eliminate ageism.
- Quality of life.
- Involvement in care.
- Staying healthy.
- Equal access to services.
- Dignity and autonomy.
- Knowledge and skills of staff.
- Information about illness and treatment available.
- Advocacy.

Figure 1.3 Older people's priorities in healthcare

1.3 The importance of doing things differently

These reports show clearly that the problems older people face have persisted for decades. The people who care for this generation of older people are not the same people who cared for older people in the mid-twentieth century but the problems identified remain unaltered.

What you can learn from these reports is that, if you continue to care for older people in the same old ways, you'll obtain the same old unsatisfactory results. If you are to do things better you must do things differently.

The reports highlight that older people do not conform to the stereotypes that many of us hold. Older people are not endlessly patient and they do mind waiting. Older people do notice poor standards of care and are well aware of the limitations of the people who are caring for them. Older people want to be treated with dignity and respect. They want to know what treatment and care are available and to make their own decisions about the treatment and care they receive.

Older people are not all the same any more than we are all the same. Older people are just like us. If you are to offer care that meets their needs you must recognise their individuality and also the way age and illness can change their ability to communicate their needs and wishes to you. You need to develop partnerships with older people and their families if you are to learn from the past and look to a more positive future.

1.4 The government's quality strategy

The current government used the slogan '24 hours to save the NHS' in its 1997 election campaign. On election the government promised to 'hit the ground running' and to introduce national policy changes that improved care.

Improvements were to be delivered using a framework called *clinical governance*. This term was first used in the government white paper, *The New NHS. Modern, Dependable*. It outlined the government's aims to end the internal market and the culture of competition and to introduce a culture that nurtured staff and valued innovation. It defined clinical governance as 'an initiative to improve clinical standards of care at local level' (Department of Health, 1997). It has also been defined as 'about patients/carers receiving the right care, at the right time, from the right person in a safe environment' (McSherry and Pearce, 2002).

Clinical governance recognised that organisations varied in their ability to deliver quality services. Some organisations delivered poor-quality services; some delivered excellent-quality services. Some organisations have excellent departments flourishing against the odds in poor-quality organisations. Some excellent organisations have a few departments that deliver poor services. The aim of clinical governance was to learn lessons from excellent organisations and to improve quality in poor organisations. Figure 1.4 illustrates this.

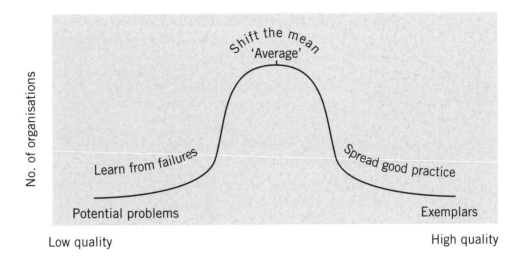

Figure 1.4 The aims of clinical governance
Source: From Scalley and Donaldson (1998)

In 1998 the government described clinical governance as 'a framework to ensure accountability for the quality of services provided' (Department of Health, 1998). Clinical governance is often thought to be very complex and hard to understand when it is in fact very simple. There are six principles that define clinical governance (see Figure 1.5).

- To provide high-quality care to all patients regardless of gender, culture or age.
- To establish national standards that are tailored to the needs of the local population.
- To place the patient at the centre of services and to develop collaborative working between acute, community and social services.
- Ensure efficient high-quality services are delivered.
- Establish strong cultures that guarantee high-quality clinical care to all patients.
- To enhance public confidence in the NHS.

Figure 1.5 The six key principles of clinical governance
Source : Adapted from Department of Health (1997; 1998)

The implementation of clinical governance is complex and requires major changes in NHS culture as well as high-level management skills. The government has set in place a number of organisations and structures to monitor performance and enable organisations to deliver quality services.

1.5 The Commission for Health Improvement

Clinical governance is about control, regulation and responsibility. If government is to control the quality of healthcare it needs to inspect organisations, find out what their strengths and weaknesses are and be able to impose sanctions on organisations that are not delivering. The Commission for Health Improvement (CHI) was set up for this purpose. Figure 1.6 illustrates its role.

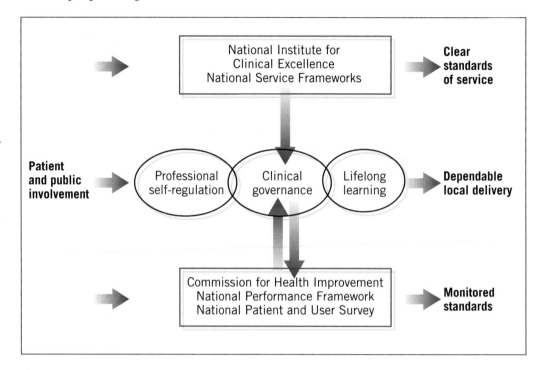

Figure 1.6 The Commission for Health Improvement

The CHI currently inspects all NHS trusts and assesses them using the following criteria:

1 Evidence-based practice.
2 The dissemination of good ideas in practice.
3 Quality improvement processes.
4 Use of high-quality data to monitor clinical care.
5 Clinical risk-reduction programmes.
6 Learning from complaints.
7 Dealing with poor performance.
8 Implementation of professional development programmes.
9 Leadership skill development.

Each year NHS trusts receive a star rating that is dependent on how they have met certain targets. An organisation can be awarded no, one, two or three stars. All CHI reviews are published and freely available on the CHI website. The organisation is

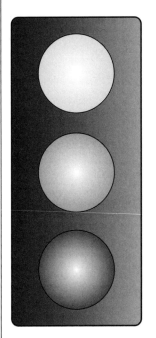

Excellent organisations

Greater freedom to develop local services. Increased funding to enable service development. Power to set own pay rates, automatic access to capital resources, decreased monitoring and inspection. Opportunity to become a 'foundation hospital'

Organisations with room for improvement

Help from intervention teams from excellent organisations. Spending plan must be agreed with regional office

Poor organisations

Help from intervention teams from excellent organisations. Modernisation agency will oversee spending

Figure 1.7 Traffic light system

required to draw up a plan to rectify any deficits within the organisation. This is also published and monitored by the CHI. Organisations are classified using a traffic light system (see Figure 1.7).

Performance indicators are now given such credence that they can make or break careers and determine the level of clinical freedom and resources an NHS trust receives.

The CHI also carries out fast-track reviews if there are concerns about an organisation or part of that organisation. CHI reviewers are seconded from NHS trusts in other areas. Reviewers carry out the review and then return to their normal jobs within the NHS.

1.6 The Commission for Healthcare Audit and Inspection

A super-regulator – the Commission for Healthcare Audit and Inspection (CHAI) – was created in April 2004 (known as the Health Care Commission). The aim of this body is to help improve the quality of healthcare by providing an independent assessment of the standards of services provided to patients, whether provided by the NHS or privately.

CHAI has taken on the functions of the following organisations:

- The Commission for Health Improvement (CHI).
- The National Care Standards Commission (in respect of private and voluntary healthcare).
- The Audit Commission (in respect of national studies of the efficiency, effectiveness and economy of healthcare).

CHAI is also expected to take over the functions of the Mental Health Act Commission. This body has new functions:

- Providing an independent assessment of complaints.
- Assessing the arrangements in place to promote public health.
- Acting as the leading inspectorate in relation to healthcare.

CHAI will seek to help providers to share the benefits from good practice and to help them to identify and address deficiencies in services at an early stage. If organisations are found wanting CHAI has the power to recommend franchised management, suspension or closure of any service.

1.7 The National Institute for Clinical Excellence

All healthcare treatments are not evidence based or effective; for example, an estimated 25 per cent of hysterectomies are carried out unnecessarily. The National Institute for Clinical Excellence (NICE) is responsible for assessing new and existing guidance and treatment and for providing evidence-based guidance. NICE reviews aim to ensure that clinicians have information that enables them to provide effective evidence-based care. Some of this guidance, such as inappropriate removal of wisdom teeth or tonsils, leads to reduced costs whilst others, such as prescribing new drugs, increase costs.

1.8 Care homes

Care homes provide continuing care for some of the most vulnerable older people. In England, care homes were regulated by the National Care Standards Commission. The National Care Standards Commission regulated care homes to National Minimum Standards. There are 38 standards, and each standard has a number of elements. These standards cover seven areas:

1 Choice of Home.
2 Health and Personal Care.
3 Daily Life and Social Activities.
4 Complaints and Protection.

5 Environmental Standards.
6 Staffing.
7 Management and Administration.

The National Care Standards Commission employed professional inspectors who work full time for the commission. People who worked for the Care Standards Commission on a full or part-time basis are not able to work within care homes. This system is very different from that used by the CHI.

There have been criticisms of the professional inspectorate model. The main criticism is that inspectors rapidly lose touch with day-to-day practice and this can make it difficult for them to inspect. Now work as an inspector is becoming viewed not as a long-term post but as a short period in a nursing career.

1.9 The Commission for Social Care Inspection

In April 2004 the National Care Standards Commission ceased to exist. It was replaced by the Commission for Social Care Inspection (CSCI). This new body brings together the work once undertaken by the Social Services Inspectorate, the SSI/Audit Commission Joint Review Team and the social care functions of the National Care Standards Commission. All care homes, including those offering nursing care, will now be designated 'social care'. In some areas of England there are reports that people who are not nurses are inspecting nursing care. If non-nursing inspectors consider that there are problems with nursing care they ask a nurse inspector to visit. It is not yet clear if the CSCI will continue this practice.

The new inspectorate will fulfil the following roles:

● Carry out local inspections of all social care organisations – public, private and voluntary – against national standards, and publish reports.
● Register services that meet national minimum standards.
● Carry out inspections of local social service authorities.
● Publish an annual report to Parliament on national progress on social care and an analysis of where resources have been spent.
● Validate all published performance assessment statistics on social care.
● Publish the star ratings for social services authorities.

1.10 A regulatory muddle

Independent and voluntary sector provision is now inspected separately from NHS provision. From April 2004, private hospitals are inspected by the CHAI and independent care homes by the CSCI. Older people who move from hospital to a care home for rehabilitation and then return home have the standards of care they receive inspected by two different bodies working to two different standards. People living in care homes on a long-term basis might find that the home they live in has to meet National Minimum Standards. When the older person receives NHS care from a GP or from the hospital outpatients department, those care providers have to meet different standards. This muddle of differing regulations affecting the same older person is very much against the spirit of the National Service Framework for Older People, with its emphasis on co-operation and collaboration and breaking down barriers.

In the future government may realise the importance of older people benefiting from the same standards of care regardless of where they live.

1.11 National Service Frameworks

If you are to improve the quality of care you need standards to measure that care. It is important that any standards set are evidence based so that you know that what you do is effective.

National Service Frameworks (NSFs) are a set of evidence-based standards that have been written by experts in consultation with representatives of people who are likely to require these services. NHS organisations and social services departments must meet these standards. Care homes are not directly affected but NSF standards will impact on the care that care home residents receive. The NSF for Older People is particularly relevant. However, the National Service Frameworks for Diabetes, Mental Health and Coronary Heart Disease are also of importance.

1.12 The National Service Framework for Older People

Currently, older people are the largest group of healthcare consumers. The NHS spends £10,000 million on older people. Social services spend £5,216 million annually. The NHS spends 40 per cent of its budget on people over the age of 65 and two thirds of NHS beds are occupied by older people. The oldest of the old consume the greatest amount of resources per head. Social services spend 48 per cent of their budgets on older people. Yet despite all this spending there are real concerns about the quality of care older people receive. There are concerns that, despite the expensive technology (such as hip replacements following falls), older people do not benefit from health and social care interventions. The NSF aims to change this by ensuring that interventions are effective and evidence based and that older people remain in good health for longer. The aim is to reduce the period of disability to increase the years of active healthy life.

1.13 NSF Standards

The NSF has outlined eight standards. These are illustrated in Figure 1.8.

The standards are evidence based and have been drawn up by experts from NHS hospitals, universities and social services. They aim to offer care that is seamless at the point of delivery regardless of where that care is delivered. Unfortunately not a single representative of the independent sector was consulted, despite the fact that the vast majority of care for older people is delivered in care homes and by independent sector home-care teams (Nazarko, 2002). The standards are to be introduced gradually and there are a series of milestones that organisations must meet by specific times.

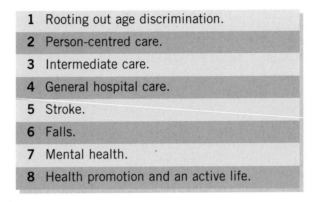

1 Rooting out age discrimination.
2 Person-centred care.
3 Intermediate care.
4 General hospital care.
5 Stroke.
6 Falls.
7 Mental health.
8 Health promotion and an active life.

Figure 1.8 The eight NSF standards

Rooting out age discrimination

This standard makes it clear that setting age limits for eligibility for services is unacceptable. Services are to be delivered on the basis of clinical need and likely benefit from those services. Under this standard it would be unacceptable to place an age limit on haemodialysis but it would be acceptable to choose the person most likely to benefit from haemodialysis.

This is a challenging standard because ageism permeates every aspect of our society. Older people are forced to retire; even government committees have age limits. Age discrimination, unlike racial and sexual discrimination, is not illegal. However, education can enable people to understand that differences do not make some people less valuable and less worthy of respect than others. The NSF recognises this and states that health and social care organisations should provide additional training for staff to enable them to develop a greater understanding of the needs of older people. This will foster more positive attitudes.

The government require the appointment of NHS non-executive directors who will support the implementation of the NSF. Health and social services are required to appoint clinical or practice champions to lead professional development across the organisation.

There will be policy reviews to identify and tackle areas of age discrimination including, hopefully, issues such as why residential care for older people is more poorly resourced than that of young people.

IMPLICATIONS

NHS acute and primary care trusts are required to appoint an non-executive director to support the implementation of the National Service Framework for Older People. Health and social services appoint clinical or practice champions to help the organisation to lead professional development across the organisation. Relevant policies and procedures that may discriminate on the basis of age will be identified, examined and rewritten by a newly set-up scrutiny group.

Nurses working in community and care home settings will find that services that were not available to older people, such as some stroke rehabilitation centres, will now be open to older people. Older people who require medical treatment should no longer face discrimination because of their age.

Reflect on practice

It is easy to change policies and procedures but much more difficult to change attitudes and approaches. Observe practice in your workplace quietly and make a note of ways in which you consider older people or certain older people are treated differently. What can you do to influence practice and prevent discrimination?

Person-centred care

This standard aims to ensure that older people receive appropriate and timely care *across sectors*. It affirms the core values of professionals who have struggled to ensure that older people do not fall through the chasm between health and social care. This standard is about dignity and choice, recognising differences in culture and values and delivering care that is tailored to those values. This standard is about fundamentals, such treating people with dignity and respect and meeting fundamental needs in ways that enable the person to maintain dignity and self-respect.

The standard requires staff to be courteous at all times and to use the older person's preferred form of address. Staff are required to communicate effectively and to provide sensitive care that preserves a person's privacy and dignity. People with long-term conditions are to be encouraged to develop expertise in their own care.

This standard aims to encourage health and social services to work together and sets out proposals for integrated care trusts. This aims to integrate health and social care and to provide integrated services to deliver equipment and continence services.

IMPLICATIONS

In some organisations the documentation required to put this standard into effect will need reviewing. For example, if you are to address a person by his or her preferred name, you will need a document that shows you what this is. The NHS and social services are working towards a 'single assessment process' and any new documentation should take this into account. Care homes are not yet included within the single assessment process.

The Essence of Care toolkit

If services are to be improved they must be audited and reviewed. NHS organisations are using *Essence of Care* as a quality improvement tool. This is a toolkit that provides good practice standards in:

1 privacy and dignity;
2 personal and oral hygiene;
3 continence (bladder and bowel care);
4 food and nutrition;
5 pressure ulcers;
6 principles of self-care;
7 record-keeping; and
8 the safety of patients with mental health needs.

This toolkit allows teams of staff caring for older people to assess their own practice, and to review areas for improvement and audit when improvements have been carried out (Department of Health, 2001a). Essence of care is widely used in NHS settings and is now being used by care homes to audit the quality of care.

It is no longer acceptable to treat NHS patients differently because of where they are receiving care. The results of this standard are already being seen. Once, nursing home patients were not eligible for continence pads and continence services; they are now able to access these in the same way as older people living in their own homes.

Intermediate care

This standard aims to prevent unnecessary hospitalisation, to ensure that hospital care delivers maximum benefits and that discharge delays are minimised. It aims to maximise a person's ability to live independently.

Currently, an estimated 20–25 per cent of people admitted to care homes could be successfully rehabilitated if rehabilitation services were available. This standard aims to increase the number of intermediate care places by 5,000. It also aims to decrease the number of permanent care home places by 50,000.

This standard aims to prevent unnecessary hospital admission. People admitted as emergencies occupy nearly 60 per cent of NHS beds. Most of the people admitted as emergencies are older people. Around half the people aged 75 or more were admitted for 'symptoms, signs and ill-defined conditions'.

The research also found that 20 per cent of older people occupying hospital beds could be discharged if alternative facilities were in place (Department of Health, 2000). The NSF aims to reduce these unnecessary admissions by providing:

- intensive support, such as 'hospital at home', within the person's home;
- step-up care in community housing, very sheltered housing and care homes; and
- specialist assessment and equipment.

This standard also aims to cut unnecessary or premature permanent admission to care homes by assessing a person's rehabilitation potential prior to considering permanent admission to a care home.

It also aims to ensure that older people have access to rehabilitation services before decisions are made regarding their need for permanent care. The person may have rehabilitation within an intermediate care unit or at home. A range of intermediate care settings are currently being developed. Some intermediate care is provided in specially designated wards in acute and community hospitals; some is provided in nursing homes and some within residential homes.

The aim of most intermediate care schemes is to move the person through care settings as he or she improves. The person might have two weeks of intermediate care in an NHS community hospital, two weeks in a care home and two weeks at home. Some homes are already contracting with primary care trusts to provide intermediate care beds.

The effects of the standard might be as follows:

- Staff working in intermediate care settings may require further education and updating to enable them to practise rehabilitative nursing. The skills required to rehabilitate are different from those required in acute and continuing care settings.
- There might be increased demands for district nursing. District nursing will be more intensive and providing care on the district will take longer. District nursing services will face increased demands for 'out-of-hours care', and district nursing teams will need to develop higher levels of expertise in caring for more acutely ill older people and will need to increase the flexibility of their services.
- Staff caring for older people in acute wards will also find the workload more intensive because the least dependent and most stable older people will be cared for in the community.
- Care home staff may find that the dependency of permanent residents rises further as only the most highly dependent of older people are admitted.
- People living in care homes may receive services that were difficult to obtain previously. Therapy services and specialist nursing services should be more readily available and there will be increased support within homes to avert the need for hospital admission.

General hospital care

This standard aims to ensure that older people receive specialist care to enable them to recover fully from illness and accident. It recognises that timely and appropriate care is crucial. It aims to ensure that waits in accident and emergency departments are minimised and that hydration is maintained. It aims to reduce the risk of pressure damage whilst the person is awaiting admission and aims to reduce admission waits to a maximum of four hours.

This standard recognises the important role specialists have to play in the care of older people and states that hospitals must form specialist teams comprising consultant geriatricians, physicians and nurses, occupational and speech therapist, dieticians, social workers and physiotherapists.

It emphasises (as the other standards do) the importance of staff development. Hospitals are required to profile staff and audit their skills in caring for older people. When gaps in staff education have been identified, the hospital must put in place education to address these.

CASE STUDY — Staff development

Laura Edwards is matron of the Haven nursing home. She attended a conference on the role of specialists in caring for older people. She was interested to hear of how nurse specialists and nurse consultants were making a difference to the care of older people in other parts of the UK. Laura began to wonder why her local hospital did not employ a nurse specialist or a nurse consultant in older people, especially as the hospital's reputation for caring for older people was poor. When Laura attended another study day she met the director of nursing at the hospital and asked. She was told: 'It's not a priority for the trust. We have a very young population and are concentrating on acute specialities.'

Reflect on practice

What does this tell you about the hospital's priorities? Do you think that nurses caring for older people in this hospital are valued? How might this mindset affect the ability of staff to provide quality care for older people?

IMPLICATIONS

This standard could be seen as significant because it places gerontology and gerontological nursing at the heart of hospital care. It should encourage the growth of specialist teams in acute hospitals and also in primary care trusts that commission and provide services to older people. There is already an increase in the number of nurse consultant posts, although some employers are finding it difficult to recruit nurses with the appropriate qualifications and expertise. The number of clinical nurse specialist posts will also increase. In the future there will be clear career pathways for nurses caring for older people with the option to specialise as a clinician or a manager.

The Royal College of Nursing launched its second faculty project in gerontological nursing in 2004. The first faculty project, in accident and emergency nursing, set clear standards on how nurses could develop from novice to expert in their field. The second project will include core competencies for nurses with different levels of expertise. In education it will ensure that universities that are not yet organising specialist elderly care placements for students will do so. It will also increase the demand for post-registration education in gerontology.

Expert nurses within care homes may find that their skills are in demand within the NHS. In London there are currently three nurse consultants in the care of older people field; two of them were previously nursing home matrons. Care homes will be able to access nurse consultants and clinical nurse specialists who can support them in practice and offer educational opportunities to nursing home staff.

Stroke

There are two elements to this standard. The first is to reduce the incidence of stroke by treating risk factors in primary care settings. The second is to ensure that when people have a stroke they benefit from integrated stroke services to maximise recovery. This standard states that all acute hospitals must have specialist stroke units. These units will follow care pathways to ensure that the effects of stroke are minimised.

The standard recognises that stroke recovery can take years and will ensure that rehabilitation programmes are put in place to maximise recovery in hospital and in community settings.

IMPLICATIONS

This standard will impact on primary care teams. GPs and practice nurses will have a greater role to play in identifying people at risk of stroke and of minimising risk factors through encouraging lifestyle modification and prescribing medication. Nurses who do not have community nursing qualifications can now take extended and supplementary prescribing courses. Prescribing courses are run by universities and are at degree level. The courses are run on a day-release basis over three or six months. Students must pass a written examination and are examined on their ability to diagnose and treat patients. The prescribing course has credits at degree level that can be used towards gaining a degree.

The government aims to have 10,000 qualified nurse prescribers by 2005. Nurse prescribers can see patients independently, and diagnose and prescribe medications from the nurse prescribers' formulary. Nurses who have completed the supplementary prescribing course can use a patient management plan to prescribe all the drugs within the British National Formulary. In the future nurse prescribers will play an increasing part in promoting health and in treating people with diseases such as hypertension to prevent complications (such as stroke).

People living in care homes might in the future be visited by a nurse prescriber from the patient's local GP practice, who will check blood pressure and adjust medication if this is required. Hospital staff will be responsible for setting up specialist stroke units in hospitals that do not yet have these.

Reflect on practice

How will this standard impact on hospital services, in particular on the new specialist stroke units?

Falls

There are two elements to this standard. The first is to reduce the number of falls that result in serious injury. The second is to ensure that people who have sustained a serious injury receive effective treatment and rehabilitation.

The standard identifies diagnosis and treatment of osteoporosis as the cornerstone to reducing the number of falls that lead to fracture. Osteoporosis is endemic in the population: one third of women and one twelfth of men over the age of 50 have osteoporosis. The standard aims to reduce the incidence of osteoporosis through lifestyle modification and to diagnose and treat osteoporosis effectively. The standard recognises there are many risk factors for falls and instructs NHS trusts that have not yet set up falls services to do so. These clinics will investigate the reasons people fall and will treat the risk factors.

This standard also aims to improve the NHS's current poor record in rehabilitation following fracture by offering evidence-based care.

IMPLICATIONS

Primary care teams will have the responsibility for reviewing medication and ensuring that older people are not exposed unnecessarily to the hazards of polypharmacy. Medication management is particularly important in older people. Although older people make up only 8.5 per cent of the total population they consume 43 per cent of all prescribed medicines. Ninety percent of people aged 75 and over take prescribed medicines: the average older person living at home takes four different medicines and the average person living in a nursing home takes eight different medicines. People often do not take medications as prescribed – fewer than 51 per cent of adults in developed countries take life-saving medication as prescribed. Older people may have major problems taking prescribed medication: medications can harm as well as heal and they can interact and cause problems. It is important to ensure that older people receive medicines that they really need, and given in the right dose at the right time.

Older people who are receiving four or more prescribed medications must have a documented medication review every six months. Pharmacists can now take extended and supplementary prescribing courses at universities and can, like nurses, become prescribers. This review may be carried out by a prescriber (nurse, pharmacist or GP) or by a non-prescribing pharmacist who recommends changes to the person's GP.

GPs are busy and, as increasing numbers of nurses and pharmacists become prescribers, they will probably take responsibility for medication reviews.

Staff in care homes may find that medications are formally reviewed by non-GP prescribers. Some reviews have been carried out in nursing and residential homes. These reviews showed that 50 per cent of prescribed medications required review. The most common change (47 per cent) was to discontinue medication. Two thirds of medications discontinued were stopped because there was no indication for prescription. Long-term follow-up shows no deterioration in health after discontinuation of medication.

Some hospital and community staff will be responsible for setting up falls-prevention clinics and using care pathways to provide evidence-based care. Staff working in hospitals, community settings and in care homes will be able to refer patients who are falling to specialist falls clinics so that the reasons for falls can be identified and, where possible, treated.

Community staff will be responsible for hospital-at-home schemes that aim to rehabilitate and reduce risk factors to prevent further falls.

Mental health

There are two elements to this standard. The first is to promote good mental health in older people. The second is to treat and support older people with dementia and depression. This standard recognises that other mental health problems, such as schizophrenia, also occur and can be dealt with within the mental health national service framework.

This standard provides evidence-based care pathways for the treatment of acute confusional states, depression and dementia.

IMPLICATIONS

One of the problems nurses face in caring for people with dementia is that they work in buildings that are poorly designed and ill-suited to caring for this group of people. Local hospitals are to receive funding to enable them to convert Nightingale wards into specialist dementia units.

The standard emphasises the importance of specialist teams to support nurses working in general wards, in community settings and in care homes.

Health promotion and active life

This standard aims to prevent or delay the onset of ill-health and disability by encouraging people to live a healthy and active life. It aims to identify any barriers to healthy living and to place healthy living within a cultural context for the older person. It aims to reduce the impact of illness and disability on health and wellbeing.

This standard aims to encourage older people to remain physically active, to eat a healthy diet and remain well nourished and to have immunisations. It also requires NHS organisations and local councils to work together to take stock of all existing services and to work out what services might be needed in the future. Nurses might be involved in developing disease-prevention and health-promotion programmes in all settings.

IMPLICATIONS

This, the final NSF standard, could be said to break new ground because it promotes wellbeing rather than adopting the traditional approach of treating sickness.

1.14 The challenges of clinical governance

Clinical governance is often seen as an issue that affects senior management and is of little relevance to those who provide direct care to older people. This is a mistaken view. Clinical governance is of great relevance to clinicians and provides an effective framework that can enable you to improve. The literature discussed here and listed in the further reading section at the end of this chapter will allow you to identify key issues in the care of older people. These are as follows:

- Ageism and inequitable access to care and rehabilitation services.
- Poor standards of care.
- Unprofessional conduct, including rudeness and neglect.
- Poor understanding of the needs of older people.
- Lack of expertise in the care of older people.
- Lack of involvement in care.
- Poor discharge planning.

Change management
Do we know
how to put it right?

Standards
Do we know what is the
right thing to do?

Monitoring
Are we doing
it correctly?

Professional qualities
Do we have appropriate
skills, knowledge and attitude?

Figure 1.9 Clinical governance and the evaluation and improvement of services

Clinical governance can be used to examine these and other issues and to evaluate and improve services (Figure 1.9).

 1.15 Conclusion

We live in interesting and challenging times. Life expectancy has increased, and many of the diseases that rapidly led to disability and death are now treatable. Older people can now live longer than ever before. Our challenge is to ensure that the healthcare required in those additional years is quality care. We cannot deliver quality if we do not see through the patient's eyes and provide care that meets the patient's needs. The problems that nurses face in their efforts to deliver quality care are finally being addressed through a quality framework known as clinical governance. Clinical governance gives you the tools and the ammunition to professionalise the care of older people. The challenge is to retain your sensitivity and compassion as you strive to offer research-based care. At the moment clinical governance is thought only to affect the NHS but, if we can get it right, its effects will ripple though all settings where older people receive care. Before the establishment of CHAI, many private hospitals had already adopted clinical governance. From April 2004, those that had not were compelled to adopt it to meet the CHAI standards.

Care homes are regulated by the CSCI and are not at this stage required to adopt clinical governance. In reality care homes are already being affected by many aspects of clinical governance, such as the implementation of the National Service Frameworks. The National Service Framework for Older People affects homes caring for older people because the people in homes are NHS patients as well as care home residents.

In the future the CSCI might be absorbed into CHAI and care homes might then be required to adopt clinical governance. The government might choose to require homes to implement it sooner because increasing numbers of people in nursing homes might be paid for by the NHS under continuing care criteria.

Key Points

○ Ageism affects older people's ability to access high-quality care.

○ Older people are vulnerable to poor-quality care.

○ There have been concerns about the quality of care older people receive since the 1940s.

○ Clinical governance provides a clear framework to assess quality of care and to improve standards.

○ The regulation of care differs depending on where the care is provided and who provides it.

○ Professionals must involve patients in the planning and delivery of care if they are to provide sensitive high-quality care.

References and further reading

SECTION 1.1

Adelman, R.D., Green, M.G. and Chana, R. (1991) 'Issues in physician–elderly patient interaction', *Ageing and Society*, 11: 127–41.

Butler, R.N. (1969) *Testimony: Subcommittee on Retirement and the Individual*. The US Senate Special Committee on Aging, 15 July 1969. US Senate, Washington, DC.

Levin, J. and Levin, W.C. (1980) *Ageism and Discrimination towards the Elderly*. Wadsworth, Belmont, CA.

Lookinland, S. and Anson, K. (1995) 'Perpetuation of ageist attitudes among present and future health care personnel: implications for elder care', *Journal of Advanced Nursing*, 21: 47–56.

SECTION 1.2

Denham, M.J. and Lubel, D. (1990) 'Peer review and services for the elderly patients', *British Medical Journal*, 1: 635–6.

Health Advisory Service 2000 (1998) *'Not because They are Old': An Independent Inquiry into the Care of Older People on Acute Wards in General Hospitals*. Health Advisory Service 2000, London.

Help the Aged (2000) *Our Future Health. Older People's Priorities for Health and Social Care*. Help the Aged, London.

Help the Aged (2002) *Hospital Care Problems in Hospital Care. Help the Aged Policy Statement June 2002*. Help the Aged, London.

Martin, J. (1984) *Hospitals in Trouble*. Blackwell Science, Oxford.

Nicholls, S., Cullen, R. and Halligan, A. (2000) 'Clinical governance: its origins and its foundations', *Clinical Performance and Quality Health Care*, 8:172–8.

Norton, D., McClaren, R. and Exon-Smith, A.N. (1962) *An Investigation into Geriatric Nursing Problems in Hospital*. Research Report NCCOP (reprinted in 1979). Churchill-Livingstone, Edinburgh.

Warren, M. (1946) 'Care of the aged chronic sick', *Lancet*, i: 841–3.

Wells, T. (1980) *Problems in Geriatric Nursing*. Churchill-Livingstone, Edinburgh.

SECTION 1.4

Cook, M.J. (2001) 'Quality in action', in Hyde, J. and Cooper, F. (eds) *Managing the Business of Health Care*. Balliere Tindall, London.

Department of Health (1997) *The New NHS. Modern and Dependable. A National Framework for Assessing Competence* (consultation document). Stationery Office, London.

Department of Health (1998) *A First Class Service. Quality in the New NHS*. Stationery Office, London.

Ferguson, B. and Lim, J.N.W. (2001) 'Incentives and clinical governance. Money following quality?', *Journal of Management in Medicine*, 15: 463–87.

McSherry, R. and Pearce, P. (2002) *Clinical Governance. A Guide to Implementation for Health Care Professionals*. Blackwell Science, Oxford.

Scally, G. and Donaldson, L.J. (1998) 'Clinical governance and the drive for quality improvement in the new NHS in England', *British Medical Journal*, 317: 61–5.

Scott, A. (1998) 'Clinical governance relies on a change in culture', *British Journal of Nursing*, 7: 940.

SECTION **1.5**

Charnock, S.A. (2001) 'Who's afraid of clinical governance?', *Nursing Times*, 97: 34–6.

Department of Health (2002) *Delivering the NHS Plan*. Department of Health, London (available at **http://www.doh.gov.uk/deliveringthenhsplan/deliveringthenhsplan.pdf**).

Ferriman, A. (2002) 'Milburn announces setting up "foundation" hospitals', *British Medical Journal*, 324: 132.

SECTION **1.6**

House of Commons (2002) *The National Health Service Reform and Health Care Professions Act*. Stationery Office, London.

SECTION **1.7**

National Institute of Clinical Excellence (2001) *Summary of Guidance Issued to the NHS in England and Wales*. Issue 3. NICE, London (available available at **http://www.nice.org.uk**).

National Institute of Clinical Excellence (2002) *Summary of Guidance Issued to the NHS in England and Wales*. Issue 5. NICE, London (available available at **http://www.nice.org.uk**).

SECTION **1.11**

Department of Health (1999) *National Service Framework for Mental Health*. Stationery Office, London.

Department of Health (2000) *National Service Framework for Coronary Heart Disease*. Stationery Office, London.

Department of Health (2001) *National Service Framework for Older People*. Stationery Office, London.

Department of Health (2002) *National Service Framework for Diabetes: Standards*. Stationery Office, London.

SECTION **1.12**

Department of Health (2000) *Shaping the Future NHS: Long Term Planning for Hospitals and Related Services* (consultation document on the findings of the National Beds Inquiry). Department of Health, London (available aavailable at **http://www.doh.gov.uk/pub/docs/doh/nationalbeds.pdf**).

Health Advisory Service (2000) *Not because They are Old. An Independent Inquiry into the Care of Older People on Acute Wards in General Hospitals*. HAS, London.

Help the Aged (1999) *Dignity on the Ward. Promoting Excellence in Care. Good Practice in*

Acute Hospital Care for Older People. Help the Aged and University of Sheffield's School of Nursing and Midwifery, London.

SECTION 1.13

American Geriatrics Society, British Geriatrics Society and the American Academy of Orthopaedic Surgeons Panel on Falls Prevention (2001) 'Guideline for the prevention of falls in older people', *Journal of the American Geriatric Society*, 49: 664–72.

Audit Commission (1994) *A Prescription for Improvement. Towards more Rational Prescribing in General Practice*. Stationery Office, London.

Broderick, E. (1997) 'Prescribing patterns for nursing home patients in the US. The reality and the vision', *Drugs and Aging*, 11: 255-60.

Department of Health (2000) *Shaping the Future NHS: Long Term Planning for Hospitals and Related Services* (consultation document on the findings of the National Beds Inquiry). Department of Health, London (available at **http://www.doh.gov.uk/pub/docs/doh/nationalbeds.pdf**).

Department of Health (2001a) *Essence of Care*. Department of Health, London (available at **http://www.doh.gov.uk/essenceofcare**).

Department of Health (2001b) *Medicines and Older People. Implementing Medicines-related Aspects of the NSF for Older People*. DOH, London.

Furniss, L., Burns, A., Craig, S.K., Scobie, S., Cooke, J. and Faragher, B. (2000) 'Effects of a pharmacist's medication review in nursing homes. Randomised control trial', *British Journal of Psychiatry*, 176: 563-7.

Furniss, L., Craig, S.K. and Burns, A. (1998a) 'Medication use in nursing homes for elderly people', *Journal of Geriatric Psychiatry*, 13: 433-9.

Furniss, L., Craig, S.K.L., Scobie, S., Cooke, J. and Burns, A. (1998b) 'Medication reviews in nursing homes: documenting and classifying the activities of a pharmacist', *Pharmacology Journal*, 261: 320-3.

Harris, C.M. and Darjda, R. (1996) 'The scale of repeat prescribing', *British Journal of General Practitioners*, 46: 649-53.

Nazarko, L. (2002) 'A catastrophe waiting to happen', *Nursing Management*, 9: 30-5.

Purves, I. and Kennedy, J. (1994) *The Quality of General Practice Repeat Prescribing*. Department of Primary Health Care, University of Newcastle upon Tyne.

Ryan, A. and Jaques, I. (1996) 'Medication compliance in older people', *Elderly Care*, 9: 16-20.

World Health Organisation (2003) *Adherence to Long Term Therapies. Evidence for Action*. WHO, Geneva.

CHAPTER 2

What level of care are you providing now?

Introduction

No nurse comes to work to provide a poor service. No nurse comes to work to provide care that is less than excellent. Poor services do exist and sometimes care is provided that is less than excellent. One of the problems that affects professionals is that they see things through the eyes of a professional and not through the eyes of a patient. As professionals you are at home in the ward or care home; you know where things are and what the routine is. The older person has a completely different perspective and is in an alien environment. The older person with an arthritic hip may be well aware of how difficult it is it to get up from the low toilet seat whilst you, the professional, have no idea that this is a problem. The older person with poor eyesight may curse the small print in the menu and find it difficult to choose food but, unless you ask, you will never know the problems people using your services experience.

Practice development is an important part of nursing because no service is ever perfect or meets exactly the needs and aspirations of those who use it. Sometimes well planned and well delivered services deteriorate over the years, not because standards slip but because the service does not change. Even the best of services needs to evolve over time. Client groups change, sometimes because of advances in treatment. In the 1980s, AIDs was a terminal illness and many organisations concentrated on providing palliative care. Now retroviral therapy has prolonged life, most of the hospices have closed and organisations concentrate on chronic disease management and prevention. Sometimes expectations change. In the 1980s a generation of older people requiring long-term care were delighted to move from Nightingale-style geriatric wards to nursing homes where they shared a room with two or three other people. Now older people expect to have a single room and, preferably, an en suite toilet when they move to a care home.

If we are to continue to meet expectations our services must evolve and change like everything else in the world. There are dangers, though, in introducing change for change's sake. Our perspective as professionals is not the same as the perspective of the older person, who may be unwell and may have chronic diseases such as arthritis or visual impairment that affect the ability to relate to staff and the care environment. If we are to meet the needs and aspirations of the people we aim to care for we must consult them and find out what we can do to make meaningful improvements to services. Our reality is not the older person's reality.

The most effective way to find out what level of services we are offering now and what would really make a difference to the older person is to use multiple methods to gain a full picture. This chapter explores how we gain a whole systems view of quality. It explains how to use tools such as Essence of Care to enable you to work out where your service is now and where you want to go.

It is fairly easy to work out what needs to be done to improve services – the difficult part is changing practice and measuring what difference you have made. This chapter explains how you can set goals that are SMART (Specific, Measurable, Attainable/Achievable, Realistic and Time-bound) and how you can work with your team to improve care and make everyone on the team feel he or she is doing what he or she came into nursing to do – provide care he or she can be proud of.

Aims

2.1	What is quality?	2.10	How to use clinical benchmarks
2.2	Quality assurance		
2.3	Continuous quality improvement	2.11	Produce and implement an action plan
2.4	A whole systems approach	2.12	Reviewing achievement
2.5	Complaints	2.13	Sharing success or reviewing the action plan
2.6	Learning from complaints		
2.7	Benchmarking	2.14	Understanding the patient's perspective
2.8	Essence of Care		
2.9	Who should use clinical benchmarks?	2.15	Walking and listening
		2.16	Conclusion

2.1 What is quality?

Although quality is a term that is often used, it is one that most of us find difficult to define. People delivering and receiving healthcare have different values and perceptions of healthcare. David Garvin describes five different types of quality. These are illustrated in Table 2.1.

Table 2.1 Garvin's definitions of quality

Transcendent	Innate excellence. This implies that quality is a simple property that defies analysis. We recognise it when we experience it but we cannot define it or reproduce it at will
Product based	Precise and measurable
User based	Meets individual consumer preferences. The standards vary according to individual wants and needs
Manufacturing based	Product meets specific design or specification standards
Value based	Product or service is based on expectations of price or cost

2.2 Quality assurance

In the 1980 Donabedian identified three approaches to the evaluation of quality of care. These are assessment of structure, processes and outcomes. Structural assessment focuses on settings where care takes place and includes staffing levels, qualifications of staff, facilities and administrative support. The assumption is that if the setting is good, quality of care will follow (Donabedian, 1986). National Minimum Standards are concerned with structural assessment.

The process of care is concerned with technical competence and humanist aspects. This is the medical audit approach and involves the development of criteria by a panel of experts. It inevitably excludes consumers who are presumed to be technically incompetent. The National Service Frameworks have been formulated using a process approach. It could be argued that the inclusion of users groups in the reference group is tokenistic.

Outcome assessment focuses on patient outcomes, such as death, disease, disability, discomfort and dissatisfaction. The assumption is that increased or improved care reduces the incidence of unfavourable outcomes. The indicators used to determine Star Ratings are outcome measures. Donabedian (1994) considers that no one aspect of the evaluation is of greater importance than the others.

2.3 Continuous quality improvement

Continuous quality improvement (CQI) was built on the quality assurance work of the 1980s. It reflects changes in the way organisations are now managed. In the 1980s quality assurance was considered to be the preserve of the specialist. Only specialists could measure and manage quality. CQI recognises that quality of care is everyone's business and that the only people who have the power to move practice forward are the people who practise. Table 2.2 illustrates the differences between quality assurance and CQI.

Table 2.2 Differing approaches to quality

QUALITY ASSURANCE	CONTINUOUS QUALITY IMPROVEMENT
Detects errors, deficiencies and areas of non-compliance	Determines requirements and expectations
Fixes blame and responsibility	Identifies processes and improvement opportunities
Reactive; investigates after the event	Proactive; focuses on prevention
Responsibility of separate specialist team	Responsibility of all staff
Inspires fear; teams and organisations may be found wanting	Inspires hope; teams and organisations can more forward together

2.4 A whole systems approach

John Godfrey Saxe's poem (based on an Indian fable) illustrates the dangers of looking at only one aspect of quality. As you can see from the poem, six blind men looking at only one aspect of an elephant obtained an inaccurate and distorted view:

It was six men of Indostan

To learning much inclined,
Who went to see the Elephant
(Though all of them were blind),
That each by observation
Might satisfy his mind.

The First approached the Elephant,
And happening to fall
Against his broad and sturdy side,
At once began to bawl:
'God bless me! but the Elephant
Is very like a wall!'

The Second, feeling of the tusk,
Cried, 'Ho! what have we here
So very round and smooth and sharp?
To me 'tis mighty clear
This wonder of an Elephant
Is very like a spear!'

The Third approached the animal,
And happening to take
The squirming trunk within his hands,
Thus boldly up and spake:
'I see,' quoth he, 'the Elephant
Is very like a snake!'

The Fourth reached out an eager hand,
And felt about the knee.
'What most this wondrous beast is like
Is mighty plain,' quoth he;
"Tis clear enough the Elephant
Is very like a tree!'

The Fifth, who chanced to touch the ear,
Said: 'E'en the blindest man
Can tell what this resembles most;
Deny the fact who can
This marvel of an Elephant
Is very like a fan!'

The Sixth no sooner had begun
About the beast to grope,
Than, seizing on the swinging tail
That fell within his scope,
'I see,' quoth he, 'the Elephant
Is very like a rope!'

And so these men of Indostan
Disputed loud and long,
Each in his own opinion
Exceeding stiff and strong,
Though each was partly in the right,
And all were in the wrong!

Moral:
So oft in theologic wars,
The disputants, I ween,
Rail on in utter ignorance
Of what each other mean,
And prate about an Elephant
Not one of them has seen!

There are a number of methods that you can use to find out what level of care you are currently providing. Each method has its limitations and, if you wish to build up a full picture, it's important to use several methods. Let's examine each method and their advantages and disadvantages.

2.5 Complaints

Most complaints are about poor communication, poor staff attitudes and incorrect or poor-quality care. Older patients are more likely to complain about services than younger people are (Webb, 1995). Older people are also more likely to complain about nursing care. Older people may tend to complain more about nursing care than younger people because they are more vulnerable to the consequences of poor care. John Tingle's (2002) analysis of a report of complaints investigated by the Health Service Ombudsman reveals that professionals sometimes fail to learn lessons from complaints and continue to make the same mistakes. He comments:

> *The common error in these cases and in many others reported by the HSO over the years is the failure of staff and management to think reflectively about the environment of care in which they are practising. These cases show that there is an urgent need for staff to stand back and reflect on the quality of care that is being provided in their speciality and to think whether it can be improved. Proactive rather than reactive care management should be the order of the day. It should not take an HSO investigation to instigate the changes*

that have been noted above. Such changes should be made as a matter of course, through everyday healthcare quality control exercises that should be in operation in all trusts.

A lack of complaints may not mean that you are providing a service that meets the needs and expectations of the people you care for. It may simply reflect low expectations on the part of the people you care for. There are many influences on the patient's overall experience of health care (see Figure 2.1).

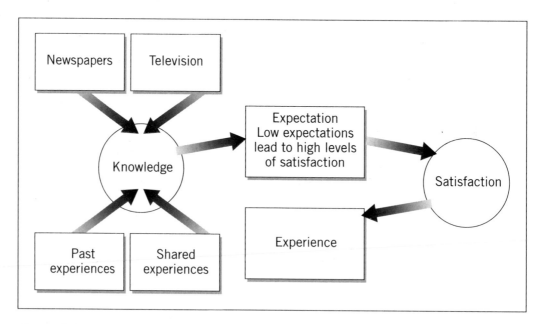

Figure 2.1 Factors influencing patient satisfaction

Professionals are often shocked when they receive a complaint. They can label the person who has complained as deviant ('everyone else appreciates our service – look at these thank-you cards') or difficult ('I knew we'd have problems with Mrs Smith and her family – we couldn't do anything right'). It is difficult for older people and their families to complain and it is estimated that for every complaint there are another nine dissatisfied people who did not complain.

People do not complain for two main reasons:

- Sometimes people feel that it is not worth bothering because no one will take any notice of their complaint and that it will not make any difference.
- Sometimes people fear making a complaint. It is relatively easy to complain about poor service in a restaurant or shop. It is much more difficult to complain about care if you are dependent on staff to care for you or may have to return to a ward in the future.

People also fear that if they complain staff will be less attentive or make life difficult. Mr Kowalski's case illustrates this.

CASE STUDY — The difficulties of complaining

Mr Tadeus Kowalski was admitted to the ward a year ago for rehabilitation following hip replacement in an elective orthopaedic centre. He has now had a second hip replacement and there are plans to transfer him to the ward again for rehabilitation. Mr Kowalski and his family said they did not want him to return to the ward. Mr Kowalski has Parkinson's disease and said that, although his medication should have been given three hourly, it was often late. This caused him great distress and impeded his recovery. In his notes there are several entries indicating that he, his wife and family have asked for him to keep his own medication as his medication has not being given on time.

Reflect on practice

How could you alleviate Mr Kowalski's concerns and enable him to accept the rehabilitation that he requires post-operatively? What lessons can you learn from this? How might you improve communication between staff and the older people they care for? What education might staff need on Parkinson's disease? What changes might you consider to enable competent patients to self-medicate whilst in hospital?

There are many influences on the patient's experience of healthcare (see Figure 2.2).

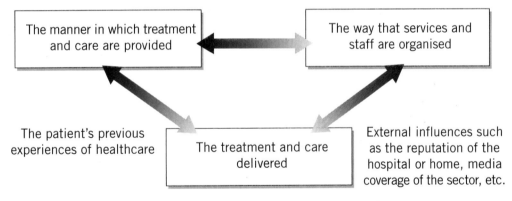

Figure 2.2 Influences on the patient's experiences of healthcare

In Mr Kowalski's case the way that drug rounds were organised at 8 am, midday, 2 pm, 6 pm and 10 pm were incompatible with his need to take antiparkinsonian medication every three hours. His expectation was that the ward, like the orthopaedic centre, would tailor the dispensing of medication to his needs. The ward did not do so. This affected his ability to participate in rehabilitation and slowed his recovery.

2.6 Learning from complaints

Complaints are important. They provide information from the patient's perspective. This information may highlight a 'one off' situation where needs were not met or it may reveal information about hidden problems. Sometimes a series of complaints over months or years have a theme. They may highlight issues such as lack of staff or a culture where patients are batch processed and given exactly the same treatment and care regardless of whether these meet individual needs. Often complaints are dealt with on an individual basis and valuable information about a service may not be identified.

Reflect on practice

Analyse complaints about your workplace over the last year. Read details of investigations and responses. What do the complaints tell you about the service provided? Are there are recurrent themes? Have the issues identified been addressed? If not, develop an action plan to address these.

2.7 Benchmarking

A benchmark is a measurement of the overall performance of an organisation, team or individual against the best achievable standard for a product or service. Sometimes nurses consider that benchmarks are complex. They are really quite simple tools that enable you to understand what standards you should deliver and what standards you are currently delivering.

Benchmarking enables you to audit services, compare them to similar care settings and to develop strategies for improvement. Audit tools have been used in healthcare settings for decades (Warzynski, 1996). There are hundreds of audit tools: some have been produced commercially, some have been designed by staff working in particular healthcare settings. Many of these tools are well designed and research based. They are of limited use in enabling professionals to compare care in different settings because it is impossible to compare and share practice if everyone is using different tools.

2.8 Essence of Care

In 2001 the Chief Nursing Officer at the Department of Health launched a benchmarking tool called 'Essence of Care'. This was designed by patients, carers and professionals working together to agree and describe good-quality care. Although it contained useful benchmarks, many practising nurses found it very complex and difficult to use. In 2003 a new, more user-friendly version was launched. This new version comes in a small folder and has a CD-ROM with all documentation on this.

There are now nine benchmarks covering nine areas of care (NHS Modernisation Agency, 2003). Figure 2.3 provides details of these.

1 Communication.
2 Continence.
3 Hygiene.
4 Nutrition.
5 Pressure ulcers.
6 Privacy and dignity.
7 Record-keeping.
8 Safety.
9 Self-care.

Figure 2.3 Essence of care benchmarks

2.9 Who should use clinical benchmarks?

Some nurses working in non-NHS settings may be unaware of Essence of Care; others may have been put off by the first version; and others may consider that they are only relevant to NHS settings. Essence of Care benchmarks are equally relevant in NHS hospitals, rehabilitation centres, care homes, day centres and community settings. They focus exclusively on fundamental care and can enable nurses to develop and share practice. The communication benchmark, for example, has eleven factors or standards. Figure 2.4 illustrates the benchmark and indicators for Factor 1.

Factor 1: Interpersonal skills

Healthcare personnel do not have the necessary interpersonal skills to communicate with patients and/or carers

Benchmark of best practice
All healthcare personnel demonstrate effective interpersonal skills when communicating with patients and/or carers

To communicate effectively, particular attention needs to be paid to the patients' or carers' hearing, vision and other physical and cognitive abilities, as well as to their preferred language and to the possible need for an interpreter.

Indicators of best practice for Factor 1
To stimulate discussion about best practice in your comparison group, you might find it helpful to consider whether:

- all healthcare personnel uphold the principles of common courtesy, especially when faced with challenging questions or working under pressure
- measures are in place to assess and provide feedback on the interpersonal skills of healthcare personnel
- the individual communication needs of patients and/or carers that require specific and/or specialist interpersonal skills are met.

Figure 2.4 The benchmark and indicators for Factor 1

As you can see, this factor is relevant to all healthcare settings.

2.10 How to use clinical benchmarks

Essence of Care described practice development as a series of steps. You may find it more useful to consider practice development as a circular process (see Figure 2.5).

At the first stage you need to decide what aspect of practice you wish to examine. You may decide to examine a particular aspect of practice because there are concerns that practice requires development.

Stage 1
What will you examine?
What is best practice?

Stage 2
Assess practice in your clinical area

Stage 3
Produce and implement action plan

Stage 4
Review achievement. Did it work?

Stage 5
Review action plan if it didn't work. Share practice if it did

Figure 2.5 Using clinical benchmarks to develop practice

CASE STUDY — Benchmarking

Corrine McCullough, a clinical nurse specialist in infection control, was concerned about continence care within her workplace. The 400-bed acute hospital did not employ a continence adviser. She worked with colleagues to benchmark continence care and presented her work to senior nursing staff and to the trust board. As a result of this the trust agreed to fund a continence adviser's post.

You may decide to examine a particular aspect because you now have people in post who have particular skills who can help you develop practice. When you have decided what aspect of care you wish to examine, you need to agree best practice. If you were, for example, examining continence care you might agree that admission records should ask trigger questions to discover any bladder or bowel problems. You might also agree that people with continence problems would have a documented assessment and a care plan with details of continence care.

At the second stage you must decide how you will assess practice in the clinical area. Your assessment strategy might include scrutiny of patient records to check for use of evidence-based guidance. These are process-based assessments and have limitations. If the documentation states that Mrs Jones, at risk of pressure sores, has her position changed two hourly then the organisation is complying with standards. However, auditors may be monitoring a myth. Although the documentation demonstrates compliance, observation of practice can demonstrate that the documentation is largely fictional (Schnelle, 1994). Observation of practice and patient surveys or interviews can overcome such weaknesses and give a more accurate view of practice.

It is important to consider barriers to best practice. Staff knowledge on the prevention of pressure sores might be low because the organisation does not employ a tissue-viability nurse specialist. Documentation might assess risk but the organisation might lack guidance on what should be done when risk has been identified. The organisation might use an inaccurate assessment tool that indicates large numbers of people are at risk, and there might not be enough pressure-relieving equipment or staff time to provide care.

At this stage you can compare and share practice:

- If you work in a hospital you can compare and share practice with another ward that deals with similar patients.
- If you work in a care home that is part of a large group, you can compare with another home.
- If you work in a care home that is not part of a corporate chain, you can network with other homes in your area.

Most organisations find that they excel in certain areas, provide care that is average in others and that there are certain areas where practice is poor. The aim of networking is to share what you have achieved in areas where you excel and learn from others where practice improvement is required. The aim is to make good practice common practice.

2.11 Produce and implement an action plan

Stage three (see Figure 2.5) is a crucial stage in benchmarking. Sometimes nurses are so enthusiastic about planning change that they make a number of errors.

It is important to define the problem accurately. You may find that staff lack skills to promote continence and that older people who are admitted are provided with incontinence pads without any effort being made to find out what the problem is and to seek solutions. It's easy to define the problem as 'Staff lack the skills to promote continence'. If you were to do this your action plan might look like Figure 2.6.

PROBLEM	CHANGE REQUIRED	HOW
Staff lack skills to promote continence	Staff develop fundamental skills in continence care	All staff to have a study day on continence care
	Staff are aware of when to refer to continence adviser	Work-based learning on continence promotion

Figure 2.6 Initial action plan

This action plan is flawed. The goals are not specific, the changes outlined are not measurable and the plan does not build in any way of evaluating the change. There is no timescale and no one is identified as being responsible for the changes. The above plan has been set up to fail.

When you have defined the problem, set your goal. The goal statement can be vague: 'Staff develop fundamental skills in continence care.' It is important to break this goal statement into objectives. Objectives should be written in simple language so that all members of the team understand them. Objectives break the goal statement down into a set of achievements necessary to meet the goal.

Objectives are concrete statements describing what you are trying to achieve. Objectives should be written in a way that enables you to find out if you have achieved these at the end of a specific time. A well written objective will be Specific, Measurable, Attainable/Achievable, Realistic and Time-bound (**SMART**):

● **S**pecific: An objective should address a specific target or accomplishment. Goals must be realistic and attainable by the average nurse.
● **M**easurable: Establish a standard that indicates that an objective has been met. Goals are an important tool in the grand scheme of reaching your philosophy and your organisation's vision. Relevant goals provide staff with direction and have a great impact on performance and morale. Staff know what they are doing, why they are doing it and what impact their activities have.
● **A**ttainable: If an objective cannot be achieved, then it's probably a goal. The best goals require staff to stretch a bit to achieve them, but they aren't extreme. Goals are neither out of reach nor below standard performance. Goals that are set too high or too low become meaningless, and staff may ignore them.
● **R**ealistic: Limit your objectives to what can realistically be done with available resources. If you set unrealistic objectives staff will become demotivated. If you are unable to set a goal because of lack of resources, you may use the results of your work to bid for increased resources.
● **T**ime-bound: Achieve objectives within a specified time frame. Objectives must have starting points, ending points and fixed durations. Commitment to deadlines

helps staff to focus their efforts on the completion of the objective on or before the due date. Objectives without deadlines or schedules for completion tend to be overtaken by the day-to-day crises that invariably arise in an organisation.

The government is increasingly using SMART objectives in its work to modernise health services. If you look at the National Service Framework for Older People you will find that the work required has been broken down into a series of milestones or time-bound objectives. Figure 2.7 is an example checklist for SMART objectives.

Do the objectives describe concrete achievements and outcomes that support the stated goal?	☐
Are your objectives **S**pecific – does your objective specify an achievement?	☐
Measurable – does your objective have a measurable outcome?	☐
Attainable – is it possible to obtain your specified objective?	☐
Realistic – is the proposed objective attainable within the constraints of available resources?	☐

Figure 2.7 A SMART checklist

If you use SMART objectives the action plan becomes more specific, understandable and attainable. Figure 2.8 is an example of such a plan (see page 42).

You now have an action plan that gives you information about where practice is now, where you want it to be, what you have do to achieve what you want and when you have to have it completed by. When you have carried out your action plan you can move on to stage four.

2.12 Reviewing achievement

Stage four is the stage at which you review your achievements towards best practice. You need to check if the changes made have resulted in improved care at the bedside. Have the changes made a difference? It is essential to be honest. People shy away from admitting that planned changes have not improved care. It's worth remembering that not all efforts are successful. Quality is a journey not a destination. Even when you have not succeeded you learn lessons and move forward.

The only people who never fail are those who never try. Some years ago when I managed a nursing home we attempted to introduce a bowel management programme to reduce the use of laxatives and promote normal bowel action. It was a spectacular failure and the team was dispirited. We examined the reasons for this failure (inadequate planning and inadequate consultation with patients and professionals), dusted ourselves down and started again. We introduced a successful

GOAL	OBJECTIVE	MEASUREMENT	TIMESCALE	RESPONSIBILITY	SUPPORT/ RESOURCES
To enable staff to develop fundamental skills in continence care	Nurse admitting patient will record details of continence status	Audit of admitting documentation	By 1st June 2004	Richard Jones, ward manager	Additional training on documentation for all nursing staff ½ study day
	Primary nurse or case manager will ensure that level two continence assessment is carried out if admission details indicate continence problems	Auditing of documentation	By 1st September 2004	Richard Jones, ward manager, Dawn Smith and Peace Odige, ward sisters	One day training on level two continence assessment organised by Cissy Smart, continence adviser. Two sessions ward-based learning for each member of staff
	Every patient with continence problems will have a plan of care to address issues	Auditing of care plans. Observational study	By 1st October 2004	Richard Jones, ward manager, Dawn Smith and Peace Odige, ward sisters & registered nurses responsible for particular patients	Additional training on planning and managing care for all nursing staff ½ study day

Figure 2.8 An extract from an action plan

programme that was widely adopted by other homes and was later incorporated within national guidance on bowel care. If we had not tried, failed, acknowledged and examined our failure we would never have succeeded.

2.13 Sharing success or reviewing the action plan

Stage five requires different actions depending on the outcomes of stage four. If practice has not improved or if it has not improved as much as you planned, it's time to review the action plan. You need to ask why you have not succeeded:

- Were the objectives unrealistic?
- Was the time frame too short?
- Did you choose the right objectives?
- Did you have sufficient support?

It's important to take time and to plan further action if your project has not delivered the required outcomes.

If practice has improved it's time to share this. Colleagues in other parts of the organisation or in other healthcare settings may be grappling and trying to develop ways to improve practice and would welcome your advice and experience. You can share informally by holding a lunchtime briefing for other practitioners. You could make this a celebration and invite a company to sponsor the lunch. If you have succeeded it is because your team have worked hard – celebrate their achievement and thank them for their efforts.

You may decide to write about the triumphs and tears involved in changing practice and to submit this to one of the nursing journals. Nursing journals are always keen to publish articles from practising nurses about practice improvement and will help you to shape an article.

You might even decide to enter the project for one of the nursing awards schemes. *Nursing Standard* and *Nursing Times* both run awards, and details of how to enter are published in the journals.

The next step is to return to the beginning of the cycle and to decide on your next practice improvement project.

2.14 Understanding the patient's perspective

A service that aims to meet the needs of patients can only meet those needs if staff engage with patients and find out what the service is like from the patient's perspective. The service might appear to be meeting patient needs but unless you ask the patient you will never know. There are lots of ways to gain patient views and multiple methods provide a fuller picture. You might like to consider some of the following.

Suggestion boxes

You can put suggestion boxes around the home or ward. Design a card that invites people to write their suggestions or comments about services. Put notices up inviting comments and suggestions and give details of the scheme in admission literature.

CASE STUDY – A suggestion scheme

Laura Edwards, the deputy manager of the Oaks, a 40-bed nursing home, introduced a suggestion scheme. The suggestion card asked: 'What single thing could we do to make life better for you?'

Laura found that the male residents felt neglected. The home had an activities programme that catered predominately for the female residents. There were bingo sessions, knitting, cookery, painting and other activities. There were film shows twice a week, normally showing romances or comedies. The male residents had no interest in these things. The single most important improvement to their quality of life was the availability of Sky Sports so that they could watch Premiership football and live cricket.

The home took out a subscription to Sky Sport and a small lounge was used to enable residents to watch sport.

Subscription to a sports channel was the direct result of a suggestion scheme

Patient interviews

Patient interviews can enable you to understand things from a patent perspective. You can interview a small sample of patients to find out what are the best and worst things about your service. Laura Edwards interviewed male residents of the Oaks to find out what else could be done to improve the activities programme. She found that male residents felt very isolated in the overwhelmingly female environment of the home. Every member of staff (apart from the gardener) was female and 'clueless' about sport. Male residents found that there was no one they could talk to about day-to-day interests such as football. They also found the activities 'boring' and trips to the seaside and a National Trust garden uninteresting.

Laura and her team asked the residents to form a small group to suggest ways to develop different activities. The home introduced trips to the local cricket club to watch cricket, and organised local volunteers to visit and befriend residents.

The problems that Laura uncovered were solved easily and with a minimum of effort. When Ruth Prior interviewed patients she found that her work cut across boundaries. It took two years before all the problems identified were resolved (see case study below).

Ruth discussed her findings with her managers and, with their support, built a multidisciplinary team to resolve the problems identified. The solutions to the problems took over two years to implement fully but improved the assessment process and efficiency in the department. The actions included the following:

- Designated car-parking space close to the outpatients department for orthopaedic patients and others with mobility problems.
- Informing patients of how long the assessment would take.
- Developing a comprehensive assessment that involved nursing, physiotherapy and occupational therapy. Providing patient information.

CASE STUDY – Interviewing patients

When Ruth Prior was appointed as sister in the outpatients department she decided to conduct a series of interviews on patients who visited the department for preoperative assessment. The patients were being assessed before hip and knee surgery. Ruth found that the assessment met the organisation's needs but not the patient's. The problems patients identified were as follows:

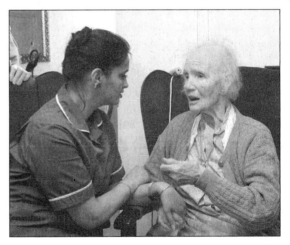

Patient interviews can enable you to understand things from a patient perspective

- They had no idea how long the assessment would take (average 3 hours 20 minutes). They worried that they had not paid for sufficient time in the hospital car park but could not leave to top up the meter.
- The assessment took too long.
- The only professional they were able to ask questions of was a doctor.
- The doctor was rushed.
- The appointment involved a long walk to X-ray.
- There were long waits in X-ray.
- There was no opportunity to talk to a nurse or a physiotherapist.

- Cutting down on time spent in assessment by relocating part of the X-ray department and improving staffing.
- Involvement of community therapists and nursing staff when potential problems were identified.

Reflect on practice

Consider what you currently do to find out how patients perceive your service and how you can improve the service. How can you find out which aspects need improvement?

2.15 Walking and listening

The amount of paperwork nurses are required to complete appears to grow each year. Nurses at ward and home-manager level often have budgetary responsibility, are responsible for recruitment, for writing reports and for many other tasks. When faced with these pressures it's very easy to become isolated and to loose touch with what is happening at the bedside. It's important that you work with the team, deliver care, and are accessible to patients. Learn to delegate some of the paperwork so that you can spend time working with patients, keeping in touch with the day-to-day issues that staff face (Adair, 1988).

2.16 Conclusion

No care setting is perfect – the ways that care is delivered and the people whom you care for are changing. Expectations of care are also changing. The way we deliver care must change if the needs and expectations of older people and their families are to be met. To improve practice means using multiple methods to enable us to work out where our service is now and how it needs to develop in the future. It is important to spend time evaluating aspects of service and planning change before implanting change.

Key Points

○ Practice development is an important part of nursing practice.

○ Professionals and patients may have differing perspectives about the quality of services.

○ You must consult patients if you are to deliver meaningful service improvements.

○ Multiple methods provide a realistic picture of current service quality.

○ Objectives should be SMART.

○ Practice development improves patient satisfaction and staff morale.

References and further reading

Section 2.2

Donabedian, A. (1980) *Explorations in Quality Assessment and Monitoring. Volume One.* Health Administration Press, Ann Arbor, MI.

Donabedian, A. (1986) 'Standards for quality assessment and monitoring', *Quality Research Bulletin*, 12: 99–108.

Donabedian, A. (1994) 'The epidemiology of quality', *Inquiry*, 22: 292.

Section 2.5

Tingle, J. (2002) 'Health professionals keep making the same mistakes', *British Journal of Nursing*, 1: 414.

Webb, B. (1995) 'A study of complaints by patients of different age groups in an NHS trust (research indicates that older patients are twice as likely to complain as younger patients)', *Nursing Standard*, 9: 34–7.

Section 2.7

Warzynski, D. (1996) 'Nursing's quality report card outcomes project', *STAT Bulletin*, July: 30–6.

Section 2.8

Department of Health (2001) *Essence of Care.* Department of Health, London.

NHS Modernisation Agency (2003) *Essence of Care. Patient-focused Benchmarks for Clinical Governance.* London, NHS Modernisation Agency (all tools are downloadable from: **http://www.modern.nhs.uk**).

Section 2.10

Schnelle, J. (1994) 'Quality of care in nursing homes.' Presentation given at a special session on staffing and the quality of care at the annual general meeting of the Gerontological Society of America, Atlanta, Georgia, November.

Section 2.15

Adair, J. (1988) *Effective Leadership.* Pan Books, London.

CHAPTER 3 Moving forward

Introduction

Every nurse who wishes to make a difference and move practice forward needs to develop change management skills. If nurses do not develop the skills required to change practice, time spent identifying areas for improvement is meaningless (see Onion and Walley, 1998).

To become a change agent you must change and develop new skills and the confidence to deal with the barriers to change.

Change is complex and, sometimes, our efforts to fix one problem lead to several other problems developing. There is no perfect formula for managing change: it is, like nursing, part art and part science. In the real world, managing change is not a set of clear-cut stages that people enter and leave at defined intervals. The real world is messy and the unexpected happens. It's not possible to plan for every eventuality. This chapter examines management theory so that you will be able to use it to plan change in real-world settings.

Change requires careful planning because, even with the best of planning and the most sensitive implementation, some people will oppose change and do everything within their power to make you go away so that things can settle down. Change is threatening and people fear it because they fear the loss of the old comforts and certainties. When you ask people to change you are asking them to invest an enormous amount of faith in you and your ideas. What if you are wrong?

You must plan change carefully and ensure that it fits in with the organisation's objectives and culture. Change should make things better, not destroy good parts of an organisation or harm the morale of good people.

Change is not something that you can do alone and, if you try to impose change, even for the best of reasons, you will face resistance. This chapter examines what power is, what types of power there are and how you can use the levers of power to change practice. It explains how you can help and support staff in times of change.

If you are to manage change successfully, you need to cultivate support at all levels of the organisation and to demonstrate that the changes you have helped introduce are effective. This chapter aims to enable you to introduce change effectively and sensitively so that others will wish to adapt to the changes.

Aims

3.1 What is change?

3.2 Planned change

3.3 The theory of change management

3.4 Theory to practice

3.5 Responses to change

3.6 The use of power

3.7 Dealing with barriers to change

3.8 Supporting staff through change

3.9 Conclusion

3.1 What is change?

Change is:

> *Any planned or unplanned alteration in an organisation, situation or process (Lippitt, 1973).*

The world is changing, and the world has changed beyond all recognition in recent times. People adapt to change in every aspect of their lives: sometimes they embrace change; sometimes they accept it reluctantly. The reasons for embracing or resisting change are related to the type of change.

Bennis and colleagues (1976) identified different types of change (see Table 3.1.)

Table 3.1 Types of change

TYPE	FEATURES
Haphazard	Random, unplanned, that's just the way things turned out
Coercive	Imposed change, imposed targets, imposed legislation
Developmental	Change naturally occurs as people, teams or organisations develop
Spontaneous	Occurs in response to uncontrollable events
Planned	Intentional, thought-out process with equal power distribution between participants

Our willingness to embrace change often depends on the type of change introduced and the way it is introduced.

Reflect on practice •

Consider a coercive change that has been introduced in your workplace. Why was the change introduced? Who was responsible for the change? How was the change received? Could this change have been introduced in a planned way?

3.2 Planned change

Many aspects of change are outside our control. Sometimes change just happens. Sometimes change is imposed on organisations and teams. There are often political reasons for coercive change: the government of the day may wish to be seen to be doing something about a problem identified in the media or of concern to voters. The Care Standards Act is an example of imposed change. You may not believe that some of the issues identified improve quality of care but if the care home is to remain registered it must meet these standards. Government targets, such as a maximum of four hours waiting in accident and emergency departments, are another example of imposed change.

Developmental change occurs as individuals, teams and organisations develop. Many new nursing roles, such as that of nurse practitioners or nurse consultants, are the results of developmental change within the nursing profession.

Spontaneous changes are the result of unpredicted, unplanned events. For example, an event such as an older person with dementia leaving a ward might lead a trust to improve its security and change its Missing Person's Policy.

The only change that you have any control over is planned change. This is defined as:

> *An intended, designed or purposive attempt by an individual, group, organisation or social system to influence directly the status quo of itself or another organisation (Lippitt, 1973).*

Planned change is not often welcomed with open arms because it implies that current practice is not good enough. People are often comfortable with the status quo, even if the system is not perfect – at least everyone knows what it is and where he or she stands. Change is uncomfortable and the first rule in planning change is not to make things worse than they already are. If you examine the theories of change management you can begin to understand what processes are involved in successful change.

3.3 The theory of change management

Change management theory was first described by Lewin over 50 years ago. Lewin (1951) described three steps in the change process:

1 Unfreezing.
2 Moving to a new level.
3 Refreezing.

Unfreezing is the term Lewin used to describe the recognition that all is not perfect, that there may be problems in the old way of doing things and that there may be better ways to practise. This may be a time of considerable stress. It is not easy for caring staff to recognise that they provide care that is less than the best possible. Staff may feel threatened and undervalued. They may feel that examining the need for change denigrates their work and themselves.

Inexperienced change managers can increase stress and cause fear and uncertainty if they use threats or coercion to force staff to examine practice. The aim of change management is to enable people to see the reasons why change might be needed, not to cause fear and uncertainty.

Moving to a new level is the second phase of change. Participants look at old problems with fresh eyes and begin to diagnose problems and develop a range of possible solutions. At this stage participants gather information, discuss and discard options, develop and refine strategies and begin to change practice.

Refreezing is the term Lewin uses to describe the final stage. The new behaviours and ways of working are fully integrated into day-to-day practice.

Rodgers (1962) built on Lewin's theory of change management. Rodgers identified additional factors influencing change. These were the people participating in the change and the environment in which the change takes place. Figure 3.1 illustrates Rodger's theory of change.

Figure 3.1 Rodger's theory of change

Rodgers believed that participants in the change process could initially accept or reject the proposed change. Participants who initially adopted the change could later reject it. People who had initially rejected the change could later adopt it. Rodgers considered that the effectiveness of change depended on whether participants were keenly interested and were committed to working towards it.

Rodgers and Shoemaker (1973) built on this work. They identified five factors essential for the successful implementation of planned change:

1 relative advantage
2 compatibility
3 complexity
4 trialability
5 observability.

Relative advantage

This describes how much better the new way of doing things will be over the old way. Sometimes the new way is more efficient, and commercial firms may be attracted to measures that give them cost-saving advantages. In healthcare, relative advantage may be judged differently. Participants may judge the advantage of the new idea in terms of treating patients more quickly or more effectively. Change managers who are keen to introduce changes must be careful not to overstate relative advantage because participants can then develop unrealistic expectations that cannot be fulfilled.

Compatibility

This describes how the proposed change fits with the organisation's values, habits, expectations and past experience of the participants. A proposed change that fits well with the values, ways of working and expectations of participants will be viewed as less threatening and more acceptable. A proposed change that does not fit well with the participants may be rejected. It may be adopted if participants can be encouraged to adopt a new set of values and attitudes, but this will take much longer. Sometimes ideas from other countries (such as the United States, where there are different value systems and there is no national health service) may be rejected because they do not fit with healthcare or general culture.

Complexity

This described how difficult the change is to understand and use. If you are introducing a very complex change that participants may have difficulty understanding or using, they are likely to reject this. Participants may find it difficult to admit that they do not understand what is required or what the likely benefits of such change are. One of the challenges of change management is to convey changes in simple ways so that they can be easily understood and adopted by participants.

Trialability

This describes the way a new idea can be trialled. If you wish to change patient documentation or shift patterns, is it possible to conduct a small trial? Trials reduce the risk of failure. If you are trialling new documentation participants may feel more able to point out pitfalls and omissions. If a change is presented complete then participants are less likely to point out pitfalls. Trials enable you to refine ideas and correct omissions before the large-scale implementation of change. Trials also make certain groups of participating staff feel special, and they often act as ambassadors for the change.

Observability

This describes how visible the benefits of the change are to participants and to onlookers:

- Did the introduction of new documentation reduce the time nurses spend on paperwork?
- Can those using the documentation and others see the benefits?
- Do nurses now have more time to spend with patients?
- Have patients and their families noticed?

The easier is it for participants and observers to see the results of the change, the more likely it is that others will adopt this change.

Reflect on practice

Can you think of a change that was trialled and readily adopted because the benefits of this change were so clear to everyone involved? What lessons can you learn from this? Was the change clearly planned? Were the benefits explained? Who was most enthusiastic about the change: the person who thought of it or those who adopted it?

Nurses are used to identifying problems and working with others to seek solutions

Lippitt (1973) states that no one can escape change but that the key question is: 'How do people handle change?' Lippitt states that the key to handling change is to develop a carefully thought-out strategy for intervention, identifying seven stages:

1 Diagnosis of the problem.
2 Assessment of motivation and capacity for change.
3 Assessment of the change manager's motivation and resources.
4 Selection of progressive change objectives.
5 Choosing the appropriate change manager role.
6 Maintenance of the change.
7 Termination of the helping role.

Lippitt's theory fits well with nursing practice. Nurses are used to identifying problems and working with others to seek solutions. Let's examine Lippitt's theory in more detail.

Diagnosis of the problem

If you are to diagnose a problem accurately you need to keep an open mind. It's important to look at all the detail and avoid jumping to conclusions. Sometimes you think you know what the problem is before you fully examine it. If you use a blinkered approach you can misdiagnose the problem and any efforts to solve it will be doomed to failure.

I investigated what the most important factor was in providing enabling care in nursing homes. I thought that it would be the educational levels of nurses and staffing levels but found that it was the leadership of the matron/manager that made the greatest difference (Nazarko, 1997). My findings suggest that if a home wished to improve the quality of care it should invest in leadership training for matron/managers.

If you wish to move practice forward it is important to involve everyone who will be involved later on in the process in diagnosing the problem. The level of involvement will vary at this stage. Some staff may be involved in benchmarking whilst others are informed that this is taking place. Involve key people within your organisation who have the power and influence to support you in the future at this stage.

The more information you can gather at this stage the more likely it is that you will accurately diagnose the problem.

Assessment of the motivation and capacity for change

Change is uncomfortable. It requires people to examine practice critically and to make efforts to change. At this point the change agent needs honestly to assess the people involved in the change process and the environment in which the change will take place. You can assess the people involved using a chart such as the one shown in Figure 3.2.

NAME	CAN DO/WILL DO	WILL DO/ CAN'T DO	CAN DO/ WON'T DO	CAN'T DO/ WON'T DO

Figure 3.2 Assessment of individual capacity for change

This chart gives you some indication of what work needs to be done with individuals to enable or persuade them to adopt the change. Some people may need education, training and support to help move practice forward. You may have to work with others to find out their objections and to work to overcome these. You may find that some people will not engage in the change process.

The change agent also needs to assess the organisation's capacity for change:

● What are the organisation's rules and policies?
● Does the change fit in with these?
● Will the organisation's policies and values support or hinder the change?
● What resources are required?
● Have you informed and do you have the support of senior managers for the change?

You may find it helpful to list the possible problems and to identify possible solutions to these problems. You can then draw up a list of the potential costs and benefits of each solution.

Assessment of the change manager's motivation and resources

This stage requires change managers to be honest and self-critical:

● How are you viewed within the organisation?
● Are you considered to be a radical or a maverick?

- Are you respected and trusted?
- Do you have colleagues and senior members of staff who will support you in your efforts to change?

The level of support you can command may depend on whether others share your view that there are problems to be solved. Sometimes others share your views but not your priorities. The organisation may have more pressing matters to attend to so, although you may be supported, the level of support may not be what you would wish:

- How do others view the proposed change?
- Are certain sections of the workforce unsupportive, sceptical or openly opposing the proposed changes?

If you have developed a team to introduce changes it is important that you are speaking as one and giving the same messages and working in the same way.

Selection of progressive change objectives

This is the planning stage of change. If at all possible you should begin with a small trial. This will enable you to concentrate on one small area, to work with others to identify and to iron out any problems. When the trial is completed you must spend time carefully and critically evaluating the benefits of the change. (Sometimes changes have unexpected benefits as well as unexpected problems.) You can then refine the proposed change before introducing it more widely.

Sometimes if the initial project was constrained by lack of resources but you can demonstrate benefits, senior people in the organisation can make additional resources available. Senior staff have to make a case for resources and a well planned, executed and evaluated trial can make it easier for them to help you improve practice.

Choosing the appropriate change manager role

Change managers come in many forms and have many roles. The change manager may be an expert practitioner who teaches and motivates staff. The change manager may gather information and work with staff to develop solutions. He or she may help staff to find information, diagnose problems and find their own solutions. Successful change management requires change managers who are clear about what their role is in improving practice. This enables staff to work out what their roles are in the change management process. If everyone is clear about roles there is less risk of misunderstanding and improved communication.

Maintenance of the change

Beginnings are tender things and should be nurtured carefully. Participants may begin the change process full of enthusiasm but this may fade and the old ways of doing things may re-emerge. The change manager needs to monitor change, to nurture staff and to remind them of how far they have come and how much they have achieved. Do not forget to keep managers informed about progress.

When practice development is established it is time to share practice with others in the organisation. The people who have participated in the change process have gained expertise and can help others who wish to introduce change to do so.

Termination of the helping role

This is the final stage in the process. The change manager slowly withdraws from the situation, leaving participants to continue to maintain the developments introduced. The change manager is usually available if staff require advice but is no longer actively involved in the change process.

Reflect on practice

Can you think of two recent examples when you were asked to change practice within your workplace? Were you involved in all aspects of the change process? Was the change planned well? How could it have been improved?

3.4 Theory to practice

Theories and techniques on how to change organisations abound. These theories are based on the successes and failures of individuals who introduced change in a particular organisation at a particular time with a certain set of people. The assumption is that others can learn from the triumphs and tribulations of these people. This assumption is flawed because change never repeats itself in the same way. It is related to its time, the people experiencing it and the culture of the organisation. There are no magic formulae for introducing change. So how can you move from theory to practice?

The theory outlined in this chapter provides a framework to enable you to manage change. In the real world change is not a clean, clear linear process – life gets in the way. The messages from the theory are as follows:

- Diagnose the problem as accurately as you can. Sometimes the problem you see is only one symptom of a bigger problem.
- Involve participants in all aspects of the change process.
- Ask if this is the right change for this organisation.
- Ask if it is the right time to introduce this change – timing is important. Sometimes the right idea is rejected because the organisation is not yet ready to embrace it.
- Plan and prepare for the change but be flexible: things have a way of turning out differently from how you planned them.

The only way to become good at managing change is to begin to change practice. No one can teach you how to do this – it's something that you can only learn from experience. It is important that you acknowledge that introducing change is a learning process for you, your colleagues and the organisation. You do not have all the answers, you will make mistakes and you will rely on colleagues to help you make successful change.

Be humble and be knowledgeable enough to know that you do not know all there is to know about this change. Be open to suggestions; the true test of having the support of your colleagues is when they point out shortcomings in the change and make suggestions to enable you to succeed as a team. If you give the impression that the change is cut and dried and not open to suggestion, you will alienate those who are willing and able to support you in moving forward.

If you are open and people point out shortcomings, others will be quick to defend you, saying: 'Well, she said it's not perfect, we're developing it. How do you suggest we get over this problem?'

Change is unpredictable and sometimes well intentioned actions lead to unforeseen and unwelcome changes (Harris et al., 1999). Sometimes when people wish to introduce change they become very emotionally attached to the change – the innovation is 'their baby' and is defended even when it is clear that things are not going as planned. As in parenthood it becomes easier to share your baby second time round: you're more relaxed and realise that others won't damage your baby – they may even be more experienced than you and can help you through difficult times.

3.5 Responses to change

People are creatures of habit. People take the same route to work each day, shop on the same day each week, use the same supermarket because they can find their way around it easily. There's a comfort and security in old habits. When 'they' move the milk or the eggs in the supermarket we get annoyed because it disrupts our routine and is inconvenient.

When you initiate change it's different. If I rearrange the furniture in the bedroom I am happy with the change but my husband grumbles: 'Why did you have to change things? I liked them the way they were?' I expect him to be aware of the advantages of moving things. My husband will settle down and quietly accept the changes – as a wife I can get away with such things but as a change agent in the workplace my actions would be unacceptable. The power dynamics within my home and my workplace are different.

Power can be defined as 'the capacity to produce or prevent change' (Sullivan and Decker, 1997). People often think of power as a given: you either have power or you do not. Power is much more complex than this. Power is a relationship that is exercised in a particular context (Foucault, 1972). The power that you are able to exercise varies in different settings. As a nurse consultant I can ask a ward manager to ensure that a patient's observations are checked four hourly and to let me know if a pyrexia does not resolve. I know that this will be done. As a mother I can ask my 16-year-old daughter to tidy her room. There is little prospect that this will be done.

Power is the strongest possible method of influence – when you use power you will affect others. The use of power can enable you to improve practice but it is important to use the appropriate source of power and to use it wisely and well. Let's look at the different types of power and how they can be used and misused (Benton, 2000).

Legitimate power

This is the power that comes with a particular position. It is often known as role power – the power that you use comes from the role that you occupy. There are limits to this power, and these limits are described in the person's job description and are usually clear in the way people work on a day-to-day basis:

- A ward sister or care home manager may have the power to work within an agreed budget or to order items up to a certain limit but may have to refer more expensive items to a more senior manager.
- You may have the power to ask someone to do something because the person is more junior to you.
- The staff nurse can use position power in requesting that the healthcare assistant does something.

The power comes with the particular role.

Position power must be used wisely. People will do things because the sister, matron or head of care has asked them to, but if they are fully engaged in the process they will give more than if they are required to do something.

Reward power

This is also known as resource power. This is the power to reward people or to withhold rewards. This covers a huge range of issues from thanking someone and complimenting him or her on a job well done to appraising salaries or deciding if someone is ready for promotion.

Coercive power

This is the power to order that things be done. It goes hand in hand with the power to punish people who do not comply. Coercive power is ultimately destructive. It prevents people from sharing good ideas. It prevents people from being open and honest. It prevents people from abandoning things that are not working. Coercive power teaches people how to avoid punishment. It can generate great resentment and a negative backlash.

Expert power

Expert power is the power that comes from having knowledge and expertise in a particular area. Experts have highly developed knowledge of their area. Expert power must be acknowledged if it is to function properly. If someone says he or she is an expert he or she will not gain expert power. If staff believe that a person has expertise in a particular area then the person will have expert power.

Information power

Information is an important source of power. This information may be about government policy, organisational policy or debates raging within government or the organisation. Such information can give you leverage to introduce practice changes. If, for example, government policy requires self-administration of medicines and the organisation has received a number of complaints regarding administration of medicines, this information is useful to you if you wish to develop practice in this area.

Information about the people involved in the change process is also important. If you find out that one of the staff nurses who is reluctant to change worked with your predecessor to introduce change but was unsupported, you may be able to work out ways to help her become involved in this change. Information power enables you to have your finger on the pulse of the organisation and to tailor practice development so that you will receive support.

Connections

This is the power that comes from having a wide network. Connection power enables you to tap into your network and learn how practice is developing in other parts of the UK or even internationally. Networks can support the change agent: they help you share good practice and help you avoid the pitfalls that others have encountered. Networking is about sharing, supporting, influencing and being influenced.

Personal power

Some people have the ability to light up a room. Some people draw others to them and staff will follow such people to the ends of the earth. This power is sometimes known as charisma or personal magnetism. People often think that those with personal power were born with it and were born to lead. This is seldom the case. Personal power is usually earned because of the person's actions, thoughts and deeds. Personal power is based on respect and trust. People chose to be led by a person with this power because they believe that the person knows what to do and will do what is right.

3.6 The use of power

Power is a subtle thing. It is a two-way process. It cannot be used unless those who it is to be used on acknowledge it and are willing to behave accordingly. Power can be abused. The person with reward power can use it unjustly to promote favourites. The person's power is then perceived by others to be tainted and diminished because the person has lost the respect of the team. The team may in the future be less ready to acknowledge the person's power.

In some cases the use of power can unleash negative power. If power is the means to make things happen, negative power is the means to prevent things happening. A person might call a meeting to discuss changes but everyone might be unavailable. The person might suggest a change but everyone might object. People might agree to implement a change but nothing happens. If the person protests, staff might ask for clarification or say that they have lost the forms on which information is to be recorded.

Staff may feel so strongly about the unfairness of a change that they leave or ask someone more senior to intervene. A recent report in *Nursing Times* illustrates such a situation (O'Dowd, 2003).

CASE STUDY – Negative power

Lothian University Hospital employs 5,000 staff. Staff are entitled to apply for a car-parking permit. This costs £250 a year. Permits are awarded on a points system that takes into account where people live, public transport and childcare responsibilities. Only 1,500 staff have been awarded parking permits. Staff who do not have parking permits must pay £10 for six hours' parking.

On one level this is about resource power: more than three quarters of staff who work at the hospital are unable to obtain parking permits. Staff are also concerned that the charge for parking permits has doubled and is higher than at other local hospitals. This is perceived as unfair.

Staff have used their negative power to oppose the change by:

- Complaining to their trade unions.
- Complaining to the press.
- Complaining to the Scottish Health Minister.
- Leaving their posts and going to work in another hospital.

The report in *Nursing Times* suggests that staff may be successful in changing practice as the Scottish Executive are reviewing guidance on car-parking charges.

Negative power is more likely to be used if people feel that they are being treated unfairly or have not been adequately consulted about change.

Can you think of a situation when staff used their negative power to block change? Why was the change blocked? Why did staff feel so strongly that they used their power to prevent things from happening? What lessons can you learn from this?

3.7 Dealing with barriers to change

When you ask people to change you're asking them to take a leap of faith. Iacovini (1993) describes this as follows:

> *For many the experience is like standing at the end of a chasm and being challenged to jump to the other side – with nothing in-between but fog.*

If you understand the root of possible resistance to change, you can plan for it and overcome it before it becomes a significant obstacle. There are a number of reasons why people opposes change. Let's examine these in detail.

Self-interest

Sometimes the status quo serves a particular individual well. The person may have status and gain self-esteem though that status. The proposed change may threaten the person's status and self-esteem.

CASE STUDY – Self-interest

Jo Malone is the registered manager of the Cedars. She has worked for the company for 12 years. Jo works 50 hours a week and comes into the Cedars on her days off to check that everything is okay. Staff are required to consult Jo about every aspect of care in the Cedars.

Marion Davies, the newly appointed regional manager for the Evergreen group of care homes, is aware that things will have to change at the Cedars. Staff turnover is high and registered nurses do not feel that they are able to practise autonomously. They are required to consult Jo about every aspect of practice.

The company has decided to encourage staff to develop their practice by making the sisters at the Cedars responsible for a particular floor of the home. The sisters will lead a team of registered nurses who will be responsible for planning and managing the care of a particular group of patients.

Jo is violently opposed to this change and runs Marion, the change manager, down to everyone who enters the home. She questions her expertise, encourages staff to disregard Marion's requests and does everything that she can to undermine Marion. She tells Marion that she has seen regional managers come and go over the years but that she remains the home manager.

The home is Jo's life, and the changes signal a loss of the old certainties and the possible loss of her power and status within the home. Jo needs the home to need her as much as she needs it. Empowering the sisters, Jo fears, will lead to her becoming less needed in the home.

Reflect on practice

What levers of power would you use to encourage Jo to work with you? How might Jo use negative power to oppose the changes? How could you have planned change to encourage Jo to embrace the change?

Fear of the unknown

Change is frightening, and some people fear change more than others. Some people may be fearful of change because of past experience. The person may have been unsupported during change and worried about his or her ability to take on new roles and responsibilities. Education and support can help people to overcome their fear of change and to work with you.

Differing perceptions

Some people may believe that you are doing the wrong thing. A person may feel that you have misdiagnosed a problem or overstated an issue or have chosen an inappropriate solution. It is important to listen to this person: he or she may have a point – he or she may see things that you do not see or see them in different ways. Respect this person, listen to his or her views and form your own conclusions. If you are not able to agree with the person explain that, although you disagree, you respect his or her opinion.

Suspicion

Some people may not trust you or trust your motives. They may feel that you have a 'hidden agenda' and that the real reason for the proposed change is not the one that you have stated.

Conservatism

Sometimes people may oppose change because they have been in post for a long time and are unaware of how other organisations are changing. The person may feel that there is no need for change or that you have yet to prove your case. If people have been in post for a long time and have become isolated from the mainstream, attending conferences or visiting other organisations that have successfully introduced similar changes may help the person to feel more comfortable about changing practice.

3.8 Supporting staff through change

When you introduce change you can, if you're not careful, denigrate the achievements of staff. Staff can feel that in asking them to change you're finding them wanting and saying that they and their work are not good enough. It's important that staff realise that change is a sign of strength not weakness. Change involves putting aside the old certainties and stepping out into the unknown. This is a time of uncertainty and loss. It is natural for people to resist loss.

People don't resist change – they resist loss: loss of security, competence, territory, power or direction. There are four essential things you can do to help colleagues through a period of change:

1   Tell people the truth.
2   Involve everyone in planning.
3   Explain 'why' and instil a sense of urgency.
4   Break it into steps.

Change is all around us in organisations – whether planned or unplanned, voluntary or involuntary. In this context of change, many people feel lost and seem to resist the changing reality around them.

To overcome this resistance, be truthful and share as much information about the change as you can. Explain why change is happening. Help establish a need for, even an urgency for, change. People are more apt to participate in a change effort if the pain of change is less than the pain of maintaining things as they are.

Identify people who can help champion the change. Get your team involved in affecting change by involving them in the planning of the change and design of new processes and procedures that affect them.

People often are overwhelmed by large-scale change, so break down a large initiative into smaller, more manageable steps. Create the possibility of small wins. This can

Explain why change is happening

help avoid the common situation when staff are engaged with the idea of change but lose momentum when change appears to take hold slowly. Breaking down the change initiative into small steps helps signal progress too. Emphasise that not everything is changing; some things are staying the same. This will help people to anchor the change into stable, secure parts of their working lives.

Keep in mind that people with certain behaviour styles are more resistant or fearful of change than others. When introducing change in your team, keep an eye out for those who are concerned about the change, and try to get them involved in shaping the new reality as much as possible.

Most people journey through stages of change – denial, resistance, exploration and commitment – and there are particular signs you can watch for as you help your team embrace the changes taking place. Figure 3.3 outlines these.

Signs of denial	**How to help**
• Expressions of anger, fear, sadness • Extreme scepticism: 'I'll believe it when I see it' • Oversimplification of the change required: 'This will be easy' • Focus on how good things used to be • Withdrawal from the team	• Provide people with information about the need for change • Explain what to expect and things they can do • Give them the time to let the reality of the change sink in, then meet to talk things over
Signs of resistance	**Avoid letting resistance derail the change by**
• Expressions of blame, anxiety, anger, depression, loss • Accusations about the organisation's intentions: 'This organisation doesn't care about staff' • Refusal to engage in new ways: 'They can't make me do it' • Negative attitudes about the potential for change: 'This will never work'	• Listening to, and acknowledging, the feelings about the changes taking place • Not trying to talk people out of their feelings or telling them to change • Keeping talking so they'll tell you how they are feeling; get feelings out • Providing information and being patient
The signs that people have moved out of denial and resistance into the exploration stage	**Harness and lever the renewed energy by**
• Attention shifts to the future • Lots of energy but lack of focus: 'Let's try this...' • Over-preparation, confusion, chaos • Buy in to the new way of doing things: 'This isn't so bad...'	• Focusing on setting priorities and planning simple steps for success and training • Praising and supporting leaders • Holding brainstorming, visioning and planning sessions

Signs that change is being committed to, accepted and embraced include	To help build on the team's commitment:
<ul><li>Better teamwork, focus and co-operation</li><li>Positive energy</li><li>Focus on the future</li></ul>	<ul><li>Set longer-term goals, beyond six months</li><li>Concentrate on team-building</li><li>Celebrate success</li><li>Recognise and acknowledge those who have changed. Tell them that you are aware of how much effort they have put into the change</li><li>Learn from experience by reflecting on what worked well and what could have been improved</li></ul>

Figure 3.3 The diagnosis and treatment of barriers to change

Be patient; any idiot can force through rapid change if he or she is unconcerned for the people involved or the costs of that change. If you wish to introduce incremental, lasting change that builds and continues to improve practice, you have to be patient and sensitive to people's hopes and fears.

3.9 Conclusion

Successful change management requires careful planning. It also requires the knowledge that things do not always work to plan. Change management requires expertise, but you cannot gain expertise in change management unless you introduce changes. The way forward is to plan what you can, gain support for the changes, trial new ideas and be receptive to the ideas of others. Flexibility is one of the most important features of successful change management.

Key Points

○ Management theory teaches that change is complex.

○ Change requires careful planning.

○ Proposed changes should fit with the organisation's objectives.

○ Changes should fit with the culture of the organisation.

○ Change managers cannot do it alone – cultivate support at all levels of the organisation.

○ Be pleasant and respect colleagues at all times.

○ Share the change and encourage and enable others to contribute to the change.

References and further reading

INTRODUCTION

Onion, W.R. and Walley, T. (1998) 'Clinical guidelines: ways ahead', *Journal of Evaluation in Clinical Practice*, 4: 287–93.

SECTION 3.1

Bennis, W.G., Benne, K.D. and Korey, K.E. (1976) *The Planning of Change*. Holt, Rinehart & Winston, New York.

Lippitt, G. (1973) *Visualising Change: Model Building in the Change Process*. University Associates, La Jolla, CA.

SECTION 3.2

Lippitt, G. (1973) *Visualising Change: Model Building in the Change Process*. University Associates, La Jolla, CA.

SECTION 3.3

Lewin, K. (1951) *Field Theory in Social Science*. Harper & Row, New York.

Lippitt, G. (1973) *Visualising Change: Model Building in the Change Process*. University Associates, La Jolla, CA.

Nazarko, L. (1997) 'Quality of care in UK nursing homes.' MSc dissertation, South Bank University, London, unpublished.

Rodgers, E. (1962) *Diffusion of Innovations*. Free Press of Glencoe, New York.

Rodgers, E. and Shoemaker, F. (1973) *Communication of Innovations*. Free Press of Glencoe, New York.

SECTION 3.4

Harris, J., Gordon, P., Plamping, D. and Fischer, M. (1999) *Elephant Problems and Fixes that Fail*. King's Fund, London.

SECTION 3.5

Benton, D. (2000) 'Assertiveness, power and influence', *Learning Disability Practice*, 3: 32–6.

Foucault, M. (1972) *The Archaeology of Knowledge*. Tavistock, London.

Sullivan, E.J. and Decker, P.J. (1997) *Effective Leadership and Management in Nursing*. Addison-Wesley, Menlo Park, CA.

SECTION 3.6

O'Dowd, A. (2003) 'Parking charges cause nurses to quit', *Nursing Times*, 99: 8.

SECTION 3.7

Iacovini, J. (1993) 'The human side of organisational change', *Training and Development*, January: 65–8.

CHAPTER 4

Underpinning structures: risk management

Introduction

Hospitals and care homes are dangerous places for older people. Older people are especially vulnerable to the risks of adverse incidents. The older person who might have impaired vision or an unsteady gait is more at risk of falling than a younger person. If an older person falls, he or she has a greater chance of fracturing a bone than a younger person. The older person is at risk of becoming 'deconditioned' and loosing ability, not because of illness but because of nursing and medical practice. The older person is also at risk of developing problems because of the risks of the treatment provided.

Every person who receives healthcare has the right to expect that the organisation providing healthcare will do everything possible to reduce the risks of poor outcomes. The person who is admitted because of a chest infection may be immobile and at risk of pressure sores, but the organisation and the people in the organisation delivering care should do everything possible to minimise the risks of pressure sores and other harm. This chapter explains your legal obligations and what we can learn from reports on adverse incidents. It aims to enable you to understand the risks of healthcare.

Hospitals and care homes delivering healthcare are required to have risk management policies. The organisation that you work for will have policies and procedures on assessing risk and reducing risks. These policies and procedures are worthless pieces of paper unless nurses at the bedside who deliver care make risk assessment a reality for patients. This chapter aims to enable you to use risk assessment in day-to-day practice and to enhance the quality of care you deliver by assessing and minimising risk.

The key purpose of healthcare is to enhance health but it is increasingly evident that aspects of healthcare services are detrimental and even dangerous to those who use them (Milligan and Bird, 2003). Treatment errors account for 98,000 deaths a year in the USA (Kohn, 2000). More people die as a result of medical error than of breast cancer, road traffic accidents, HIV and AIDS (Woods, 2000). This estimate does not include people treated in the community.

The report, *An Organisation with a Memory* (Department of Health, 2000), acknowledges that adverse events occur in around 10 per cent of admissions and that service failures can have serious consequences for individual patients. This report breaks new ground in that it proposes not merely that individuals are held to account for their actions but also that organisations should put in place systems that reduce the likelihood of service failures. The report states that the NHS has a body of knowledge relating to adverse incidents in secondary (hospital) care but lacks detailed information about primary care where greater numbers of patients are treated. It proposes that the strategies outlined in the report are adopted by primary trusts but omits to mention the independent sector. Research (Nazarko, 2002) suggests that the percentage of adverse events is 'markedly higher' in older people and that 'many injuries are the result of substandard care'.

Healthcare is also hazardous to those who deliver care. The healthcare sector has high rates of ill health. In 2001–2, 199,000 staff believed that their illness was caused by their work or made worse by it. Healthcare workers have the highest rates of mental illness, spine and back problems, dermatitis and infections than any other sector (Health and Safety Executive, 2002).

Organisations have a legal duty to assess risk and to reduce those risks whenever possible. In practice, many organisations introduce policies, but the responsibility for assessing and managing risk on a day-to-day basis rests with nurses at the bedside. Sometimes busy nurses are not always aware of the importance of managing risk. It might seem like just one more thing to be done. Risk management is an important issue and is ultimately about providing an environment that is as safe as possible, as well as about enhancing the quality of care.

Aims

4.1 What is risk?

Risk has been defined as:

- 'The possibility of incurring misfortune or loss.'
- 'To be exposed to danger or loss.'
- 'To be vulnerable.'

Life is full of risks. You take risks every time you get out of bed, every time you step in the car, every time you cross the road. If you decide to cower under the duvet, you merely exchange one set of risks for another. You can't avoid risks entirely but what you can do is reduce the probability that major problems will occur. In order to do that you need information. Decisions are only as good as the information on which they are based.

4.2 Why identify and classify risk?

Ward managers, managers of registered homes and nurses in charge of a shift in hospitals and care homes must be able to identify and manage risk. There are three reasons why nurses must manage risk. These are to protect patients, to protect staff and to manage well. In 1998 the UKCC stated:

> *The ultimate aim of risk management is the promotion of quality.*

In 2002, 249 people were killed in workplace accidents, 27,477 people suffered major injury and 127,084 suffered an injury that kept them off work for more than three days (Health and Safety Executive, 2002).

Whilst everyone would agree that life is about risk and without risks life would be dull and impoverished (Counsel and Care, 1993), it's clear that risk must be managed. Life is about responsible risk-taking and about weighing up costs and benefits. If professionals are to manage risk they must be able to identify it and measure it. If you can't measure something then you can't manage it.

4.3 Can you manage risk?

It's important to recognise that no ward or care home can ever hope to offer a totally safe environment (Counsel and Care, 1992). No ward or care home should be expected to offer a totally safe environment. Instead, the organisation should develop policies that identify potential risks and work with older people, families and staff to determine the acceptable level of risk.

No organisation can ever hope to offer staff a totally safe environment. Organisations cannot ever eliminate the chance combination of circumstances that lead to an accident. People with responsibility for health and safety have to strike a balance between offering an enabling environment and a safe environment. In order to do this managers and staff must develop policies that identify potential risks and work together to determine acceptable levels of risk.

4.4 Hazards

A hazard is the potential to cause harm or damage:

> *Hazard identification is the systematic consideration of all the equipment, processes, activities etc associated with your work and that of others in the home, that may cause anyone personal injury or ill health or that may cause damage to property (Tullett, 1996).*

Hazards can potentially harm older people, staff, relatives and other visitors. Organisations often have policies stating that the organisation will carry out risk assessments but, if you read these policies carefully, most will require individual managers of wards and care homes to carry out these assessments. If you are the manager of a ward or care home you are probably responsible for identifying risk, working out how important these risks are and taking appropriate action. If you are a registered nurse working in a ward or care home you may be required to help with formal risk assessments. You will certainly be responsible for identifying risks that you come across in your day-to-day work and helping others to reduce the risks.

If you work in an acute NHS trust, a primary care trust or are part of a nursing home group, your organisation will employ one or more people as risk managers. You should ask for help in learning how to identify and manage risk. Some organisations will run study days on this. If you work in a care home that is not part of a large group and feel that you require further training, you should ask for this as part of your professional development.

It is important that you are able to identify hazards that older people may face when they have been admitted. Table 4.1 gives details of some possible hazards that older people may face.

Table 4.1 Some potential hazards to older people

HAZARD	CAUSE	CONSEQUENCE
Abuse	Staff, relatives, other patients or residents	Physical and psychological harm
Alteration in room layout	Staff, relatives, other patients or residents	Physical and psychological harm
Changes in floor level	Design of ward or care home	Falls, injury
Chemicals left out	Staff	Skin damage, ingestion
Fire	Equipment, staff, other patients or residents, relatives	Physical and psychological harm
Floors strewn with obstacles	Staff, other patients or residents, relatives	Falls, loss of mobility

HAZARD	CAUSE	CONSEQUENCE
Hot water, exposed piping, radiators	Design, management	Injury or death
Inappropriate care	Staff, relatives	Loss of independence, neglect
Inadequate, absent lights	Poor maintenance, design	Falls, injury
Manual-handling techniques	Staff, relatives	Falls, dislocations, injury
Medication	Staff, GPs, relatives	Adverse reactions, illness
Poorly maintained furniture	Staff, management	Falls, injuries
Poorly maintained equipment, e.g. wheelchairs with flat tyres, broken brakes	Staff, management, outside agencies	Falls, injuries
Stairs	Design, management	Falls, injuries
Wet floors	Staff, other patients or residents, relatives	Falls, injuries

As you can see from Table 4.1, older people are at risk not only from staff practice but also from the actions and inactions of other patients or residents and relatives. One older person may wet on the toilet floor exposing others to the risk of falls or injuries. A relative may bring in medication for her mother's pain and give it, exposing the older person to many risks.

Reflect on practice

Check how many accidents involving residents or patients there have been in your workplace over the last three months. What percentage of these have been falls? Are there any common themes in the accidents? Have you identified any hazards and taken action to deal with these?

Health and safety in the workplace must be a team effort

The workplace is also hazardous to staff. Table 4.2 (see page 74) outlines some of the risks staff are exposed to in the workplace.

As you can see from these tables, if a care environment isn't safe for staff, it isn't safe for patients. Patients can be put at risk by other patients as well as staff. Staff can be put at risk by thoughtless or overworked colleagues who fail to report hazards. Staff can be put at risk by managers who fail to take health and safety seriously. Managers can be placed in impossible situations by staff who think health and safety is solely a management responsibility. Health and safety in the workplace must be a team effort.

Table 4.2 Some potential hazards to staff

HAZARD	CAUSE	CONSEQUENCE
Abuse	Patients or residents, relatives, manager, other staff	Physical and psychological harm
Alteration in room layout	Patients or residents, relatives, other staff	Physical harm
Biological hazards	Contact with body fluids, infected material	Hepatitis and blood-borne infection
Changes in floor level	Design of the home	Falls, injury
Chemicals	Working practice, poor ventilation	Skin damage, inhalation
Fire	Equipment, staff, patients or residents, relatives	Physical and psychological harm
Floors strewn with obstacles	Staff, patients or residents, relatives	Falls, loss mobility
Inappropriate staff care	Manager, organisation's care home inspectors	Stress, illness
Inadequate, absent lights	Poor maintenance, design	Falls, accident, injury
Manual-handling techniques	Inadequate equipment, space, training, inadequate staffing, culture where equipment provided is not used	Injury, stress, burnout
Needle-stick injury	Poor practice, inadequate facilities and equipment	Infection, illness, injury
Poorly maintained furniture	Staff, management	Injuries
Poorly maintained equipment, e.g. wheelchairs with flat tyres, broken brakes	Staff, management, outside agencies	Injuries
Stairs	Design, management, care home inspectors	Falls, injuries
Wet floors	Staff, patients or residents, relatives	Falls, injuries

 ## 4.5 Hazard identification

If you are to provide a safe care environment you need to identify the hazards in your workplace. Use Table 4.3 as a template for this.

Your identification will be more specific than that in Tables 4.1 and 4.2 and may look similar to that shown on page 75.

Table 4.3 Template for hazard identification

HAZARD	CAUSE	CONSEQUENCE

HAZARD	CAUSE	CONSEQUENCE
Uneven floor by bed 12	Dent in floor	Person using a Zimmer frame or walking stick could stumble and fall if he or she places his or her frame or stick in the dent in the floor
Older people could come in contact with dangerous chemicals	Lock on domestic's cupboard broken	Confused people could splash chemicals on skin, in eyes or drink them. Potential for serious injury
Poorly maintained wheelchair	Defective wheelchair brakes Mrs Jones' wheelchair	Mrs Jones could fall whilst transferring, staff could be injured assisting

Reflect on practice

Use Table 4.3 as a template and work with your colleagues to identify hazards in your workplace. How many potential hazards can you find? How likely are these hazards to cause harm? Which of these hazards do you consider to be the most dangerous and why?

4.6 Risk evaluation

When you have identified hazards, the next step is to determine the level of risk. Is the level of risk high, medium or low? Figure 4.1 illustrates the risk assessment process (see page 76).

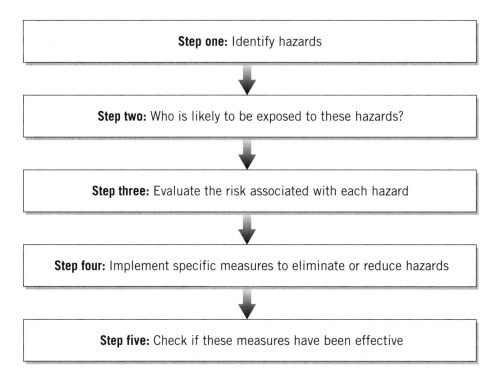

Figure 4.1 The risk assessment process

Managers carrying out risk assessment can feel overwhelmed. You may identify twenty or thirty potential hazards in one area such as an older person's room. The older person might slip on a vinyl floor. She might fall off her chair. She might fall out of bed. She might slip in the ensuite toilet and bang her head on the grab rail. Suddenly an environment that you thought was fairly safe and designed for the needs of the older person becomes filled with what you might view as potential death traps. Where do you start? How do you begin to prioritise?

4.7 Risk ratings

Assessing the level of risk as high, medium or low enables you to begin to prioritise. Take the example of Mrs Norton. You could ask: 'Is she likely to fall off the chair?' The difficulty with this approach is that, although something might be very likely to happen, the consequences might not be very serious. Mrs Norton might be well padded, the chair might be low and her bones might be strong. If so then she is unlikely to sustain serious injury from slipping from the chair.

Assessing the risk and the severity makes it easier for you to determine priorities. If Mrs Norton is lucid and mobile and has good muscle control she is at low risk of falling from the chair and her risk likelihood is 1. If she is well padded, has strong bones and is in reasonable health, the consequence is at most minor injury. If you multiply the likelihood (1) by the possible severity (2), at most, then, her risk rating is 2.

If Mrs Norton is frail, has poor muscle control and mobility problems perhaps because she has suffered a stroke and has a tendency to lean forward in her chair, she is at high risk of falling out of the chair. Her risk likelihood is 3. If she is thin she is more vulnerable to major injury such as a fractured femur because she has less subcutaneous fat over vulnerable areas such as her hips. If she has a history of previous fracture, such as a fractured neck of femur, her bones are very likely to be osteoporotic and vulnerable to fracture. In this case Mrs Norton is at risk of major injury if she falls. If you multiply the risk likelihood of 3 by the consequences of 3 you have a risk rating of 9. Mrs Norton is highly likely to fall from her chair and highly likely to fracture if she falls. Table 4.4 shows how this works.

Table 4.4 Risk rating

RISK LIKELIHOOD	CONSEQUENCE SEVERITY	RISK RATING
High = 3	Death/major injury = 3	3 x 3 = 9
Medium = 2	Minor injury = 2	2 x 2 = 4
Low = 1	No injury = 1	1 x 1 = 2

You can use this method to draw up a risk scale. This scale enables you to get risk into perspective. Some things might be very unlikely to happen and only have minor consequences. They are not a priority. Some things, such as the likelihood of a frail Mrs Norton falling from her chair, might be highly likely to happen and have potentially very serious consequences. These must be your first priority. Table 4.5 illustrates this.

Table 4.5 Risk scale

RISK RATING	POTENTIAL CONSEQUENCES	PRIORITY
3 x 3 = 9	Highest risk, most serious consequences	Urgent, highest possible priority
3 x 2 = 6	High risk, serious consequences	High priority
2 x 2 = 4	Medium risk, less serious consequences	Medium priority
1 x 3 = 3	Low risk, most serious consequences	Medium priority because of the severity of consequences
2 x 1 = 2	Medium risk, less serious consequences	Medium priority
1 x 1 = 1	Low risk, less serious onsequences	Low priority, but don't ignore

Using a risk scale gives you the ability to determine what you need to sort today and how to prioritise all the other risks within the environment. You can then draw up a table to enable you go through the workplace identifying risks and determining priorities.

4.8 Control measures

Identifying and measuring risk gives you the ability to begin to manage that risk. You must deal with high, severe consequence risk urgently. Control measures aim, wherever possible, to eliminate risk.

If Mrs Norton has a risk rating of 9 you must given this your urgent attention. You might consult colleagues who have expertise in physiotherapy, falls or risk assessment to help you work out how to reduce the risks. Some of your actions might be as follows:

- To provide Mrs Norton with a 'helping hand' aide so that she can pick things up that she has dropped without putting herself at risk of falling out of the chair. This action reduces the likelihood of Mrs Norton falling.
- Providing a special chair designed to support people who have had strokes. This action reduces the likelihood of Mrs Norton falling.
- Ensuring that Mrs Norton receives physiotherapy to increase her muscle strength and co-ordination. This action reduces the likelihood of Mrs Norton falling.
- Asking her doctor to consider prescribing medication to treat her osteoporosis. This action reduces the consequences of Mrs Norton falling.
- Providing a high-protein, high-calorie diet to enable Mrs Norton to gain weight. This will help to increase the amount of subcutaneous fat and reduce the risk of fracture. This action reduces the consequences of Mrs Norton falling.
- Providing hip protectors to protect her hips from risk of fracture in the event of a fall. This action reduces the consequences of Mrs Norton falling.

The actions above might reduce Mrs Norton's likelihood of falling from 3 to 2. These actions also reduce the risks of Mrs Norton suffering severe consequences from a 3 to a 2. Her risk rating is now risk 2 × severity 2 = 4. These actions have reduced Mrs Norton's risk rating from 9 to 4. You have not eliminated Mrs Norton's risk but it has been significantly reduced.

It would have been possible to eliminate risk entirely by forbidding Mrs Norton from sitting in a chair and confining her to bed. That would have been inhumane, would have impeded her recovery and adversely affected her quality of life. You would also have exchanged one set of risks for another. If you had persuaded Mrs Norton to stay in bed she would been at increased risk of developing a chest infection, pressure sores, urinary tract infection and incontinence.

Effective risk management is often about balancing risks with quality of life. Mrs Norton's quality of life would have been dreadful had she been on bed rest. If you had done nothing to reduce her risks she might have fallen and fractured her femur and never recovered.

Risk reduction can avoid incidents such as the one outlined below that caused the death of an older woman.

A Nottswoodshire care home and its director were fined a total of £17,000 at Bridgetown Crown Court on 2 September 2003 for breaching health and safety legislation. Springmeadows Care Homes Ltd, 4 The Avenue, Nottswood – owners and operators of Springmeadows House Nursing Home, Oakley, Nottswoodshire – was fined £10,000 plus £5,569.18 costs for breaching Section 3(1) of the Health and Safety at Work, etc., Act 1974 (HSWA) in failing to ensure the health and safety of persons not in its employment.

Mr Rasheed Aggarwal, a director of Springmeadows Care Homes Ltd, was also fined £7,500 and £15,000 costs for breaching section 37(1) of the HSWA, in that the offence was committed with his consent or connivance, in relation to the same incident. This fine was the fourth highest imposed on a director in recent years for a breach under Section 37(1).

The Health and Safety Executive (HSE) prosecution followed an incident on 26 July 2001 in which an 85 year old resident, Mrs Rosemary Lord, sustained serious burns to her legs whilst she was sleeping in her bed at Springmeadows House Nursing Home. The burns arose from contact with the hot surface of a radiator, which was located next to the bed. Mrs Lord contracted a wound infection and died on 30 August 2001.

The case was heard before Bridgetown Crown Court on 2 September 2003. The company and the director entered guilty pleas to the charges.

After the hearing, HSE investigating inspector Alan Martin said: 'This sad incident could have been easily prevented. Care homes and hospitals should be well aware of the risk that hot radiators and pipework present to vulnerable, elderly people.

'This case serves to remind directors of the need to ensure that their organisations manage risks to health and safety effectively.'

This tragic case occurred in a nursing home but could just as well have occurred in an NHS hospital. Many older NHS hospitals have exposed pipework and radiators that could injure an older person.

4.9 Evaluation

When you have identified risks and introduced measures to reduce risk it is important to evaluate. Evaluation enables you to find out if your policies are working. Sometimes staff can become very aware of the hazards of healthcare because you have worked with them to increase awareness and to change practice. Sometimes people slip back into the old ways of doing things. Sometimes you don't notice changes in the workplace – reviewing risk assessments enables you to pick up those subtle changes that might otherwise be missed.

Environmental risk assessments should be carried out annually, or more often if there are significant changes within the workplace. Assessments of the risks to individual patients should be carried out on an individual basis and should be ongoing. If a person is admitted who is especially vulnerable, perhaps the person is blind or like Mrs Norton at high risk of falls, then an individual risk assessment should be carried out.

Reflect on practice

Check when your workplace last had an environmental audit. What risks were identified? Have actions been taken to address these risks? If not, what can you do to address them?

4.10 Health and safety in the workplace: legal aspects

There are several laws governing health and safety in the workplace. These are as follows:

- Common law.
- The Health and Safety at Work Act 1974.
- The Management of Health and Safety at Work Regulations 1992 (amended 1994).
- The Control of Substances Hazardous to Health 1988 (known as COSHH).
- The Reporting of Injury, Disease and Dangerous Occurrences Regulations 1995 (known as RIDDOR).
- The Fire Precautions (Workplace) Regulations 1997.
- The Manual Handling Operations Regulations 1992.

This part of the chapter outlines the duties and responsibilities of this legislation that apply to our work.

Common law

Common law has evolved over the last 1,000 years and is unwritten. Under common law, each of person has a 'duty of care'. Employers, statutory bodies and professionals who breach this duty may be sued for negligence. In negligence claims, the person suing must prove that:

- the company/person had a general duty of care to prevent foreseeable injuries;
- the failure to prevent injury was negligent; and
- this failure caused the injury.

The case study below illustrates how negligence claims can work.

CASE STUDY — Negligence claims

A resident's bath oil was spilt on a vinyl 'non-slip' floor. The care assistant bathing the resident accompanied the resident to her room. She did not mop up the bath oil as she was busy; anyhow, it was the last bath of the morning. Soon the domestic would come to clean the bathroom. Unfortunately, the domestic didn't come soon enough. The resident's elderly visitor, noting that the bath oil had not been brought back from the bathroom, went to fetch it. She slipped on the floor and fractured her femur. She sued the home for negligence. Her solicitor argued that the home was negligent in failing to prevent a foreseeable accident. The nursing home settled out of court on legal advice.

The duty of care that professionals are required to display is that of a reasonably competent nurse. The employer also has a duty of care. If the employer is aware of shortcomings in an employee's performance and the employer's inactions place patients at risk, the employer is liable. The next case study illustrates this.

CASE STUDY — Duty of care

Veronica Gibbs has just been appointed modern matron and is responsible for the older people's wards in the acute trust. The deputy director of nursing tells her about an incident that occurred before her appointment.

There were concerns about nurse Green's performance. Her ward manager told the modern matron she was concerned about nurse Green's ability to give medication safely. Neither assessed the risks of the situation or put in place any measures to reduce the risk.

Nurse Green gave a patient who was allergic to penicillin unprescribed Amoxicillin in error. The patient suffered an allergic reaction. The patient and her family accepted an apology from the trust and the assurance that controls had been put in place to prevent a recurrence of such problems. If the patient had wished to sue she would have been likely to succeed.

The deputy director of nursing asked Veronica to prepare a report for the trust board, outlining what controls have been put in place to prevent such problems occurring in the future: 'I'm sorry to put you on the spot, Veronica. I know that you've only just started but the board would like to know why the problem occurred, why it wasn't dealt with and what we have done to ensure that this sort of problem does not occur in the future.'

Reflect on practice

Imagine that you are Veronica Gibbs. What do you think went wrong? Why do you think that the ward manager and the modern matron did not act in this situation? What do you think needs to be done to reduce the risks of such problems happening in the future?

There are many points to be learnt from this case study. First, the hospital had a general duty of care to prevent foreseeable injuries, and the failure to prevent such injury was negligent. The patient had told staff that she was allergic to penicillin. This was recorded on the front of her drug chart. The patient was given a red identity band that she wore on her wrist. This stated that she was allergic to penicillin. This was one of the controls in place to alert staff to this patient's allergy. A reasonably competent nurse would be expected to check a patient's allergy status before giving the first dose of an antibiotic. A reasonably competent nurse would also be aware that Amoxicillin is penicillin. Nurse Green's manager and the modern matron had serious concerns about nurse Green's ability to dispense medication safely. There was a high risk that nurse Green would make an error in dispensing medication.

A solicitor would argue that the managers' failure to address concerns regarding nurse Green's performance was negligent. It is often difficult for lawyers to prove what is known as causation – that is, that the action or inaction caused the harm. In this case it is very clear that the action of giving a penicillin to an allergic patient caused the patient to go into anaphylactic shock. The patient could well have died if other nurses had not acted promptly.

People whose actions have contributed to their injury may be found 'contributory negligent' and any damages awarded may be reduced. This is discussed in more detail below in the context of manual handling.

Reflect on practice

What actions would you take if you had concerns about a colleague's practice? Are you aware of your organisation's policies in such circumstances? Why do you think that staff sometimes do not act when they have serious concerns about a colleague's practice?

The Health and Safety at Work Act 1974

The Health and Safety at Work Act was introduced in 1974. This Act is the main piece of health and safety legislation and it outlines broad principles concerning health and safety. Other more recent legislation is more specific.

The key points of the Act are as follows:

● The Act is a piece of criminal law.
● People who fail to comply with the Act can be prosecuted, fined or jailed if found guilty.

The Health and Safety at Work Act emphasises that health and safety is the responsibility of the employer and the employee and that they must work together to promote health and safety in the workplace. It outlines the responsibilities of the employer and the employee. The organisation that you work for will have a written health and safety policy that meets the following requirements.

The *employer's* responsibilities:

● Those who employ more than five people must prepare, review and revise a written health and safety policy. This should acknowledge and comply with legislation.
● Employers must ensure the health and safety of employees at work and other people on the premises.
● Employers must display a certificate of employer's liability insurance.
● Employers must display the poster 'Health and Safety Law – What You Should Know' or distribute leaflets giving this information.

Bridgetown Primary Care Trust

1. HEALTH AND SAFETY POLICY STATEMENT

1.1   The Trust recognises its responsibilities for the health and safety of all its employees and for anyone who may be affected by its activities. The Trust is committed to establishing and maintaining safe working conditions for all its employees by establishing a reasonably acceptable level of safety throughout the Trust.

1.2   The Trust will take all reasonable steps to comply with legislative requirements of the Health and Safety At Work etc. Act 1994, all regulations under the Act and European Directives. As a minimum the Trust will comply with all relevant statutory provision and codes of practice.

1.3   The Chief Executive is ultimately responsible for health and safety throughout the Trust with the Director for Primary Care Development as the lead Director.

1.4   The Chief Executive is responsible to the Trust Board for arranging to ensure the application of the Health and Safety Policy throughout the Trust.

1.5   All Corporate Directors are directly responsible for the implementation of the Trust Health and Safety Policy in their directorates.

1.6   The implementation of this policy will be delegated as a management function and monitored for its effectiveness to ensure that the Trust engages in its activities in a manner designed to provide the health and safety of all those who may be affected.

Health and safety policy statement

- Employers must ensure that employees receive adequate and appropriate information, instruction and training to carry out their work safely.

The *employees'* responsibilities:

- Employees must comply with legislation and ensure that their actions do not adversely affect others.
- Employees are entitled to sue their employers if they have been injured in the course of their work.

Self-employed people (such as the window cleaner in a care home or contractors working for the NHS) must comply with legislation and ensure that their actions do not adversely affect others.

Manufacturers and *suppliers* must ensure that their products are safe when used properly. They must provide health and safety information about their products.

The Management of Health and Safety at Work Regulations 1992

The Management of Health and Safety at Work Regulations were introduced in 1992. These were amended in 1994 by the Management of Health and Safety at Work (Amendment) Regulations. These regulations are more specific than the 1974 regulations. It is these regulations that require employers to carry out risk assessments. The key points of the regulations are as follows.

Employers are required to:

- Assess risks associated with the business to determine how to eliminate or minimise those risks. If the organisation delivers healthcare, the risks associated with its activities, such as accident prevention, would be different from those of a building company. Each organisation is responsible for identifying the general and specific risks.
- Take action to eliminate or minimise risk.
- Appoint 'competent persons' to help meet the requirements. This can be the manager or a member of staff. If no one within the organisation has the skills, consultants can be used.
- Ensure that temporary staff (including agency staff) are informed of any health and safety information and/or the skills necessary to do their job.
- Consider the capabilities of each individual to do his or her work safely.

Employees are required to:

- Adhere to the instructions, policies and procedures laid down by their employer.
- Report any shortcomings in the employer's arrangements. For example, if there are instructions that Mrs X is to be moved using the hoist but the hoist is broken, this must be reported to the employer.

NEW AND EXPECTANT MOTHERS

The workplace can damage the health of mothers and that of their unborn children (Salvage et al., 1998). Research shows that working long hours, working shifts, heavy physical labour and stress can affect pregnancy (Williams, 1996). The 1994 amendment regulations recognise that new and expectant mothers are particularly vulnerable in the workplace. Employers must carry out a specific risk assessment that includes the risks to expectant and new mothers and to mothers who are breast-feeding. The Health and Safety Executive (1997) have produced guidance on this.

Reflect on practice

What health and safety information do you provide to newly recruited or agency staff coming to work in your workplace? How might you improve this?

The Control of Substances Hazardous to Health (COSHH) Regulations 1988

COSHH regulations distinguish between the hazards and risks of substances commonly used in the workplace. The manager's responsibilities under COSHH are to:

- Identify hazardous items. Some common kitchen hazards are bleach, disinfectant, descaler and dishwasher powder.
- Identify how these items could affect health. The manager must ensure that potentially harmful substances (such as bleach) are labelled. He or she must also maintain a file of the chemicals used (and the action to be taken) in case of splashing or swallowing. Your suppliers can provide this information.
- Devise secure storage systems. The manager must ensure that potentially hazardous substances are stored under lock and key. For example, bleach should not be stored under the sink and staff should not leave cleaning trolleys where they are easily accessible.
- Train staff. Staff who have previously worked in non-healthcare settings or in healthcare settings where patients are less vulnerable may not fully appreciate the dangers of leaving hazardous chemicals (such as toilet cleaner) in areas where confused and vulnerable older people receive care.

The Reporting of Injury, Disease and Dangerous Occurrences Regulations 1995 (often referred to as RIDDOR)

RIDDOR legislation is not specific to care environments. It was, in fact, drafted with the building industry in mind. Under Riddor, employers (or designated managers) must report the occurrences (as listed below) to their local Health and Safety Executive (Health and Safety Executive, 1996). Your organisation's health and safety policy should make your responsibilities under Riddor clear. The legislation distinguishes between incidents that lead to death or major injury, over three-day injuries, diseases and dangerous occurrences.

Many accident forms now prompt managers to fulfil RIDDOR obligations. However, some older accident forms used in the NHS and within care homes do not.

DEATH OR MAJOR INJURY OF A MEMBER OF STAFF, THE PUBLIC OR A SUBCONTRACTOR

In the case of death or major injury requiring hospitalisation, the manager must telephone the HSE and details will be taken. This should be followed up with a completed accident report on form F2508 within ten days of the occurrence. Relevant reportable injuries are as follows:

- Fracture other than to the fingers, thumbs or toes.
- Amputation.

- Dislocation of the shoulder, hips, knee or spine.
- Acute illness requiring medical treatment where there is reason to believe that this resulted from exposure to a biological agent or its toxins or to infected material.

OVER THREE-DAY INJURIES

If an accident occurs (including an assault) connected with work and the employee or contractor is unable to work for three days or more, a completed accident report form must be sent to the HSE. This three-day period includes non-working days. If a member of staff injures his or her back and has one day off sick before his or her two days off, you should check if he or she is taking his or her days off as usual. If this person does not report that he or she is taking days off as usual and not as sick leave, you should report the incident to the HSE.

DISEASE

If a doctor informs you that an employee is suffering from a reportable work-related disease, you must send a completed disease report form (F2508A) to the HSE. Relevant examples are as follows:

- Skin diseases such as occupational dermatitis. Current HSE opinion is that this includes latex allergy and hand dermatitis.
- Infections such as hepatitis, tuberculosis, legionellosis and MRSA.

DANGEROUS OCCURRENCES

This near-miss clause compels mangers to report occurrences that could have but did not cause serious injury. If a wall collapsed and narrowly missed hitting someone, this should be reported. The HSE should be telephoned and a completed form (F2508B) should be completed within ten days. Relevant examples are as follows:

- Unintended collapse of a wall or floor at a place of work.
- A chandelier falling from the ceiling.
- Explosion or fire causing suspension of normal work for over 24 hours.
- Collapse of load-bearing parts of lifts.

RECORDS

Employers must keep records of any injury, reportable disease or dangerous occurrence. You can comply with the legislation by keeping copies of the report forms in a file, by recording details on a computer or by maintaining a written log. Check what your organisation's policy is for recording.

The Fire Precautions (Workplace) Regulations 1997

In the past, the local fire officer determined safety regulations concerning fire. The fire officer visited and decided which particular measures were necessary to comply with fire safety regulations. On 1 December 1997, the new regulations came into force. These implemented part of the general fire safety provisions of the European Framework and Workplace Directive.

The regulations specify minimum fire-safety standards in places where people work. In situations where the employer does not have control over part of the workplace, this is the responsibility of the person who has control. If an employer leases an office in a block, the landlord or letting agent would have responsibility for common areas outside the employer's control, such as stairs and hallways. In healthcare environments employers' responsibilities are:

- risk assessment;
- fire detection and warnings;
- means of escape;
- provision of fire-fighting equipment;
- planning for an emergency; and
- training staff.

RISK ASSESSMENT

Some organisations may employ a member of staff or a consultant to carry out most of these functions. In some organisations managers may be responsible for these. Managers, however, are already required to assess health and safety risks. Fire safety can either be incorporated into this or carried out separately. You need to keep a formal record and determine if your current arrangements are satisfactory. If you need to change anything, record any proposed changes. You need to inform staff of any changes. Ensure that staff have access to this in case they need to refer to it.

It is important that managers in all healthcare environments maintain a record of staff training. If a trainer is carrying out the training, you will need to ensure that all staff have training and receive regular updates. A record enables you to check easily and ensure that everyone is up to date.

Moving and handling

Only one group of workers – those working in the building industry – are more likely than nurses to be injured at work. Most nursing staff are at high risk of back injury. Research carried out in 1996 found that 80,000 nurses injured their backs every year (Royal College of Nursing, 2000). In 2002, 97,555 staff had a work-related injury causing them to be off work for three days or more, and around half these injuries were back injuries. The rate of back injury has fallen by around 20 per cent since 1996 (Health and Safety Executive, 2002). Employers, managers and staff have legal responsibilities to ensure that patients and staff are not injured during moving and handling.

Legislation requires an assessment of all moving and handling tasks. Guidance issued in 1996 states that 'other than in an emergency' nurses should no longer manually handle patients. However, a recent RCN survey showed that there is a high level of non-compliance with the 1996 recommendations: 55 per cent of NHS trusts indicated a success score of between 51 and 80 per cent in implementing the recommendations. The reasons given included lack of training, poor knowledge or understanding and equipment not being suited to patient needs. Negative peer pressure (64 per cent) and lack of policy enforcement and resources (79 per cent) were cited as the most significant reasons. As a result, 68 per cent of respondents reported bad practice due to lack of risk assessment, 65 per cent reported non-use of equipment, 71 per cent the continued use of condemned lifts and 77 per cent failure to follow safe systems of work (Royal College of Nursing, 2002). This research emphasises that training and education are not enough – they must be supplemented with risk assessment and major changes in the way nurses work.

LEGAL ASPECTS

Legislation aims to prevent workers becoming injured at work. The relevant legislation is the Health and Safety at Work Act 1974 and the Manual Handling Regulations 1992. The manual handling regulations aim to prevent back injury by evaluating handling tasks and reducing or eliminating the need for manual handling. Employers have legal duties to:

> *So far is reasonably practical, avoid the need for employees to undertake any manual handling operations at work which involve the risk of their being injured.*

The Manual Handling Operations Regulations 1992

These regulations are supplemented by guidance from the Health and Safety Executive (1992; 1998) and the Health and Safety Commission (1992). Let's examine the key points.

Weight limits

Neither the regulations nor the guidance contain any weight limits. These documents state that there is no threshold below which handling must be regarded as safe.

Assessment

All manual-handling regulations must be assessed. In a care home or ward, this means that every operation that involves lifting must be assessed:

All settings should have a designated manual-handling co-ordinator

- Do you know how much a laundry bag full of damp towels, etc., weighs? How will it be moved?
- How much do the boxes of incontinence pads weigh?
- Where are staff expected to store things like incontinence pads? Remember, lifting upwards is dangerous.

The guidance contains numerical scales to simplify the assessment of minor tasks.

Every individual who requires manual handling should be assessed. This manual-handling assessment should include weight, factors affecting handling and the methods to be used to handle patients. Ideally, a care home should have a designated manual-handling co-ordinator responsible for assessing manual handling.

Training

Employers have a legal duty to provide training to enable staff to move patients and avoid injury. The latest recommendations are that all staff receive classroom-based training on induction. The training required will depend on the previous level of training but should be between two and five days. Regular refresher training is required. The recommendations on this have now changed, however. The latest recommendation is that staff have a one day a year refresher course every two years (Hignett, 2001; Royal College of Nursing, 2002).

Written records of staff training should be kept. These should include details of handouts and information supplied to staff, including what is not acceptable within the ward or care home (for example, certain types of manual handling).

Equipment

The employer is required to provide a range of equipment to enable staff to handle patients and other loads safely. The range of equipment available may include: hoists, standing hoists, transfer boards and sliding sheets. Under the legislation, the employer could argue that the provision of equipment is not necessary because the cost of supplying equipment *greatly* outweighs the risk of injury. However, a risk assessment would disprove this assertion. Increasingly, insurers demand evidence of risk assessment before agreeing to insure. In 1996, the RCN legal department won more than £8.5 million in compensation for members as who suffered back injuries.

CASE STUDY — Equipment

When Sunayna Verma was appointed as matron as Lawton War Memorial hospital she was surprised at how poorly equipped the wards were. Each ward only had one hoist, and there were no sliding sheets, turntables or other equipment. Sunayna carried out a risk assessment, worked with the trust's moving and handling co-ordinator and ordered the equipment required. A few weeks after the equipment arrived Sunayna was surprised to find it in the ward storerooms still packed in its protective plastic wrapping.

Reflect on practice

Why do you think staff have not used the new equipment? How can Sunyna encourage staff to move patients safely? Can you think of any similar situations in your own workplace where staff have placed themselves and patients at risk by not using equipment? Did you raise the issue with staff and try to change practice? What barriers might you face in such situations? How could you overcome these barriers?

Recording accidents

The employer is required to introduce procedures for recording accidents, investigating causes and, when possible, setting up systems to prevent their recurrence.

Staff responsibilities

Staff have responsibilities under the regulations. These are as follows:

- Staff should co-operate with employers to enable them to develop and implement a code of practice on the handling of patients.
- To inform the employer of any situation that might present 'a serious and imminent danger' and of any shortcomings in the arrangements for manual handling. These include lack of staff, lack of equipment, faulty machinery, injuries or accidents, illness or disability affecting handling capacity. Pregnancy is neither an illness nor disability but pregnant women are more vulnerable to back injury than other workers.
- To comply with the employer's policies on moving and handling. Nurses must have access to and follow the written individual handling assessments.
- Nurses are responsible for updating assessments of patient-handling needs.
- Recording any accidents that occur and help to investigate and set up systems to prevent recurrence.

Refusing hoists

Sometimes patients or relatives refuse hoists and other handling aids. If the older person is mentally competent he or she has a right to decline to use a hoist. The employer is responsible for ensuring that staff are not injured; staff are responsible for ensuring that they take reasonable care of their own and colleagues' health and do not injure patients. In such cases a risk assessment should be carried out and discussed with the older person and, if indicated, regulators.

Agency nurses

The agency nurse is not directly employed by the home but recent court cases have found the employer responsible in such instances. The courts consider that the employer must take reasonable steps to ensure that contractors (such as agency nurses) have been trained and assessed as competent in moving and handling patients. NHS-approved agencies now ensure that the staff they employ have received appropriate moving and handling training and that this is regularly updated.

Managers and employers should ensure that they have a written assurance from the agency that they use staff who are fully trained in the moving and handling of patients.

Vicarious liability

Vicarious liability means that the employer is responsible for the actions of employees. Even if an employee breaches the employer's guidance, the employer is liable. In one case, where two nurses were lifting on the count of three and one failed to lift, the employer was found liable. In another case, where two staff lifted a patient and one injured her back, the employer was found liable. The organisation's policy, manual-handling assessment and care plan stated the patient was to be hoisted.

Contributory negligence

When nurses breach the employer's guidance, injure themselves and sue, the question of contributory negligence arises. If a nurse used a prohibited lift or lifted when she should not have done, she might be 'contributory negligent'. If she is considered 25 per cent at fault then damages will be reduced by this amount. In some cases, the employer is held to account because policies are unworkable. One employer's guidance stated that hoists must be used to toilet patients but the hoists wouldn't go through the toilet doors.

Assessing workplace manual-handling risks

When assessing manual-handling risks you must ask yourself the following questions and implement the following procedures:

- What is being moved?
- Is there a risk of injury?
- Does it have to be moved?
- Can you use mechanical aids to do this? If not, carry out a handling assessment.
- Determine the procedures needed to reduce risk to lowest practicable level.
- Implement these measures.
- Has the risk been sufficiently reduced? If not, reassess.

When you have completed your assessment you must document your findings and the measures you have taken to reduce risk. Guidance recommends that you date your assessment and carry out another assessment every year. If you have evidence to suggest that your policies are not working, you will need to reassess as soon as you are aware of this.

Assessing an individual's risk

Every patient should have a moving and handling assessment. It is good practice to complete a short assessment even on patients who do not require assistance. The assessment should indicate when the person requires help, what help is required and detail any aids that will be used. This assessment should be documented and referred to in the care plan. The assessment should be updated every six months in a long-term care setting or sooner if the individual's needs change.

Educating staff and promoting safe practice

The incidence of staff back injury is now falling, but staff still don't practise what they are taught (Swain et al., 2003). Risk assessments are meant to be used, so they must be available and communicated to all staff. Nurses are not good at documenting what they've done. NMC guidance is clear: documentation is not an optional extra – it is essential.

4.11 Documentation

Sometimes managers and staff claim to have carried out comprehensive risk assessments of work areas but say that they have not documented these. It is important to document risk assessments and actions as undocumented risk assessment is worthless. It is unlikely that you will be able to remember it later. It will be of no use to others as they will be unable to refer to it, and you have no proof that you have actually carried out an assessment. The UKCC (1998) commented that it considered that professionals had both a legal and professional duty of care. They emphasised the importance of record-keeping, stating:

> The approach to record keeping which courts of law adopt tends to be 'if it is not recorded it has not been done'.

4.12 Enforcement

In the past there has been some confusion regarding how the Health and Safety Executive work with regulators in the care home sector. In November 2002 the Health and Safety Executive and the National Care Standards Commission negotiated a memorandum of understanding to set out clearly the responsibilities for health and safety in care homes.

4.13 Summary

Everyone has a legal responsibility to ensure that the workplace is safe. What level of risk is posed by these hazards?

Employers, managers and professionals have a legal responsibility to ensure that the workplace is as safe as possible. This can be achieved by proactive work (such as risk assessment) and reactive work (such as acting after accidents have occurred). Risk assessment involves identifying hazards and determining the level of risk posed by these hazards. Risk management involves eliminating hazards, wherever possible, and acting to reduce risks when this is not possible. Auditing enables you to discover how effective your health and safety policy is.

4.14 Conclusion

Risk assessment is becoming increasingly important. Organisations that fail to assess and document risk are open to claims of negligence and malpractice. Government policy on clinical governance and National Minimum Standards in care homes will lead to an increased emphasis on risk assessment.

Key Points

○ Every older person has the right to expect that the organisation providing care will protect the person from the adverse consequences of healthcare.

○ Admission to a healthcare faculty exposes a person to risk.

○ An older person's illness and age-related changes can increase risks.

○ Organisations have a legal duty to assess risk and to act to reduce risks whilst maintaining the quality of life.

○ Staff are also at risk when delivering care.

○ Organisations have a legal duty to assess and reduce risks faced by staff.

○ Risk management is an important issue that is ultimately about enhancing the quality of care.

References and further reading

INTRODUCTION

Department of Health (2000) *An Organisation with a Memory* (report of an expert group on learning from adverse events in the NHS chaired by the Chief Medical Officer). Stationery Office, London.

Health and Safety Executive (2002) *Health and Safety Statistics. Highlights 2001/2002.* Stationery Office, London.

Kohn, L.T. (2000) *To Err is Human: Building a Safer Health System.* National Academy Press, Washington, DC.

Milligan, F. and Bird, D. (2003) 'Adverse health-care events. Part 1. The nature of the problem', *Professional Nurse*, 18: 502–5.

Nazarko, L. (2002) 'A catastrophe waiting to happen. Beating negligence in the independent sector', *Nursing Management*, 9: 30–5.

Woods, D. (2000) 'Estimate of 98,000 deaths too low, says specialist', *British Medical Journal*, 320: 1326.

SECTION 4.2

Counsel and Care (1993) *The Right to Take Risks.* Counsel and Care, London.

Health and Safety Executive (2002) *Health and Safety Statistics. Highlights 2001/2002.* Stationery Office, London.

United Kingdom Central Council (1998) *Guidelines for Records and Record Keeping.* UKCC, London.

SECTION 4.3

Counsel and Care (1992) *What if They Hurt Themselves?* Counsel and Care, London.

SECTION 4.4

Tullett, S. (1996) *Health and Safety in Care Homes. A Practical Guide.* Age Concern, London.

SECTION 4.10

Health and Safety Commission (1992) *Guidance on the Manual Handling of Loads in the Health Service.* Health and Safety Commission, Sheffield.

Health and Safety Executive (1974) *A Guide to the Health and Safety at Work Act 1974.* HSE Books, Sudbury.

Health and Safety Executive (1992) *Management of Health and Safety at Work Regulations and Approved Code of Practice.* Stationery Office, London.

Health and Safety Executive (1992/1998) *Manual Handling. Guidance on Regulations. Manual Handling Operations Regulations 1992.* HSE Books, Sheffield.

Health and Safety Executive (1996) *Everyone's Guide to RIDDOR 95* (single copies are available free from HSE Books, PO Box 1999, Sudbury, Suffolk, CO10 6FS; tel: 01787 313 955).

Health and Safety Executive (1997) *New and Expectant Mothers at Work: A Guide for Employers. HS (G) 122.* Health and Safety Executive, Sheffield.

Health and Safety Executive (2002) *Health and Safety Statistics. Highlights 2001/2002.* Stationery Office, London.

Hignett, S. (2001) 'Embedding ergonomics in hospital culture: top-down and bottom-up strategies', *Applied Ergonomics*, 32: 61–9.

Royal College of Nursing (2000) *Introducing a Safer Patient Handling Policy.* RCN, London (publication code 000 603).

Royal College of Nursing (2002) *Safer Staff, Better Care* (RCN manual for handling training, guidance and competencies). RCN, London.

Salvage, J., Rogers, R. and Cowell, R. (1998) 'Nurses and children at risk', *Nursing Times*, 94: 34–5.

Swain, J., Pufahl, E. and Williamson, G. (2003) 'Do they practise what we teach? A survey of manual handling practice amongst student nurses', *Journal of Clinical Nursing*, 12: 297–306.

Williams, N. (1996) 'Hazards to pregnant women at work', *Modern Midwife*, 3: 28–30.

Section 4.11

United Kingdom Central Council (1998) *Guidelines for Records and Record Keeping.* UKCC, London.

Section 4.12

Health and Safety Executive (2002) 'New agreement will simplify health and safety enforcement in care homes', press release E215:02, 13 November (available at **http://www.hse.gov.uk/action/content/f-mou_aa.pdf**).

Useful websites

www.qualitydigest.com (monthly magazine with columns on quality topics, articles and suggested resources).

http://www.medical-devices.gov.uk/ (has all the Medical Device Agency guidelines).

CHAPTER 5

Supportive processes

Introduction

In September 2003 the Commission for Health Improvement (CHI) published a harrowing report into the quality of care delivered on Rowan Ward in Manchester. Rowan Ward cared for vulnerable older people with mental health needs. The ward was subsequently closed but the comments of CHI's acting chief executive are telling:

> The care received by vulnerable older people on Rowan Ward was unacceptable, but we are seriously concerned that circumstances surrounding this investigation are not unique.

> CHI has completed two previous investigations into the care of older people and has continual requests for investigations in this area. The same issues keep coming up and the NHS does not seem to be learning. The care of older people nationally is very concerning. NHS managers and commissioners should take a good look at this report and ensure recommendations are embedded in their own services.

The message that must be taken from the report into Rowan Ward is that quality cannot be provided in isolation. The organisation must have structures and processes in place that support nurses in their efforts to develop high-quality care.

Management theory originally evolved from manufacturing and engineering. The early management writers described management as a machine and used engineering metaphors to describe organisations. Organisations are much more complex than mere machines, and it is more accurate to describe organisations as living things. They are much more complicated than the management charts used to try to explain them. Each box on the management chart describes a role, but that role is occupied by a person. Each person brings his or her values and expectations to a role. Each person in each role interacts with others. Organisations are not entities in themselves: they are made up of people who act and interact with each other.

Some management texts consider that organisations are rational and that you can obtain results by using a particular formula: 'Press lever A to move lever B.' The reality is that organisations are not models of rational thought but reflect the values and behaviour of those of us who work in them.

Organisations have cultures, and that culture differs in different parts of the organisation. This culture might be entirely suited to that part of the organisation. The payrolls department might have a role culture so that it is able to pay the staff properly at the end of each month. The organisation needs a payroll department that is stable and effective. Professionals caring for patients might have a task culture so that they can work effectively in a team and tailor care to patients' needs. This chapter discusses the theory of organisational culture and aims to help you apply it in the workplace.

In the rational organisation of the theorists, information flows upward and downwards in a logical way. In the real world we inhabit, information is spread more randomly. Sometimes important messages do not get heard and sometimes 'confidential' information whizzes through an organisation at lightning speed.

Although most of us do not always embrace change it is all around us and, often, it is the small incremental changes we do not notice that transform our lives. Organisations are changing to meet the changing demands placed on them.

This chapter examines the theory about team roles and about how teams function. It aims to enable you to understand how teams function and how you can support your team when changing practice. If we are to improve practice we need to plan and manage care. This chapter examines nursing theory and new developments in planning and managing care.

Aims

5.1 What is organisational culture?

Organisational culture is the key to organisational excellence...and the function of leadership is the creation and management of culture. Everyone is born into a culture and people chose to work in organisations with a certain culture.

Every organisation has its own unique culture. Most cultures have not been consciously created. They have developed and changed over time and are unconsciously based on the values of the top management or the founders or core people who build or direct that organisation. Over time individuals (particularly the organisation's leaders) attempt to change the culture of their organisations to fit their own preferences or changing marketplace conditions.

Healthcare has changed out of all recognition over the last 20 years. Once older people were viewed as passive recipients of care. The professionals knew best, and older people and their families who questioned their judgement were considered to be problems. Now it is realised that people who have had diabetes for 50 years may know a little more about the condition than a newly qualified staff nurse. It is now known that if patients are told what to do without explaining the reasons they ignore the advice. It is also known that only around 60 per cent of patients with serious medical conditions take medication regularly enough to achieve any benefit (McGavock, 1997). As knowledge has developed, strategies have been devised to improve care by working with patients as partners in care. These strategies involve changing the culture of healthcare. Staff who have been working in organisations for many years can find this change threatening and can put up barriers to change.

In Rowan Ward the care given was described as 'old fashioned' and the CHI report suggests that patients were subjected to a rigid routine. The report suggested that managers recognised that this was not appropriate and attempted to change things. Their efforts were unsuccessful and staff and managers appeared to be pitted against each other. The ultimate victims were the vulnerable patients.

Schein (1992) defines organisational culture as:

> *A deeper level of basic assumptions and beliefs that are shared by members of an organisation, that operate unconsciously and define in a basic 'taken for granted' fashion an organisation's view of itself and its environment.*

Culture is the way that things are done in an organisation. It is the unwritten rule book that is often more important and more 'real' than the official policies and procedures.

In the early twentieth century management theories described organisational cultures in terms of a machine. As our understanding of people and the cultures they work in has grown, so has the number of management theories. Schein considers that culture has three layers (see Figure 5.1):

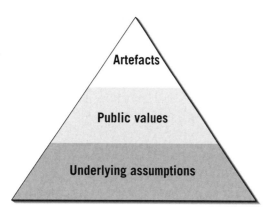

Figure 5.1 Layers of organisational culture

- *Artefacts* are the physical objects, such as the organisation's newsletter, the photograph of the employee of the month and the décor of the entrance, the organisation's processes and observable behaviour.
- *Publicly espoused values* are the values that the organisation claims to hold. These include public statements, mission statements and policy documents.
- *Underlying assumptions* are the unwritten rules and values. These are rarely articulated and may conflict with the espoused values of the organisation. Often different underlying assumptions conflict with each other.

Rowan Ward was part of Manchester Mental Health and Social Care Trust. The trust is one of the first care trusts in the county. Its mission statement states:

> We are committed to developing the participation of service users/patients and carers throughout the organisation, and to ensuring that our services and structures reflect the diverse communities of Manchester. Our aim is for the Trust to be a learning organisation, providing quality services, which supports staff development and increases job satisfaction. Our education and training strategy recognises the changing environment within which mental health services are delivered, and reflects local needs and national standards, including the National Service Framework for Mental Health.

The trust was clearly run with the best of intentions but somehow these intentions did not work through to the staff on the ward. Schein's framework may be used to explain the gap between an organisation's rhetoric and the reality of working within the organisation. He considers that culture is the outcome of the shared experiences arising from an organisation's attempts to resolve fundamental problems of adapting to the external world and achieving internal integration and consistency. This constructs a collective pool of knowledge that determines what is appropriate behaviour, directs understanding and gives guidance on how to resolve problems.

Reflect on practice

Can you think of areas where your organisation says one thing and does another? Why do you think this happens? Do you think that senior managers in the organisation say one thing and do another? Do your own words ever contrast with your actions? What effect do you think this has on the staff you manage?

5.2 Structure and culture

Some writers believe that the structure of the organisation determines its culture. These writers believe that certain structures create a certain type of culture. Roger Harrison et al. (1992) identified different types of culture that were associated with different types of organisation. Charles Handy (1995) further developed this work. They identified four basic types of cultures:

- power culture
- role culture
- task culture
- person culture.

Each culture has different characteristics. These are outlined in Figure 5.2.

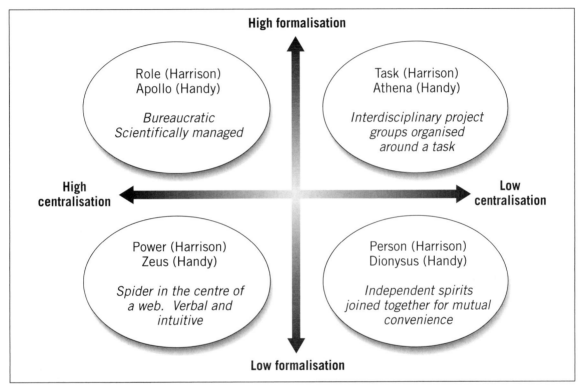

Figure 5.2 The characteristics of cultures

Let's examine each of these cultures in detail.

Power culture

Power cultures are dominated by one powerful individual. This individual can be thought of as the Sun God. All power emanates from this golden person. The person in control of the power culture can also be thought of as the spider in the centre of the web. This is an organisation built on trust. There are few policies and procedures here. In this culture you are either 'in' and viewed as loyal and trustworthy or you are 'out'. In power cultures you are judged by results and if you obtain results the power figure may not be too concerned about how you have achieved those results.

Power cultures are dynamic; they can react quickly to changes. They can provide care that is individual. At their best they are 'can do' cultures. Power cultures flourish in situations where rapid change may be required. Many organisations start off as power cultures. Nursing homes and primary care groups may start of as power cultures. If the nursing home becomes part of a group or the primary care group becomes part of a primary care trust, the culture will change.

Power cultures are dependent on the strength, ability and judgement of the person with the power. If the person with the power is weak, corrupt or lazy the organisation will struggle because other people in the organisation will be unable to help.

Staff turnover within power cultures may be high because they can be uncomfortable places to work. People who are power orientated may enjoy the buzz of working in such an organisation but others may find them too controlling and unsupportive.

Role culture

 Role cultures can be thought of as Greek temples. The three pillars underpinning the temple are policies, procedures and roles. The power lies at the pediment at the top.

Role cultures are dominated by rules, policies and procedures. Role cultures have organisational charts. In a role culture the person is secondary to the role and the person is a role occupant. The organisational chart may indicate that there is a director of nursing but not the name of the director of nursing.

Role cultures exist in large organisations. They are slow to perceive threats and good at maintaining the status quo. They provide stable steady outputs. Role cultures are suitable for organisations that carry out routine work in an unchanging environment. The culture in the Inland Revenue is a role culture. This is suitable because everyone wishes to know what the rules are and be clear about procedures. A power culture would be unsuitable because you wouldn't want every tax officer to interpret your tax allowances differently.

Role cultures are well suited to unchanging environments where stability is more important than innovation. Nationalised industries were a good example of role cultures. Role cultures can be unresponsive to individuals and expect the individual to fit into the culture rather than the culture to meet the needs of the individual. Role cultures do not tend to evolve and can be resistant to change. When change is introduced (often as the result of a threat or a perceived threat) it is often revolutionary rather than evolutionary. The NHS is dominated by role culture.

At its best a role culture is stable, fair and rational. It is predictable; everyone knows what the rules are and they are the same for everyone. Loyalty is to the organisation and there are communication channels. At its worst it is bureaucratic, inflexible and discourages innovation.

Task culture

 The task culture can be thought of as a fisherman's net or a matrix. It is a team or project culture. It is based on the collaboration of equals. Titles and roles are unimportant in task cultures. Task cultures are about ability: ability to master your own work and to work with others. Task cultures are made up of highly skilled, highly motivated people.

Task cultures can exist within healthcare settings either as the predominate culture or as a subculture. They can co-exist within a role culture. Often managers working in a role culture will form a project group to get something done. The group will pull together people with particular expertise and talent. This is a conscious or subconscious effort to introduce a task culture within a role culture.

Task cultures are also described as Athenian cultures and considered to be a feminine culture. This may be a mistaken view. Teams of doctors working within a hospital will usually work in a task culture. Teams of nurses working in a care home, a ward or department will often develop task cultures. The task culture is not limited to a single group of professionals. In the operating theatre everyone is a team member. Doctors, nurses and operating department practitioners wear the same clothes and work as a team.

At their best task cultures are flexible and adaptable. At their worst they can be seen as 'elitist'. They are focused entirely on the task at hand and may lack the ability to see the 'whole picture'. Task cultures can be unstable. They team might lack political awareness because they are so focused on their work that they fail to see and react to threats. The consultant surgeon might be wrong footed and bewildered by modernisation because of a narrow focus on surgery.

Managers in a role culture might view task cultures as expensive, elitist and petty. When resources are short, task cultures might be starved of the resources that they need to carry out their work.

People working in task cultures feel empowered. They can work creatively to seek solutions and seniority and role are less important than enthusiasm and ability. Some people may feel that task cultures make unreasonable demands of them and prefer the stability of a role culture.

Person culture

 The person culture is also described at the 'existential' or Dionysus culture. It can be thought of as a group of stars. People who chose to work in a person culture do not really want to work for an organisation at all. The organisation exists to meet the needs of the individual. The individual does not exist to meet the needs of the organisation. People who work autonomously get together to share facilities, equipment and staff. Co-ordination is for long-term convenience, but there is no 'boss'.

Management is a chore, and management functions are often shared on a rotational basis and viewed as a 'duty'. The manager has low status and is often resented. Handy points out that people may enjoy working in this kind of organisation, but managing them is difficult and exhausting. There are no usable sanctions, and professionals do not willingly receive orders. Every individual has the right of veto so that co-ordinated action might require almost endless negotiation. Barristers working in chambers, accountants working in a practice or lecturers working in a university might be part of a person-centred organisation. These individuals have many names, all of them avoiding using the word 'organisation'.

Managing a person-centred culture is challenging, to say the least. Charles Handy describes it as 'like trying to herd a group of tom cats'.

People in person-centred cultures have power bases. The star professor in the university might devote most of her time to networking, writing and research: the things that will contribute to her personal status and power. If the university gains prestige from these activities that is incidental. The professor will do what she has to do to maintain her position but no more.

General practitioners work within a person-centred culture. They do not actually work for the NHS at all but are independent contractors. Rosemary Wright outlines the problems of working within a person-centred culture:

> *This system is least problematic when each individual can do his or her own thing without impinging on others and where each individual can perfectly well survive without the organisation. The more individuals become dependent on shared facilities, the more of a managerial nightmare it becomes.*

Harrison and Handy discuss person-centred cultures in terms of highly educated professionals. Person-centred cultures can exist in less rarefied organisations. Goffman's (1961) work defines an institution as an organisation that exists to serve the needs of the people working there rather than the people who require care. His descriptions of ritualised working and ritualised practice that suits the people who work in the institution are an early example of a person-centred culture in healthcare. A more recent example is found the lessons from the Bristol inquiry into heart surgery on children (Department of Health, 2002). The Bristol inquiry is a case study into an organisation that had developed dysfunctional elements. There was a lack of leadership, poor organisation and poor communication. People working within the unit knew what was wrong but did not speak out. One brave man made a difference by speaking out. He was unable to find another post in the UK and was forced to emigrate. The prevailing culture was a person-centred or club culture.

5.3 Cultural mix

There is no one 'right' culture for an organisation. Organisations tend to develop a certain culture because it suits the environment that the organisation is working in.

New business are set up because someone had the drive to set them up. They are naturally power cultures in the early days. As the organisation becomes larger and more complex it might develop into a role culture. A person-centred culture, such as a group GP practice, might function as a person-centred culture but things might change. The practice might become larger and partners might need more help to maintain records and organise staff. The practice might develop into a role or task culture.

Organisations are not culturally pure. A large organisation such as a group of care homes or an NHS trust might function as a role culture. There are policies and procedures and rules. The culture of individual homes or wards might be very different. The ward or care home with a bullying manipulative manager might function as a power culture superimposed on a role culture. The care home or ward that prides itself in putting patients before procedures might function as a task culture.

In the real world organisations have a public culture, but all the cultures that have been discussed here can exist within the organisation.

5.4 What is the culture in your workplace?

Everyone works within a culture. Language gives the game away. Power cultures describe themselves as 'close knit' or as a 'family'. The power source is the head of the family. The power culture might have 'a boss' or directors. The role culture describes itself as an organisation and may give the game away by listing people in telephone directories by role first and name second. The role culture has managers. The task culture has co-ordinators and people who lead on certain aspects of work. The task culture has work groups and projects. The person-centred organisation does not have a boss and members value their freedom.

What is the culture in your workplace?

Handy (1988) suggests that if you want to find out what the culture of an organisation is, ask someone what his or her job is. If the person says 'I work for Tony Blair' (or another named person) the culture is probably a power culture. If the person says 'I work for Guys and St Thomas' NHS Trust' (or another organisation) the culture is a role culture. If the person says 'I work as a nurse manager for Springfield Care Homes' (or another job title and organisation) the culture is a task culture. If the person says 'I am a nurse' this indicates the person culture.

All of us have one preferred cultural style and a back-up culture. Sometimes you're not happy in the organisation because the culture of the organisation is different from your preferred working culture. Someone at home in a person-centred culture may be able to work in a task culture but would feel stifled in a role culture.

5.5 What is your preferred management style?

Try this quiz to see what your preferred management style is and how you fit within the organisation you work for. Choose one of the alternatives (A–D) listed for each question.

1 The most important part of my work is to have:
   A Lots of challenges
   B Sensitive guidance
   C A stable environment. I need to know where I stand
   D A friendly harmonious place. I can't stand backbiting

2 I want my manager to:
   A Show me what is required
   B Tell me who is on the team
   C Show me how to do it
   D Tell me why you want it done that way

3 I prefer to have:
   A An opportunity to learn new skills
   B Job satisfaction
   C Plenty of warning before things happen
   D Time to work things out

4 When under pressure and meeting resistance I say:
   A Look I'm in charge
   B So why doesn't anybody like me anymore?
   C Listen, don't rock the boat
   D Sorry, it's not my decision

5 When under pressure to produce work quickly do you say:
   A It will be quicker to do it myself
   B I don't have time for all the details
   C I'm waiting for clarification and written details
   D Hold on – let's get some more information first

How did you score?

MOSTLY AS

Your dominant management style is that of the pioneer or jungle fighter. Pioneers are pushy, produce results and are powerful, persistent, straight talking, exasperating, irritating problem solvers. Pioneers not only overstep the mark they actually refuse to acknowledge that the mark exists. Pioneers need lots of challenges, strong fair direction and opportunities to learn new skill. They need to feel competent. Pioneers are risk-takers, decision-makers, independent workers, change agents and are results orientated. The hostile pioneer is known as the dictator.

MOSTLY BS

Your dominant management style is that of the politician, socialite or game player. Politicians are smart, charming, adaptable, democratic, diplomatic, dynamic, poor on detail but co-operative and willing to help and please. Politicians need democratic guidance, lots of people contact, plenty of variety, to enjoy work and to have fun. Politicians need public recognition. Politicians are inspiring leaders, diplomats, enthusiastic workers; they are good for morale and project a positive image. The hostile socialite is known as the politician.

MOSTLY CS

Your dominant management style is that of the steady soul, the rock, the company person. Steady souls are conservative, consistent, kind, careful, calming, considerate, co-operative and conventional. Steady souls maintain a balance and are good caretakers. Steady souls need stability, to be shown how it should be done. They need to be encouraged to analyse and need plenty of warning before change takes place. Steady souls need encouragement to show their real feelings and need economic security. They are reliable, follow instructions to the letter, are loyal and task orientated. The hostile steady soul is known as the bureaucrat.

MOSTLY DS

Your dominant management style is that of the specialist, the expert, the sympathetic worker. Specialists are sensitive, systematic, supportive, self-critical and analytical. Specialists need harmony and to know why it is done. They need to use a detailed approach, to avoid criticism and to be given praise in private. Specialists hate to be 'put on the spot'. They need time to process and analyse information. Specialists work to high standards; they provide highly detailed work, make careful decisions and are highly accurate.

5.6 Which management style is the right one?

The answer is all of them and none of them. Although every manager has one or, hopefully, more preferred management styles, most managers need to use a variety.

The more management styles you can use the more versatile and effective a manager you become. You need to choose the style for the situation (Mant, 1983).

Setting up a new care home or NHS service needs a pioneer. The pioneer explores new territory and selects a team. Soon the unexplored territory settles into well trodden paths. Now the home or service needs a politician. Staff need leadership, diplomacy and tact. Teams must be influenced and inspired and it's time to begin managing your boss.

When your staff and boss have settled in the home or service, it moves on to the organisational and maintenance phase. You've got to keep to the service budget, watch morale and maintain standards. Now the manager needs to be steady and rock-like, holding the ship on course.

You've no sooner achieved stability than things change. In the care home resident dependency is up; incontinence rates and infection go up. In the NHS your new service is overwhelmed with referrals. Suddenly you've got a huge waiting list and people are beginning to grumble. Now you need to be an expert. You need to analyse problems and work out solutions. Of course when you discover that you need to introduce rehabilitation programmes, continence promotion programmes and infection control programmes, you need to be a pioneer to push them through. Management styles and effectiveness are influenced by the culture of the organisation that you work in.

Sometimes managers can use different styles at different times during the same day. One day you might come on duty and work with staff to develop care plans. Suddenly there's a crisis. Mrs Patel collapses and starts to fit. Then she stops breathing. You are in charge and you tell people what to do. You expect them to comply immediately and without question. Later, when you have dealt with the crisis, you talk things through with the staff. You explain to the junior staff what happened to Mrs Patel, why you took the action that you took and what they can learn from this. In a few hours you've used a facilitative style, an autocratic style and an enabling style.

The most important thing about being a manager is to know yourself and to manage yourself effectively. Until you can manage yourself effectively you have little chance of managing others.

Reflect on practice

What is the dominant culture within your organisation? Is the dominant culture a suitable one for the services you provide? Is there a different culture within the unit where you work? Does this culture improve the efficiency of the organisation or detract from it? How many different cultures can you identify within the organisation?

5.7 Developing an enabling culture

In the early twentieth century most management writers were men, and many gained their management experience in manufacturing and engineering. They often described organisations, the people who worked in organisations and the culture of organisations using mechanical metaphors. Now it is known that organisations, like the people who work in them, are living organisms.

Cultures can be healthy, thriving and supportive. They can also be diseased and dysfunctional. When I researched quality of care for my MSc I worked in three different care homes. One organisation was resource poor but rich in the quality of staff. Staff worked together and supported each other. They developed innovative practice because they had a culture that supported and enabled staff.

In one organisation there was a blame culture. If something went wrong the manager did not try to find out what had happened so services could be improved. She looked around for someone to blame. Everyone's worked in a blame culture. A blame culture permeates every aspect of care. In a blame culture people cover their backs and don't try new things. That might get them noticed and it's best to keep your head down in a blame culture. Rosabeth Moss Kanter (1983) completed a study of companies in America that operated role cultures and produced ten rules for stifling initiative and preventing progress (see Figure 5.3).

---

1 Regard any new idea from below with suspicion because it is new and because it is from below.

2 Insist that people who need to get your approval to act first go through several other levels of management to get their signatures.

3 Ask departments or individuals to challenge and criticise each other's proposals. Then you can just pick the survivor.

4 Criticise freely and withhold your praise. That keeps people on their toes. Let them know that they can be fired at any time.

5 Treat problems as signs of failure to discourage people from letting you know when something in their area isn't working.

6 Control everything carefully; make sure people count everything that can be counted, frequently.

7 Make decisions to reorganise and change policies in secret and spring them on people suddenly. That also keeps people on their toes.

8 Make sure any request for information is fully justified. You don't want it falling into the wrong hands.

9 Assign to lower-level managers responsibility for cutbacks and layoffs.

10 Above all, never forget that you (at the top) already know everything that is important about business.

Figure 5.3 Ten rules for preventing progress

Blame cultures are sick and dysfunctional and they must be healed before quality can be improved.

Enabling organisations to heal is very different from traditional management strategies. If the organisation is an organism there are sick parts and healthy parts. The healthy parts may be overshadowed by the diseased parts but they exist. If the entire organisation was diseased it would be unable to function. Your aim should be to identify the healthy functioning parts of the organisation and to help those parts develop and regenerate the organisation.

Reflect on practice

Think of a time when you worked in a blame culture. What effect did the blame culture have on morale? What affect did it have on the quality of care? Why do you think that blame cultures develop within organisations? How would you begin to heal the damage caused by a blame culture?

5.8 Playing by the rules?

Every so often the earth tilts on its axis and everything changes dramatically. Once people thought that the world was flat and that sailors could fall of the edge. The idea of the world being round was thought of as an eccentric theory. Then suddenly everyone accepted that the world was round. This sort of change is called a 'paradigm shift'.

The way organisations are managed is in the middle of a paradigm shift. This process began in the mid-1990s when management writers began to write about how employees didn't always play by the organisation's rules. They began to understand that organisations weren't the clean, clear-cut rational things that they perceived them to be. Organisations are like real life, not black and white but full of shades of grey. They can be as muddled, messy and as full of contradictions as real life.

In role cultures it is assumed that those at the top have the answers but that's not always true because they often don't know what the problems are. The only way senior managers can find out about problems at the coal-face is if those engaged in clinical practice tell them. Sometimes staff don't tell senior managers because they work in a blame culture and, if they explain what the problems are, they may be blamed. Sometimes staff don't tell senior managers because they don't think they'll listen; sometimes staff are just secretive (Argyris et al., 1994).

Studies show that informal adaptations can develop unplanned in the nooks and crannies (unsupervised spaces) of organisations, creating local, unofficial (and sometimes covert) solutions to operating problems not officially recognised (and often not known) at higher levels. Sometimes these informal arrangements were in line with the goals of the host organisation, as the case study below illustrates.

CASE STUDY — Sweet dreams

Mrs Joyce Williams was living independently with her husband at home. She slipped on an uneven pavement when shopping and fractured her left neck of femur. Four days after her operation she was transferred from the acute hospital to Lawton War Memorial for rehabilitation.

Mrs Williams had arthritis for many years and hadn't had a night's sleep since her accident because of backache. She was offered pain killers but these made her feel sick and constipated. Milder pain killers were useless.

Mrs Williams asked her husband to bring in her hot water bottle. She knew that applying a little heat to her back would ease her aching muscles and let her get a good night's sleep. She asked Astrid Wilson, the deputy ward manager, if it would be okay to use the hot water bottle. Astrid knew that the hospital policy (written in the 1980s) forbade the use of hot water bottles. The policy stated that they were dangerous and could cause scalds. Astrid decided to ignore the policy and use her common sense. She carried out a simple risk assessment. Mrs Williams was lucid and unlikely to remove the hot water and scald herself. She had no altered sensation; she had not had a stroke and was not diabetic and was not suffering from nerve damage. The hot water came out of the taps at a temperature far below that capable of causing scalds. The hot water bottle was in good condition, the cap fitted, the rubber wasn't perished and it didn't leak. Mrs Williams had been using a hot water bottle without incident for 20 years. So Astrid smiled sweetly and said: 'Of course you can use your hot water bottle.'

Meanwhile somewhere in the organisation the senior manager's sleep easily knowing that the policies that they had written were being followed to the letter.

Reflect on practice

When was the last time you broke the rules? Why did you break them? Did breaking the rules lead to improved quality?

Sometimes they served the goals of the subunit rather than those of the whole organisation (Blau and Meyer, 1971). The culture on Rowan Ward was different from that of South Manchester Care Trust. Rowan Ward was one of the nooks and crannies that exist in organisations and it may well have been poorly supervised. Perhaps the manager had many other areas of responsibility; perhaps the manager was preoccupied with other areas within the newly formed care trust.

Managing a Quality Service

5.9 A learning organisation

This paradigm shift led to the development of the learning organisation. Peter Senge (1990) defined the learning organisation as:

> An organization that is continually expanding its capacity to create its future. For such an organization, it is not enough merely to survive. 'Survival learning' [adaptive learning] is necessary. But for a learning organization, 'adaptive learning' must be joined by 'generative learning', learning that enhances our capacity to create.

Senge's work builds on the work of J. Edward Deming. Deming worked for many years with Japanese companies. His work stresses the importance of front-line workers, empowering them to collaborate in order to provide quality services. They do this by working in cross-functional teams, across different status levels of the firm, united 'horizontally' by a focus on giving customers what they expect.

The learning organisation is built on basic principles (Senge, 1992; Senge et al., 1994). These are outlined in Figure 5.4.

- Humans retain their childlike curiosity and drive to learn.
- People urge themselves to ever-higher standards of quality and performance in activities that are important to them – hobbies, sports, professions – and they make much (voluntary) use of feedback data.
- People fear, resist and deceive external evaluations by those in power.
- All perceptions are structured by our assumptions and categories. These mental models can be surfaced, tested, revised and reformed.
- Personal knowledge and understanding are constructed by each individual processing new information – using it, discussing it, reflecting on it, etc.
- Data are meaningless if we do not view in context.
- People tend to co-operate with people they see regularly. They meet their expectations, especially affirming the identity-self claimed by the other. This leads to tacit acceptance of a taboo on 'non-discussible' topics.
- Most workers are capable of organising and planning their own work.
- People's capabilities are vastly under-utilised in most workplaces. Their efforts to break out of those limitations are usually discouraged or punished.
- Managers who attempt to get the most out of staff will initially experience resistance because of mistust and barriers.

Figure 5.4 The principles and assumptions of a learning organisation

In a learning organisation people acknowledge that they do not know all that there is to know. They recognise that they need to co-operate and collaborate. Learning organisations make people feel valued and enable them to give of their best.

In a learning organisation, people recognise that they need to co-operate and collaborate

New streams

Learning organisations are what Kanter (1983; 1989) describes as new streams. They do things differently and do not fit well with the old ways of working. There are bound to be conflicts with the mainstream. Chapter 3 looked at compatibility and how planned changes are more likely to be successful if they fit in with where the organisation is going.

In the NHS there is a great deal of support at the highest possible levels for changing the way things are done. Government policy aims to transform the NHS, to educate staff and to enable staff to work effectively in teams. Modernisation is all about developing the NHS as a learning organisation.

In care homes there is also a great deal of support for the learning organisation. Care homes have huge incentives to enable staff to give of their best and to provide quality services. If a care home does not provide quality services, older people and their families will chose to go to a home that does provide quality services.

If you are to succeed in enabling people to admit when they don't know something and to do their best, you need to develop strong, effective teams.

> ### Reflect on practice
>
> Is the culture within your organisation changing? How much are you encouraged to use your own initiative? How does having the ability to use your own initiative affect your day-to-day practice and the quality of care that you deliver?

5.10 Teams

When you reached adulthood, you had little preparation for working in teams. In the education system people compete against each other to get the best grades in GCEs and in their assignments during their professional education. If you do not play the game and compete, you may not succeed in becoming a nurse. Sometimes you are expected to work in groups during your education but the teamwork projects are not considered real and they do not contribute to your educational success. There are no marks for teamwork when growing up. Usually the only time you work together in teams is when you're at play. People work well in teams when they're playing football, netball and other sports but even then they're competing against another team.

People are brought up to win and then, when they reach adulthood, they're expected to have the skills to co-operate.

Teamworking skills are important in the adult world yet people are seldom taught how to develop them. At all levels of your career you're expected to have the skills to be a successful team member and a team leader. The key to developing team skills is to begin to understand how teams work, what makes teams work well and what causes them to become dysfunctional.

Team roles

The team's effectiveness is dependent on the personalities of the people in the team. People tend to adopt roles within a team. Management writers have researched the relationships between the roles people adopt within teams and the effectiveness of the team. Let's look at the work of two important writers: William Schutz (1958) and R. Meredith Belbin (1981; 1996).

Schutz developed a short psychological instrument, the FIRO-B (Fundamental Interpersonal Relations Orientation-Behaviour), based on his theory, to help understand interpersonal behaviour.

FIRO-B has been used successfully in career, management, team-building and leadership development. The American and British armies have used FIRO-B in their leadership training for many years to determine how soldiers would work together in groups under battle conditions.

In teams people adopt roles that meet their own needs and the needs of other team members. Schutz's tool scores individuals and predicts which roles the individual is likely to play. Every person will adopt at least one role and many people can adopt more than one role depending on their FIRO-B profile and the interpersonal needs of the other team members.

Figure 5.5 outlines these team roles (Schnell and Hammer, 1993). An individual's FIRO-B scores can predict which team roles they are likely to play.

Clarifier	Presents issues or solutions for clarification, summarises discussion, introduces new members to the team, keeps team members up to date, provides group with facts and data
Tension-reducer	Helps move the team along by joking or clowning at appropriate moments, redirects group at tense moments, builds on common interests in the group
Individualist	Is not an active team player, sees meetings as unnecessary or distracting, may work on other tasks or hold side conversations during meetings, may not follow through or co-operate with group decision
Director	Pushes for action and decision-making, may interrupt others or monopolise the 'air-time' in meetings, may be unrealistically optimistic about what can be accomplished

Questioner	Seeks orientation and clarification, is a constructive critic of the team and its members, may use questions to postpone closure or decisions
Rebel	Struggles to establish a position within the group, may criticise others, challenges the status quo, may refuse to comply with group decisions, provides alternative ideas but may have difficulty with follow-through
Encourager	Builds the ego or status of others, is friendly, responsive, warm, diplomatic, may sacrifice the truth to maintain good relationships
Listener	Maintains a participative attitude and interest non-verbally, is involved in group goals, shows interest by receptive facial and bodily expressions
Cautioner	Expresses concern about direction of the group, relays doubts about the success of initiatives planned, shows reluctance to get swept up in group energy, provides careful analysis of potential problems, may play devil's advocate
Initiator	Suggests procedures or problems as discussion topics, proposes alternative solutions, is the 'idea person', actively encourages others to share in discussions
Energiser	Urges team towards decision-making, insists on covering the agenda, prods the team into action
Opinion-giver	States a belief or opinion on all problems and issues, offers predictions based on past experiences, works independently from the group, does not try to become part of the leader's inner circle
Harmoniser	Agrees with the group, reconciles opposing positions, understands, complies and accepts
Consensus-tester	Checks for agreement, brings closure to discussions, confronts unacknowledged feelings in the group, wants to build a close-knit, powerful team
Task-master	Tries to keep group focused on its central purpose and required outcomes, ignores social chit-chat, believes that the team members do not have to like each other to do the job, reminds the group that this is business, not a family

Figure 5.5 FIRO-B team roles
Source: Schnell and Hammer (1993)

Belbin's research into teams focused on the relationship between personality, ability and the effectiveness of management teams. Belbin defines a team role as:

A tendency to behave, contribute and interrelate with others in a particular way.

He describes a pattern of behaviour influenced by the way in which one team member interacts with another team member. Belbin identified eight team roles and devised two personality tests to identify the types of role. In his later work he changed the labels, added an additional team role (the specialist) and refined the tests. Belbin considers that everyone has one preferred team role and that most people also have a back-up role (Figure 5.6 on page 116 provides details of team roles identified by Belbin).

Co-ordinator (Chairperson)	Controls the way in which the team moves towards the group objectives by making the best use of team resources; recognises where the team's strengths and weaknesses lie; ensures that the best use is made of each team member's potential
Shaper (Shaper)	Shapes the way in which team effort is applied, directing attention generally to the setting of objectives and priorities; seeks to impose some shape or pattern on group discussion and on the outcome of group activities
Plant (Plant)	Advances new ideas and strategies with special attention to major issues; looks for possible breaks in the approach to the problems which confront the team
Implementer (Company Worker)	Turns concepts and plans into practical working procedures; carries out agreed plans systematically and efficiently
Teamworker (Team Worker)	Supports members in their strengths (e.g. building on suggestions); underpins members in their shortcomings; improves communications between members; fosters team spirit generally
Monitor Evaluator (Monitor-Evaluator)	Analyses problems; evaluates ideas and suggestions so that the team is better placed to take balanced decisions
Resource Investigator (Resource Investigator)	Explores and reports on ideas, developments and resources outside the group; creates external contacts that may be useful to the team; conducts any subsequent negotiations
Completer Finisher (Completer-Finisher)	Ensures that the team is protected as far as possible from the mistakes of both commission and omission; actively searches for aspects of work which need a more than usual degree of attention; maintains a sense of urgency within the team
Specialist	New team role added to the original work. The specialist provides knowledge and skills that are in rare supply. Single-minded, self-starting, dedicated. Contributes only on a narrow front. Dwells on technicalities

Figure 5.6 Belbin's classification of team roles
Source: Belbin (1996)

Belbin team roles can be defined as follows:

- Action-orientated roles – Shaper, Implementer and Completer Finisher.
- People-orientated roles – Co-ordinator, Teamworker and Resource Investigator.
- Cerebral roles – Plant, Monitor Evaluator and Specialist.

Which approach should I use?

Both methods work effectively and you should try them to discover which you find the most suitable. I personally prefer to mix and match. Belbin's work is useful when working with teams that I do not know well, such as strategic management groups.

FIRO theory is useful in working with a team on a day-to-day basis. It focuses on relationships within the team and helps you to develop the team.

> **Reflect on practice**
>
> Look at the team roles and decide which you feel most comfortable with. Copy the list of team roles you feel most comfortable using. Next time you attend a meeting, take your list along. Identify the roles that people in the team have adopted. Does the team have the correct balance of roles required to function effectively? If not, can you now understand why the team is not achieving what it should achieve? If the team is working well, can you now understand why?

Leading teams

A successful manager must be self-aware and must use the right style in the right place with the right people. Sometimes the manager must lead; sometimes the manager should manage; and sometimes the manager should facilitate (Weaver and Farrell, 1999). Table 5.1 explains these different management styles.

Table 5.1 Management styles

LEADER	MANAGER	FACILITATOR
Concerned with doing the right thing	Concerned with doing things right	Concerned with helping people do things
Takes the long-term view	Takes the short-term view	Helps people find a view and articulate it
Concentrates on what and why	Concentrates on how	Helps people concentrate and be clear in the here and now
Thinks in terms of innovations, development and the future	Thinks in terms of administrations, maintenance and the present	Helps people think, and helps them communicate their thoughts
Sets the vision: the tone and direction	Sets the plan; the pace	Helps people make meaning of tone and direction, and to function well at the required pace
Hopes others will respond and follow	Hopes others will complete their tasks	Hopes others will engage in the process
Appeals to hopes and dreams	Monitors boundaries and defines limits	Helps others make meaning of hopes and dreams; pushes appropriately on boundaries
Expects others to help realise a vision	Expects others to fulfil their mission or purpose	Helps others articulate a shared vision and common mission or purpose
Inspires innovation	Inspires stability	Helps people respond to things that are new and things that remain the same

Source: Based on Weaver and Farrell (1999)

How do you know which role to adopt in different situations? As a general rule you should *lead* people, *manage* tasks and *facilitate* decisions. Look at what you need to achieve. Weaver and Farrell suggest looking at the nature of the result for which you are responsible. If the task is setting direction for a group – helping group members see the bigger picture – then the leader role is best. If the task is setting limits on the work, delegating or defining deadlines, the manager role should be the choice. If the task is more complex, requiring the assistance of a number of other people to complete, the facilitator role is best. As a practical guideline, for a given work session or meeting, one primary role should be used.

It is important to adopt one style for a particular meeting or session, otherwise colleagues can become very confused. It can be difficult for them to work out what your role is and what is expected of them if you switch from a leader role outlining the vision to the manager role working out who is going to cover the late shift on Friday. Sometimes life gets in the way of this; if you have to switch roles because circumstances demand it, be clear with staff what you are doing and why you doing it. Encourage people to ask questions and clarify issues if you have thrown them with this sudden change of style.

Team development

If you are to develop your team successfully, you need to identify the roles people within the team have adopted. This will help you to understand the people whom you must involve in the change process. Chapter 3 looked at the work of Kurt Lewin. Lewin (1951) developed what he described as a force field theory (see Figure 5.7). He considered that at any one time there are forces that are driving change and forces that are restraining change. If these forces balance each other then the status quo prevails. The most effective way to introduce change is not to increase the driving forces but to reduce the restraining forces.

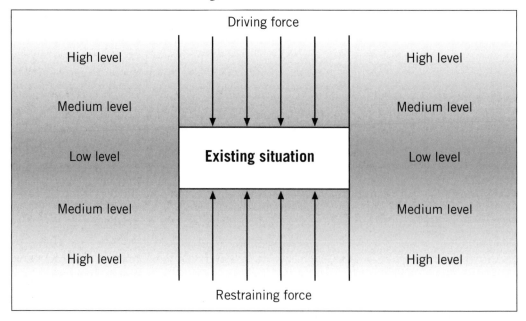

Figure 5.7 Force field theory

Lewin considers that teams go through different stages of development.

FORMING

In the forming stage, group members first come together to lay the foundation for the team. Excitement, anxiety, dependence and uncertainties are the driving motivations. The best leaders at this stage find out what the team members know and work with them to develop the team. At this stage you need to become accepted and trusted as a team leader.

Leading

Add structure to team meetings – for example, assemble a team charter. This charter should set ground rules. These should be worked out by the group but should include confidentiality and respect for other group members' points of view. Focus discussions, clarify tasks and help to define team roles. You also need to encourage learning within the group.

Watch for individuals who attempt to dominate at this stage, and invite all to participate equally. You may have to work hard to draw out some quieter members of the team who have a lot to contribute. Careful leadership prevents their voices being drowned by vocal team members. Beware at this stage of individuals who may try to hijack the group to fulfil their personal agendas.

STORMING

When groups enter the storming stage, members begin to realise the scale of the change ahead and sometimes panic. Support and help the team. Sometimes at this point, because the team has moved to a higher level of understanding, they look at current practice with horror, yet they fear that they do not have the skills to move practice forward.

Leading

Be open and honest; acknowledge the value of what has gone before. It would not have been possible to begin the change without the foundations of current practice. Sell the change as an indicator of strength not weakness. The weak thing would have been to ignore the need for change, not to begin the journey. If people feel overwhelmed, break tasks and work down into a series of small steps. People climb mountains in the same way that they bound up hills: one step at a time.

You can also help by guiding decisions and problem-solving efforts. The team is vulnerable at this point because of conflicting opinions and emotions. Enable the team to refocus by pointing out not how far they have to travel but how far they have already come.

NORMING

Norming is the stage where people get used to working with one another. You will see co-operation over competition, more acceptance and comfort in giving and receiving feedback. Nobody ever washes a rental car. The team must feel ownership at this stage of the game or they won't take care of the team.

Leading

It's hard to let go but at this stage you have to. This is the stage when you let go of your child's bicycle and watch in fear and pride as he wobbles off on two wheels. Yes it's scary, but it's part of growing up for you and for your team. Delegate more responsibility and be conscious about doing so. Praise and remind people of how far they have come and how well they have worked *together*.

PERFORMING

In the performing stage, team members are comfortable with each other and everyone is 'singing from the same song sheet'. Team performance soars and everyone's highest concern is team success.

Leading

Evaluate the work and let everyone know the results. Celebrate, go for a meal together, go bowling, tell others what you've done. Work to maintain what you have achieved and look for new goals.

Anyone can be a great team leader; all it requires is common sense, humility (no one can know it all) and the ability to help others give of their best.

CASE STUDY — Teamwork

When Winnie Douglas announced that she was retiring, the managing director of Evergreen Care Homes didn't think he'd have any trouble replacing her. Winnie had managed the Cedars for 12 years and she'd had a charmed life. No one at the Cedars had ever been dismissed. Disciplinary problems were rare. Sickness absence was low. The staff worked well together and were pleasant, kind and caring to everyone. Winnie didn't seem to do any managing at all; in fact she spent a lot of time working with staff and delivering care. She seemed to delegate everything: care assistants answered the phone and one even prepared the monthly petty cash returns.

The managing director wasn't overwhelmed with applications when he advertised, and the most suitable candidate didn't have very much experience. He wasn't too worried because Winnie hadn't really had to manage anyhow.

When the new manager started work she managed by the book. Morale plummeted, sickness rose and the staff didn't seem so happy anymore. Belatedly the managing director realised that Winnie had developed a strong team. In working with the team she was respected because her actions in working with staff and delivering care were in line with her words that patient care was important. The managing director began to examine his perceptions of management.

Reflect on practice ....

Good management, like good nursing care, is often invisible. You notice when management is poor because people don't work together, morale is poor and there is an atmosphere. Think of an area where you have worked where no one seemed to be managed but everything went well. What were the characteristics of the manager or leader in this situation? Think of an area where you worked where the quality of care and morale were poor. Can you identify the reasons why this was so? What would you do to improve such a situation?

5.11 Planning and managing care

Although nursing assessments and care plans have been used for many years, there is no legal requirement to assess needs and plan care within the NHS. Staff working in homes are now required to carry out assessments and to plan care under National Minimum Standards, and also to enable nurses to carry out assessments for eligibility for the Registered Nursing Care Contribution (Department of Health, 2001). Nurses in all settings often find it difficult to assess and plan care effectively.

Care homes' legal obligations to plan and manage care

Standard 3 of National Minimum Standards requires the home to carry out comprehensive assessment using 13 care categories including falls and continence promotion. Homes must carry out a comprehensive assessment prior to admitting a resident. The home is (for the first time) legally required to maintain care plans. This has long been good practice but has never been a legal requirement. (See the example care plan on page 122.)

Standard 4 requires the home to demonstrate its ability to meet assessed needs and deliver care that is based on good practice and clinical guidance. New standards, such as *Good Practice in Continence Services* (Department of Health, 2000), must be adhered too. New standards, such as those on prescribing and older people contained in the National Service Framework for Older People, must also be met. Failure to meet such standards could result in loss of registration. Staff are also required to document the risk assessment in relation to the prevention of falls. The care plan must be:

● reviewed at least once a month to reflect changing needs;
● drawn up in consultation with the resident;
● accessible to the resident; and
● signed by the resident (if capable); if not, it must be signed by a representative.

Standard 8 relates to maintaining health. The issue of assessing pressure sore risk and prevention and treatment of pressure sores is emphasised. The issue of preventing falls is again emphasised. Homes are required to carry out comprehensive nutritional assessments and to take appropriate action to prevent malnutrition.

DATE	IDENTIFIED PROBLEM OR NEED	AIM OF CARE	CARE REQUIRED	EVALUATION AND OUTCOMES OF CARE	DATE OF EVALUATION
1.7.04	Immobile following repair of fractured femur	To enable Mrs Jones to regain previous level of mobility	Currently unable to transfer unaided from bed to chair. Assessed by physiotherapist, requires one person to help transfer. Requires regular analgesia as fear of pain may impede transfers. To walk five metres with physiotherapist and one member of staff three times a day	Now transferring with minimal assistance of one person. Mobility improving, to walk with physiotherapist with one member of staff available to help if needed.	5th July 2004
1.7.04	At risk of developing pressure sores, Braden scale = 14, sacrum red.	To prevent pressure sores. To enable red sacrum to heal	Pressure relieving overlay on bed. Cushion supplied for chair. Encourage to change position in bed and chair. Assist to change position if unable. Observe skin for deterioration and report if this occurs.	Now moving freely in bed and able to change position in chair. Condition of skin on sacrum improved, now pink.	7th July 2004
1.7.04	Appetite poor, weight 45kg. Encourage to eat normal diet and snacks to regain weight.	To regain weight, normally weighs 50kg and has lost weight whilst in hospital	Encourage to eat meals, ensure that Mrs Jones is able to chose meals that she likes. Encourage her to eat snacks between meals.	Appetite improving now eating _ of meals provided and some snacks.	8th July 2004
1.7.04	To control pain post operatively	To prevent Mrs Jones experiencing severe pain post operatively.	Give Tramadol six hourly as prescribed. Observe Mrs Jones to ensure that this effectively controlling pain	Pain well controlled. Seen by doctor. Paracetamol prescribed regularly for pain. Tramadol now to be given only on an as required basis if paracetamol ineffective. Please observe and report on pain control.	9th July 2004.

A care plan

Standard 12 requires homes to demonstrate that routines and activities of daily living are flexible and reflect the needs and aspirations of residents. A home, for example, that forced residents to rise at 6 am would not meet this standard. A home where staff stated that every resident chooses to rise at 6 am would not meet the standard. The only way to demonstrate that you meet this standard is to state the person's preferences specifically on the person's care plan. The care plan should state: 'Mrs Jones wishes to get up at...She prefers to shower. She prefers to shower before breakfast.'

5.12 Professional requirements

Registered nurses working in all care settings are required to meet standards set by the Nursing and Midwifery Council. Standards on record-keeping state that nurses are required to complete a daily record (Nursing and Midwifery Council, 2003). In all care settings nurses are required to record assessments of a person's care requirements and their actions in meeting those requirements. How can nurses meet these requirements without becoming overwhelmed with paperwork?

Generic assessments

You can meet standards and obligations by using a generic assessment with triggers to more specific assessments. The generic assessment asks questions about every aspect of the person's health and wellbeing. If this assessment identifies problems then a more specific assessment is carried out.

Good practice in continence services identifies four levels of assessment. The assessment in the generic assessment is known as level one assessment. Level one assessment identifies problems. A specific assessment tool, such as a continence assessment, is a level-two assessment and can be carried out by a registered nurse. Level-three assessment is more specialised and can be carried out by a continence specialist. A medical or, sometimes, a nurse consultant carries out the most complex of assessments: level-four assessment. If a person does not have a specific problem and is not at high risk of developing a problem, you do not need to do a specific assessment.

Specialist assessments

If your generic assessment identifies a potential problem, such as the person being unable to move unaided and so at risk of developing pressure sores, you need to undertake a specific assessment such as the Braden or Waterlow scale. The information that you gain from your specific assessment will enable you to eliminate problems and reduce the risks of the problems that you cannot eliminate. The information you gain from the assessment will form the basis of your care plan.

5.13 Nursing models

Nursing models provide nurses with 'a frame of reference, a pattern of thoughts and activities that enables them to make explicit the art and science of nursing'. Nursing models are tools that provide a framework. This framework is used to enable you to assess need, set goals, implement and evaluate care.

The Roper Model was introduced by Roper, Logan and Tierney in the late 1970s and adapted in the 1980s and 1990s. It identifies activities of daily living that the authors consider should be used to plan care. It is the most widely used nursing model in the UK (Holland et al., 2003). Critics of this model state that it places too much emphasis on the physical and not enough on the psychological.

The Orem model is not widely used in wards or nursing homes. Orem considers that human beings benefit from nursing when they have health needs and are dependent on others. She suggests that adults in western society should be self-reliant. People should be encouraged to see themselves as self-care agents. People should only require help when a potential or actual self-care deficit becomes evident (Orem, 1971). Orem emphasises the need for nurses to collaborate with patients and to work together. Critics of the model point out that Orem assumes that patients all have the ability to make choices about care.

All nursing models have a common core. They assess the person, the environment, the person's health and nursing needs.

5.14 The principles of planning care

Care planning consists of four key areas (see Figure 5.8).

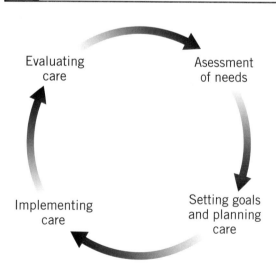

Figure 5.8 The care planning cycle

Assessment of needs

Nursing models provide structured assessment and enable nurses to identify problems that could otherwise be overlooked. You can only begin to set goals and plan care when you have accurately identified needs. Assessment is crucial to the whole care-planning process. Yet often nurses rush assessment in their haste to set goals and plan care.

Setting goals and planning care

The planning process must set specific, realistic, measurable and achievable goals.

Nursing actions should be clear and concise. Everyone in the team should be able to understand them. It's important to break down a large goal such as 'Enable Mrs Mary Evans to regain mobility' into a number of smaller, easily measured goals. Breaking down the process into smaller, more easily measured goals means that the task does not appear overwhelming and unachievable. A goal should not plan to take Mrs Jones from inability to weight bearing to walking independently with a frame. Set interim goals such as standing with a standing frame, transferring from bed to chair with help, rising unaided from a chair. Nurses and those they care for are people, and people are more motivated by a series of small wins rather than one big win. When planning care consider the following questions:

- What is the problem?
- What does the patient want to achieve?
- What can you do about the problem?
- What are the benefits of treatment/care?
- What are the costs or pitfalls of treatment/care?
- What resources (e.g. equipment and staff) are required?
- Who is the best person to deliver this care?
- How will this care be delivered?
- What do you want to achieve?
- How will you know when this has been achieved?
- When will you review treatment?

Implementing care

When implementing a plan of care consider the person's safety but do not loose sight of the person's needs, hopes and fears. It's important to work with other professionals and the person's family.

Evaluating care

The evaluation process is concerned with the outcome of the plan of care. Evaluation, like all other stages of care planning, should be ongoing but often it isn't. Nurses often shrink from evaluating care because evaluation may reveal that nurses have 'failed' to achieve their goals. The problem is not the evaluation but that the goals set were inappropriate. When evaluating you need to ask the following questions:

- Were the goals realistic and achievable?
- Was the timescale in which the goals were to be met realistic?
- Did you really have the patient's consent and active participation?
- Did you set the right priorities?
- Did you have sufficient staff to realise these goals?
- Did staff have the skills to achieve these goals?
- Was the care plan flexible and adapted to the patient's changing needs?

Evaluation is a learning process. Be forgiving of yourself and your staff. If staff are condemned for 'getting it wrong', you'll develop a culture where no one is prepared to take risks. Then all innovation will be stifled and morale will suffer.

5.15 Documentation

Nurses are poor at documenting care. This may be because they receive little training in documentation. However, there have been calls to improve training (Hocking and Shamash, 1998). Nurses are better at delivering care than documenting care. Unfortunately the world is changing and the number of complaints and litigation claims are rising. In legal terms, if it wasn't documented it wasn't done. Documentation enables you to audit care and to answer complaints effectively.

DATE	DAILY STATEMENT OF HEALTH/CHANGES IN CONDITION/ CARE NEEDS	SIG
1.7.04, 12md	Transferred from Queen Elizabeth hospital following repair of fractured femur five days ago, accompanied by daughter Janet. Mrs Jones is keen to return home to her bungalow as soon as possible but requires rehabilitation as mobility poor (see care plan).	AS
14:30	Mrs Jones consented to being seen and treated by physiotherapist. Currently unable to transfer unaided from bed to chair. Is safe to transfer with one. Has agreed to sit out of bed and to walk with physiotherapist and nurse three times a day.	JK
18:00	Small amount of supper taken, analgesia given pain free.	JN
2.7.04 07:00hrs	Comfortable night, assisted to change position in bed.	PB

Be extremely careful how you document your goals in care plans

CASE STUDY — Documentation

Anytown NHS Trust made a large out-of-court settlement when a frail, emaciated cancer patient developed a pressure sore. Nurses had done everything they could to prevent the person developing a pressure sore, including risk assessment and the use of special equipment. The trust was forced to settle out of court because they were advised they would loose the court battle. The nursing care plan stated that one of the aims of care was 'to prevent pressure sores' and they had failed.

Reflect on practice

Examine the care plans in your workplace. Do they accurately reflect the care required? Are they up to date? If they are not, why do you think this is? Is it clear who is responsible for individual care plans? Do staff consider care plans to be important? What can you do to ensure that care plans are accurate and up to date?

5.16 Beyond care planning – patient care pathways

Care plans originated in the USA in the 1970s. The world has moved on and, in the future, care plans may be replaced in some care settings by care pathways. Integrated

---

INTEGRATED CARE PATHWAY FOR THE PREVENTION AND MANAGEMENT OF FALLS

Lincolnshire Partnership
NHS Trust

The prevalence of falls increases with age, and the subsequent disability and mortality that arises indicates a serious issue in the care of older adults. This Integrated Care Pathway is for those receiving care in Older Adult's Inpatient Mental Health Services. It is intended to guide the prevention of falls and management of risk. Wherever possible the interventions are based upon evidence and best practice.

1. PERSONAL DETAILS

Name & Date of Birth: (affix ID label)	**Ward:**
	Unit/Location:
	Admission Date:

Overall Objectives of this care pathway are to
- Reduce the likelihood of falling and subsequent injury.
- Establish effective interdisciplinary working and ensure that appropriate and necessary treatments are part of post fall care.
- Determine a measure of risk by prompt and expert assessment.
- Provide an effective and evidence based treatment plan to manage the level of identified risk.

Sources and evidence which inform the content of this pathway are;
Department of Health. (2001). National Service Framework for Older People. Department of Health; London.
Effective Healthcare Research Team. (1996). Preventing Falls and Subsequent Injury in Older People. Effective Health Care. NHS Centre for Reviews and Dissemination; University of York.
Parker. M. J., Gillespie. L. D. & Gillespie. W. J. (2003). Hip protectors for preventing hip fractures in the elderly. Cochrane Library. Issue 1
Redsall. S., Cheater. F. & Juby. L. (2002). Management and prevention of falls in the elderly. The Journal of Clinical Governance. 10.215-222

Instructions for use:
Before writing in this Integrated Care Pathway, please ensure you have signed the signature sheet (overleaf). When using this document please ensure that you date, time and sign against each activity where indicated. It is important to remember that the aim of the Integrated Care Pathway (ICP) is to ensure the most appropriate care is given at the correct time. If an activity outlined in the ICP has not, for whatever reason, been completed then this must be shown as a variance. Record this at the points for variance recording. Then ensure that this is transferred onto the variance record sheet (page 4). If further action needs to be taken, e.g. the intervention needs to be repeated, then use the blank spaces in the appropriate time frame of the ICP to record this. These blank spaces can also be used to add interventions which are deemed appropriate but are not already in the ICP. These additions should also be recorded as a variance. To view an example of a completed ICP please read the ICP file which is in your ward/area.

It remains each professional's responsibility to ensure that practice is safe. This ICP is not a replacement for experienced clinical judgement and inter-disciplinary discussions. If you require further information please contact your Ward Manager, Clinical Team Leader or Care Pathway Manager.

Issue Date: 01/04/03   Version: In Use 1   Page1

An integrated care pathway

care pathways are 'structured multidisciplinary care plans, which detail essential steps in the care of patients with a specific clinical problem' (Campbell et al., 1998). They are also a means of improving the systematic collection of data for audit and promoting change in practice. If the care given should deviate from the pathway, a variance is recorded. This allows a record of what was done differently, why it was done differently and what action was taken (Johnson and Smith, 2000).

Integrated care pathways are particularly suited to some areas of work. People who are receiving healthcare move through different healthcare systems and receive care from people in different organisations. An integrated care pathway can help ensure that the person receives continuity of care and that different staff communicate effectively.

CASE STUDY – An integrated care pathway

Mrs Barbara Forbes lived alone. She had suffered from arthritis in her hip for many years. A hip replacement was organised at the local elective orthopaedic centre. Mrs Forbes' care pathway began with assessment at home by an occupational therapist. When she was admitted, staff followed the care pathway for the five days that she was an inpatient. On day three it was clear that Mrs Forbes was slow to recover. She was assessed under the pathway and it was agreed to transfer her to a care home on day five.

On day five Mrs Forbes was transferred to the care home with her integrated care pathway. The pathway indicated treatment and assessment were required during her 14-day stay in the care home. Physiotherapy was delivered by community physiotherapists, nursing care by nursing home nurses. Further assessment for home care by the community rehabilitation team was carried out. On day 19 Mrs Forbes was transferred to the community rehabilitation team with her care pathway. The pathway enabled all the people working with Mrs Forbes to deliver integrated care.

Reflect on practice

Do you think that integrated care pathways could be useful in your work area? What do you think their advantages might be? What disadvantages can you think of?

5.17 Integrated care pathways in long-term care

Staff at Oakdene (a 36-bed mental health unit for patients with complex needs) found problems with care plans. The unit had used core care plans and found that staff were often delivering completely different care from that planned. They found that core care plans were not always evidence based and often had unrealistic outcomes. They introduced integrated care pathways. They found that paperwork was reduced and staff could determine the care required at a glance (Brett and Schofield, 2002). Care pathways are research based, reduce paperwork and enable nurses and managers to demonstrate that care has been delivered. They can be used in continuing care and rehabilitation settings.

Potential dangers of care pathways

A care pathway, like any other tool, is a two-edged sword. It has the potential to improve care, as we've seen. It also has the potential to take us backwards. Care pathways can be reductionalist. Mrs Forbes' care pathway related to her hip replacement. It focused on the hip and not on the person having a hip replacement. If you are not careful in the way that you integrate care pathways you risk going backwards and seeing Mrs Forbes and others like her only as a diseased part, in her case the hip, and not as a whole person.

Those trained in the old days will remember being taught about the care of the hysterectomy without reference to the person who was having the hysterectomy. In the old days you weren't taught to think how a hysterectomy might affect a woman's perception of herself. You weren't taught to think about the difficulties she might have coping with responsibilities at home on discharge.

Now nurses are taught to care for the whole person and this is a huge step forward. There is a danger that in adopting a bright, shiny, research-based integrated care pathway we might once again revert to a medical model that did not serve people well in the past. Combining the old with the new will ensure that care pathways integrate all aspects of a person's being and are not simply disease focused.

5.18 Conclusion

Sometimes people who are new to management look to writers, teachers and experienced managers for 'the answer'. The implication is that there is only one answer and one way. Life isn't like that. There are often many answers, and the skill is to work out which answers have the greatest chance of success within a particular organisation, with a particular set of people at a particular time. The skilful manager will be aware of how little he or she knows. The self-aware manager will know that he or she does not have all the answers. Sometimes staff will have some of the answers, sometimes no one has the answers. Then the manager and the staff must set out on an exciting journey to find out what they can do to make things better. During this journey they will find out a great deal about each other and about themselves.

Key Points

○ Organisations are much more complex than the management charts used to explain them.

○ Organisations are not the model of rationality that some management writers would have you believe.

○ Organisations have a culture. That culture may differ in different parts of the organisation.

○ Information does not flow up and down within organisations in clear pathways. It flows in all directions.

○ Organisations are changing to meet the changing demands placed on them.

○ The key to providing responsive services is to develop the people in the organisation and to work together collaboratively as teams.

○ Understanding team roles enables you to understand the team better.

○ Understanding the dynamics of the team enables you to support and nurture it during its growth.

○ The sensitive manager needs to know when to let go and enable the team to go it alone.

○ Planning and managing care are an important part of effective teamworking.

References and further reading

INTRODUCTION

Commission Health Improvement (2003) 'Older people's ward "forgotten" by Manchester health services', press statement (available at **http://www.chi.nhs.uk/eng/news/2003/sep/14.shtml24).**

SECTION 5.1

McGavock, H. (1997) *A Review of the Literature on Drug Adherence.* Royal Pharmaceutical Society of Great Britain, London.

Schein, E. (1992) *Organisational Culture and Leadership* (2nd edn). Jossey-Bass, San Francisco.

SECTION 5.2

Department of Health (2002) *Learning from Bristol. The Department of Health's Response to the Report of the Public Enquiry into Children's Heart Surgery at the Bristol Royal Infirmary, 1984–1995.* Department of Health, London.

Goffman, E. (1961) *Asylums.* Penguin Books, London (reprinted 1998).

Handy, C. (1995) *Gods of Management. The Changing Work of Organisations.* Arrow, London.

Harrison, R. and Stokes, H. (1992) *Diagnosing Organisational Culture.* Pfeiffer, Mass.

Wright, R. *GPs as Managers* (available at **http://www.hoolet.org.uk/33hoolet/managers.htm**).

SECTION 5.4

Handy, C. (1988) *Understanding Voluntary Organisations.* Penguin Books, London.

SECTION 5.5

Macoby, M. (1976) *The Gamesman.* Simon & Schuster, New York.

SECTION 5.6

Mant, A. (1983) *Leaders We Deserve.* Martin Robertson, London.

SECTION 5.7

Kanter, R.M. (1983) *The Change Masters. Corporate Entrepreneurs at Work.* Allen & Unwin, New York.

Section 5.8

Argyris, C., Bridges, W., Dean, B. et al. (1994) 'The future of workplace learning and performance', *Training and Development*, special issue, May.

Blau, P. and Meyer, M.W. (1971) *Bureaucracy in Modern Society*. Random House, New York.

Section 5.9

Kanter, R.M. (1983) *The Change Masters. Corporate Entrepreneurs at Work*. Allen & Unwin, New York.

Kanter, R.M. (1989) *When Giants Learn to Dance*. Simon & Schuster, New York.

Senge, P. (1990) *The Fifth Discipline*. Doubleday, New York.

Senge, P. (1992) 'The real message of the quality movement: building learning organisations', *Journal for Quality and Participation*, March: 30–8.

Senge, P.M., Roberts, C., Ross, R.B., Smith, B.J. and Kleiner, A. (1994) *The Fifth Discipline Fieldbook*. Doubleday, New York.

Section 5.10

Belbin, R.M. (1981) *Management Teams: Why They Succeed or Fail*. Butterworth-Heinemann, Oxford.

Belbin, R.M. (1996) *Team Roles at Work*. Butterworth-Heinemann, Oxford.

Lewin, K. (1951) *Field Theory in Social Science*. Harper & Row, New York.

Schnell, E.R. and Hammer, A. (1993) *Introduction to the FIRO-B in Organizations*. Consulting Psychologists Press, Palo Alto, CA.

Schutz, W. (1958) *FIRO: A Three Dimensional Theory of Interpersonal Behaviour*. Holt, Rinehart & Winston, New York.

Weaver, R.G. and Farrell, J.D. (1999) *Managers as Facilitators*. Berett-Kochler, San Francisco.

Section 5.11

Department of Health (2001) *National Minimum Standards for Care Homes for Older People* (available at **http://www.doh.gov.uk/ncsc**).

Section 5.12

Department of Health (2000) *Good Practice in Continence Services*. Department of Health, London.

Section 5.13

Holland, A. J., Roper, N., Logan, W. and Tierney, A. (2003) *Applying the Roper–Logan–Tierney Model in Practice. Elements of Nursing*. Churchill Livingstone, London.

Nursing and Midwifery Council (2003) *Guidelines for Records and Record Keeping*. NMC, London.

Orem, D. (1971) *Nursing Concepts in Practice*. McGraw-Hill, New York.

Roper, N., Logan, W. and Tierney, J. (2001) *The Roper–Logan–Tierney Model of Nursing*. Churchill Livingstone, London.

Section 5.16

Campbell, H., Hotchkiss, R. and Bradshaw, N. (1998) 'Integrated care pathways', *British Medical Journal*, 316: 133–7.

Hocking, J. and Shamash, J. (1998) 'Poor record keeping harms patient care, says report', *Nursing Standard*, 12: 5.

Johnson, S. and Smith, J. (2000) 'Factors influencing the success of ICP projects', *Professional Nurse*, 15: 776–9.

Section 5.18

Brett, W. and Schofield, J. (2002) 'Integrated care pathways for patients with complex needs', *Nursing Standard*, 16: 36–40.

CHAPTER 6

Special skills for special people

Introduction

Older people are the major consumers of healthcare. Medical, surgical and orthopaedic wards are full of older people. Older people are also cared for in wards designated as care of older people, rehabilitation and intermediate care, in care homes and in their own homes. Yet few nurses have developed the special skills required to care for older people.

Aims

6.1   Total institutions

6.2   Gerontological nursing: the undervalued speciality

6.3   The art and science of nursing

6.4   As others see us

6.5   Articulating the value of gerontological nursing

6.6   Drivers for change

6.7   Skills required

6.8   Do specialist skills make a difference?

6.9   The place of specialist skills

6.10 Conclusion

6.1 Total institutions

My first experience of nursing older people was in 1976 when I was allocated to what was then known as the 'geriatric' hospital. The geriatric hospital was on a different site from the main hospital and it was very different from the main building. The building was old and it had concrete corridors. The main hospital had brightly lit corridors with marble flooring. The corridors of the main hospital teemed with life. The corridors of the geriatric hospital were eerily quiet. When I got to the wards I was surprised to find that they didn't use names, just numbers. The wards were arranged in blocks and numbered according to their position on the blocks: E4 was the top ward on the E block. I had entered one of the nooks and crannies of the organisation.

I had entered what Goffman (1961) would describe as a 'total institution'. Goffman considers that there are five categories of institution. The geriatric hospital was in the first category: 'institutions established to care for persons felt to be both incapable and harmless; these are the homes for the blind, the aged, the orphaned, and the indigent.'

In normal life people sleep, play and work in different places. This is not so for people who live in institutions (see Figure 6.1).

---

1   All aspects of life are conducted in the same place and under the same central authority.

2   Each phase of the member's daily activity is carried on in the immediate company of a large batch of others, all of whom are treated alike and required to do the same thing together.

3   All phases of the day's activities are tightly scheduled, with one activity leading at a prearranged time into the next, the whole sequence of activities being imposed from above by a system of explicit formal rulings and a body of officials.

4   Finally, the various enforced activities are brought together into a single rational plan purportedly designed to fulfil the official aims of the institution.

Figure 6.1 The characteristics of institutions

The patients in the lower blocks had 'failed' to recover sufficiently to return home and were having rehabilitation to enable them to return home. It wasn't clear to me how they would recover because we didn't have very many staff and only a few therapists. The patients were very dependent, and I felt totally unable to offer them appropriate care because I knew so little about caring for older people. I went to see my tutor who assured me that I shouldn't worry – all the patients needed was basic nursing care. It was hard to give even 'basic' nursing care because we were so short staffed. The patients were so much more dependent than in the surgical ward I had left but there were, nevertheless, two fewer nurses on each shift on this ward. I asked sister why and she told me that this was just the way it was. I went to see the Director of Nursing for the group. I sat outside her office for hours and was eventually shown in to see her. She was bemused and said that I seemed a sensitive soul and, if was getting so upset, perhaps I'd like to move. I said I'd stay. What I'd encountered at nineteen was ageism in action.

My placement finished, I qualified and went to work in neurosurgery and general surgery before going to work abroad for two years. When I returned I signed on with an agency. The agency was less than impressed with my stint abroad and suggested that I might be a bit rusty. So they sent me to the geriatric ward as it was 'only basic nursing'. It was anything but basic, and I knew so little and they needed so much.

In 1983 my journey to attain the skills required to care for older people began, and it continues to this day.

Older people are the major consumers of healthcare, yet few nurses have developed the special skills required to care for them. This chapter aims to explore the reasons why nursing older people has traditionally been perceived as requiring less specialist skills. It outlines the powerful drivers now in place to change the old ways and to enable staff to develop new skills in order to provide quality care.

This chapter explores the technical and humanistic aspects of caring for older people. Nursing is both a science and an art. If we are to nurse well we need to learn how to combine technical skills with an understanding of how human beings react when ill. We need not only to be able to care for a wound but also for the human being who has the wound.

The ability to understand how ageing affects individuals and to work with people who are old and ill and may be grieving for the loss of a loved one can make the difference between a person choosing to work with you to regain skills or turning his or her face to the wall and giving up. This chapter explores how, by improving skills and knowledge, nurses can truly make a difference.

6.2 Gerontological nursing: the undervalued specialty

Images of gerontological nursing are often negative. Caring for older people can be thought of as full of doom, gloom, dependency, disability and death. It doesn't have to be this way. Nurses can and do enable older people to experience a rich and full life. Tessa Harding (1997) points out that older people do not wish to be dependent:

Dependence is too often foisted on older people, not by their own circumstances but by lack of access and opportunity to remain independent.

Nurses caring for older people can and do enable older people to regain ability. It is important, though, that you value people who are not able to regain independence equally as any others. Dimon (pers. comm.) describes the care of older people as:

The holistic provision of humanistic care required by an individual in order to maintain quality of life.

Nursing does not exist in isolation from society. Nurses' values reflect the values of the society nurses live in. People recoil in horror now at the prejudices of earlier generations and the way people were discriminated against. When my parents came to England from Ireland to find work in the 1950s there were signs in newsagents' windows advertising accommodation that stated: 'No blacks, no dogs, no Irish.' Such discrimination was always immoral. It is now illegal and unthinkable but in one area – that of ageism – discrimination is alive and kicking.

The term ageism was invented by Robert Butler (1969) to describe stereotyping and discrimination based on age. He commented:

Ageist attitudes may do tangible disservice to older people. No where is this more apparent than in healthcare.

Ageism, like all discrimination, has certain features. Stereotyping is one important feature. People are grouped into a set because of certain characteristics and are labelled 'the old', 'the elderly'. When people are labelled they loose individuality and are viewed as a herd. They loose humanity and individuality. Some people in any group will have negative characteristics, and all the people in the group are assigned these characteristics. Jokes are made about the group and public opinion considers this group less valuable and less worth while than other members of society. It then becomes acceptable to discriminate against this group.

In our society it is acceptable to discriminate on grounds of age. In advertising and computing, for instance, it is difficult to get a job if you are over 40 years of age. These jobs are considered as requiring bright, enthusiastic, youthful people. The perception seems to be that the mind seizes up and can no longer produce bright, original thought after a certain age. In the UK it is not illegal to place a job advert asking for 'young dynamic people' or to discriminate on the grounds of age. People are still forced to retire when they reach a certain age. The government will comply with European Union requirements to introduce legislation to ban discrimination on the grounds of age in 2007. However, it remains that older people are often considered to be less capable than younger people and are often portrayed negatively, particularly by the media.

Reflect on practice

The next time you watch television for an evening, bear the following points in mind. Are older people less well represented than people of other age groups? Are the portrayals of older people less well rounded and more stereotypical than those of other age groups? Do you think the way older people are portrayed on television is accurate? Read your usual newspaper and make the same checks.

In the 1980s and 1990s there were concerns about the growing numbers of older people, and there were fears that the rising tide of older people would engulf the health services, making it impossible for other people to obtain healthcare

(Phillipson, 1999). These concerns were reflected in health service spending. In the late twentieth century the number of older people increased by 50 per cent but spending on health and social services fell (Nazarko, 2000). The NHS nursing home experiment (which was begun in the 1970s) was transferred from the NHS to means-tested, independent sector care, and the NHS long-stay hospitals that were free at the point of delivery were closed (Royal Commission on Long Term Care, 1999). At the same time, the link between earnings and retirement pensions was cut and the value of state pensions has continued to decline. Such policy changes could be construed as implying that older people are considered to be a burden on society rather than an asset. From this it could be argued that those who care for older people are unlikely to be highly valued.

6.3 The art and science of nursing

Nursing combines art and science. The *science* of nursing includes the ability to assess wounds, to prepare the wound bed correctly, to apply appropriate dressings and to enable the wound to heal (Collier, 2003). The *art* of nursing includes the ability to communicate with people who feel that life is not worth living, to reach out to them and to enable them to begin healing, both physically and mentally (Nazarko, 1993). Some nursing concentrates on curing people. The person with gallstones might have surgery to remove the stones or the gall bladder containing the stones. Nursing provides support whilst the patient recovers, and the patient leaves the hospital cured. It's easy to see the attraction in the curing aspects of nursing. It's clean and quick, there's a beginning when the patient enters the system ill and an end when the patient leaves cured. The technical part of nursing follows the medical model, and some nurses caring for older people disparage this model. However, there is a place for the technical aspects of nursing within the care of older people, but the caring aspects must balance the technical aspects.

In adult nursing the cure or medical model is no longer sufficient on its own because adult nursing has become less clearly defined. The person who receives gall bladder surgery may well be an older person, and this person might be vulnerable to malnutrition and loss of ability post-operatively. The science of nursing would enable you to identify that this person is at risk of malnutrition, but it is the art of nursing that enables you to communicate effectively and to provide tempting food to enable him or her to eat.

In Chapter 1 we saw that the art of nursing, of seeing the patient as a person and more than just a disease process, has somehow become neglected. A narrow disease-orientated view of nursing ill serves older people. It can lead to the 'successful' repair of a fractured femur but the patient might be left immobile, incontinent and unable to care for him or herself (Audit Commission, 1995). The failure to meet the holistic needs of older people means that older people loose their ability in acute settings so that it is not possible to discharge them home. The Royal Commission on Long Term Care identified this problem and recommended setting up rehabilitation centres to enable older people to recover fully following illness or accident. Their recommendations provide part of the solution, but the real challenge is to improve acute care for older people so that recovery times are minimised. The case study below illustrates how care that is not holistic can contribute to increased dependency.

CASE STUDY – Holistic care

Mr Amjad is 76 and was recently widowed. He normally drives, gardens and shops – in other words, he leads a reasonably active life. He has Parkinson's disease and recently developed a chest infection, which made him confused and he fell several times. His GP arranged for him to be admitted to hospital.

Mr Amjad was nursed in bed and treated with antibiotics. He was got up ten days after admission but felt very dizzy and sick. Each time the nurses tried to get him up he felt unwell and so he was returned to bed. Twenty days after admission he was well enough for discharge. Unfortunately, he had become incontinent, he was unable to sit up and he had lost the ability to care for himself or to move unaided. Staff in the ward had looked after Mr Amjad's chest but had not supplied the holistic care that he required.

Mr Amjad was transferred to Lawton War Memorial Hospital. He was sick in body and soul. The science of nursing had effectively assessed his physical problems and had enabled the team to provide the right treatment. This had revealed that he was constipated and that his bladder contained 1.3 litres of urine. He had urinary retention with overflow. Effective bowel management removed the mass of faeces that was contributing to urinary retention. Mr Amjad regained continence with effective bladder management. He felt sick and dizzy when he sat up because he had experienced a prolonged period of bed rest. He was mobilised gently and regained the ability to move independently.

The art of nursing enabled the nurses to see Mr Amjad as a person grieving for his wife of 52 years – as a person frightened and bewildered by his illness and disability, a person who wondered if it was worth the effort to get better. The art of nursing enabled the nurses to reach out and connect with Mr Amjad and to help him find his way back from sickness to health and to become healthy and whole once again.

Reflect on practice

Is equal value given to the art and science of nursing within your workplace? If not, why do you think this is so? Think of the skills that you use to care for an older person. Could you provide more effective care if you used the art and the science of nursing? What are the barriers you face when you aim to combine both aspects of nursing? How might you lower those barriers?

6.4 As others see us

There is a hierarchy within nursing. The areas where technical skills are perceived to be of prime importance are considered to be more demanding and more exciting areas for nurses to work than the areas where caring skills are perceived to be more important. A job in intensive care, renal dialysis or accident and emergency is perceived to be 'better' than one caring for older people (Stevens and Crouch, 1995). Nursing older people is a relatively unpopular option (McKinley and Cowan, 2003). Benner (1984), a nurse theorist who has written of the nurse's journey from novice to expert, illustrates her work with examples from these technical areas (Wade, 1999).

This hierarchy, however, does not make sense: nurses working in acute areas of care, where technical skills are perceived to be the most important aspect of the care, do not live in a hermetically sealed bubble. They are caring for the UK population as a whole, and that population is growing older. Many of the adults in the accident and emergency department are older people, as are many of those in the renal dialysis unit and the intensive care unit. Somehow older people and the people who care for them are considered to be of value as long as the needs are for acute technical care. When technical care given in isolation fails to deliver and the patient is considered to have 'failed' to recover, the perception of the patient changes. The patient is no longer considered to be worthy of acute care and might be labelled a 'bed blocker'. Care is transferred to lower-status nurses in step-down units, in rehabilitation, community or nursing home settings.

Senior nurse managers, nurses working in technical areas of practice and nurse educators often view the care of older people as being unskilled. These perceptions have a real impact on the quality of care older people receive. If nurse managers do not consider that older people require high levels of skilled care, the skill mix in wards caring for older people might be different from that in other areas. The wards caring for older people might have lower levels of registered nurses, and those registered nurses who are employed might be on lower grades.

Ward managers are normally employed on G grades within the NHS. In high-tech areas the manager may well have an H or I grade. In some trusts it is considered acceptable to employ ward managers who care for older people on F grades. This sends out the message that caring for older people is less skilled than other areas of nursing. If posts are downgraded there are fewer senior posts and fewer chances of promotion. Ambitious nurses may chose to work in another speciality where prospects are greater. Nurses who choose to care for older people might feel that they are being exploited and treated less favourably than nurses in other specialities. NHS pay grades and attitudes affect the pay and prospects of nurses working in care homes.

Nurse managers are responsible for drawing up job descriptions and for advertising posts. If they believe that caring for older people does not require specialist skills, this might become a self-fulfilling prophecy in that they might consider appointing unskilled people to senior positions. The case study below illustrates the problems of such thinking.

CASE STUDY — Specialist skills?

Sarah Murphy moved to London with her husband in 2003. She has 22 years' experience of working with older people (ten as a nurse manager) and has a degree in gerontology. She is studying for her master's degree on a part-time basis. When Sarah saw a modern matron's post for older people's wards advertised in her local hospital she applied. Her application was not successful. The interviewers stated that they had decided to appoint someone who lacked gerontology experience but who had good experience of acute care. They felt that the nurses on the older people's wards could learn a great deal from someone who had acute experience. One of the interviewers also said that she felt that Sarah was 'overqualified, too academic' and that the trust was looking for someone who would stay.

On her informal visit it was clear to Sarah that the trust desperately needed someone who had expertise in the care of older people and who could educate and enable staff to provide high-quality care. The difficulty was that the trust didn't recognise that special skills were required.

Reflect on practice

Do you consider that your expertise in caring for older people is valued by others outside your organisation? If not, how does this affect your ability to work with these people? Is your expertise recognised within your area of practice? If so, how does this help you to provide high-quality care? If not, how might you improve the situation?

Nurses who are responsible for inspecting the quality of care within care homes require expertise in caring for older people so that they can determine what is and what is not good practice. They also require educational skills and change management skills so that they can help educate nurses to move practice forward. Unfortunately nurse inspectors are poorly paid, and poor pay and lack of recognition of the skills required to inspect effectively make it difficult for the National Care Standards Commission and its Welsh and Scottish counterparts to attract well qualified nurses.

If nurses working in technical areas do not appreciate the expertise of nurses working with older people, they are unlikely to seek help from nurses with expertise in care of older people. This perpetuates the problems older people experience when they do not receive care that meets all their needs.

If nurse educators do not perceive the care of older people as anything other than 'basic' care that can be delivered by any nurse, they are sending the message to students that nursing older people is an unskilled and unattractive career option. Nurse educators who do not consider that older people require specialist skills are unlikely to ask nurses with specialist expertise in clinical practice to visit their universities to teach students the importance of special skills in the care of older people.

6.5 Articulating the value of gerontological nursing

Mr Amjad moved from illness to wellness because of the ability of nurses to combine curing and caring skills. Curing skills are highly valued, and the medical profession is highly valued because doctors have developed skills, knowledge and competency that are seen as doctor's work (Stevens and Crouch, 1995). Nurses who wish to be viewed as highly skilled professionals find that technical skills are highly regarded in nursing. Caring skills are more difficult to define. They are often viewed as feminine skills that come naturally to all women. This view deprofessionalises caring skills.

Good nursing is often invisible. If older people enjoy the best possible quality of life, this is often considered to be more luck than judgement. Good nursing is usually visible by its absence. If older people are to be treated as complex human beings with the same needs as younger adults, everyone must realise the need for staff with specialist skills. However, nurses who work with older people have sometimes failed to challenge the prejudice that surrounds their practice. They have not, for example, defined what advanced gerontological practice is. This is important:

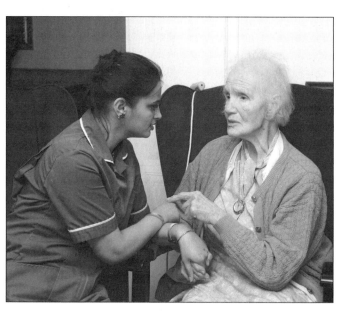

Good nursing is often invisible

If we cannot name it, we cannot control it, finance it, teach it, research it or put it into public policy (Clark and Lang, 1994).

If you are to develop practice within gerontology, you need to be able to define expert practice, to work out what skills nurses require as they move from novice to expert and what resources are required to deliver expert practice. There is much to be done. Chapter 5 examined change management, force field theory and how drivers for change can move practice forward. There are now a number of such drivers that are pushing practice forward.

6.6 Drivers for change

When the current government was elected there was widespread dissatisfaction with healthcare. People were worried about waiting lists and about older people receiving poor-quality care. Older people were having to sell their homes and to spend their life savings to pay for nursing home care. The government promised to cut waiting lists, to ensure people received care promptly and to establish a Royal Commission to examine the funding of long-term care.

The government was not going to find it easy to fulfil these promises. The number of people receiving inpatient care has grown over the last forty or more years. Demands on healthcare have grown because of advances in technology and an ageing population. Technological advances mean that diseases that were once untreatable (such as severe arthritis of the hip) can now be treated. An ageing population is the result of success in preventing premature deaths. This success means that more people live longer and require treatment for diseases that are more common in old age. Figure 6.2 shows the increase in hospital treatment since the mid-twentieth century.

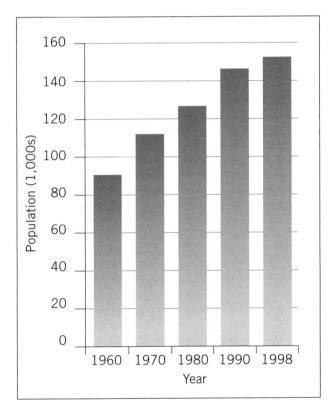

Figure 6.2 Hospital inpatient admissions per thousand of population

There are now more than five times as many people aged 85 years and over as there were in 1961. Figure 6.3 shows how the population has aged.

The government was faced with rising numbers of older people likely to require NHS treatment and, therefore, an increased pressure on NHS beds. Unfortunately the number of beds had not expanded to accommodate these changes. The number of NHS beds had fallen year on year as the need for those beds had increased (Department of Health, 2000) (see Figure 6.4).

The findings of the National Bed Inquiry presented the government with both an opportunity and a threat. The threat was that there were insufficient NHS beds to enable them to meet their promise to cut waiting lists and provide prompt treatment. The low number of beds, however, could also be viewed as an opportunity to do things differently and to provide a more effective, higher-quality care for the

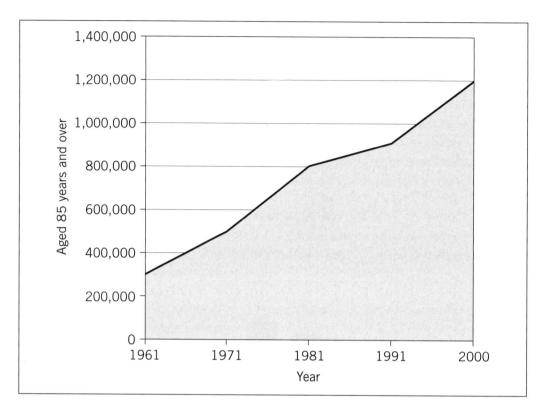

Figure 6.3 The ageing of the population

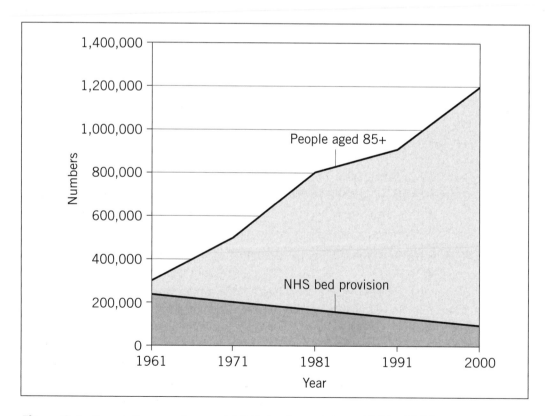

Figure 6.4 Population ageing and NHS bed provision, 1961–2000

older people who occupied the majority of NHS beds. It is known that older people often lose their ability and become dependent in hospital – the older the person, the greater the risk (Covinsky et al., 2003). Older people often enter hospital malnourished and underweight and continue to loose weight in hospital (ACHEW, 1997). The National Service Framework for Older People (NSF) and reports from other bodies highlighted the need to minimise hospital admissions, to ensure high-quality care within hospitals, to make sure that older people had access to effective rehabilitation, if required, and that they received evidence-based care in all settings.

The NSF set up standards and broke those standards down into a series of short and medium-term goals and milestones. Organisations were required to make certain changes within a particular time frame. Standard 4, for example, requires acute hospitals to set up specialist teams to ensure that older people throughout the hospital receive high-quality care. These teams should have a nurse specialist or a nurse consultant in older people in the team. Organisations have responded in different ways to the NSF: some have worked hard to meet the standards; others have not considered them a priority. London has a population of 7.1 million yet some NHS trusts do not have a single older people's clinical nurse specialist or nurse consultant. The Health Care Commission began to audit how organisations are meeting the NSF targets in April 2004. This audit drives organisations that have not yet appointed older people's specialists and consultants to do so. In organisations that have appointed nurse consultants, these nurse consultants are also working hard to drive change.

In January 2004, the Delayed Discharges Act was introduced (Nazarko, 2003). This Act aims to prevent delayed discharges by fining social services departments £150 for every day that an older person's discharge is delayed. Many NHS hospitals have received a guesstimate of the money they will need to improve their social services departments. Some of this money, however, is being used to improve the quality of inpatient care so that older people do not loose their ability whilst in hospital.

The Royal College of Nursing is developing a coherent strategy for older people. This strategy will include improving the profile of older people, changing the focus of nursing to include wellbeing and developing a framework of specialist gerontological education.

The final and, perhaps, most significant driver is that of the government. If the government is to deliver on its promise to provide an efficient, effective health service that treats people promptly, it must get the care of older people right. Currently older people are the largest group of healthcare consumers. The NHS spends £10,000 million – 40 per cent of its budget – on people over the age of 65 years, and two thirds of NHS beds are occupied by older people. Social services spend £5,216 million of their budgets (48 per cent) annually on older people (Department of Health, 2000). The government is driving forward change to ensure that this money is spent effectively. There are pressures to use funds more imaginatively to ensure that older people remain well, instead of spending money when older people have become sick.

6.7 Skills required

One of reasons why nursing older people is not considered to be a speciality may be because it differs from every other speciality. Nurses specialising in the care of neonates care for babies with particular characteristics. These neonates can develop a clearly defined range of problems specific to that age group. Gerontological nurses care for people from the age of sixty to over a hundred years. This age range alone means that there are tremendous physical and psychological variations in the people they care for.

Nurses who specialise in the care of adults have clearly defined areas of clinical practice. The cardiology nurse specialist cares for people with cardiac problems. This clearly defined area of clinical practice enables the nurse specialist to develop a deep understanding of a narrow area. The nurse specialist in adult nursing is normally expected to know a great deal about a narrow area of practice.

Nurses who specialise in the care of older adults do not have clearly defined areas of clinical practice. Older people often have a number of chronic diseases; they can also develop acute illness. Nurses who specialise in the care of older people are required to have a broader knowledge base than other nurse specialists. It is vital that nurses who specialise in the care of older people have the ability to look beyond the disease process to see the whole person. The nurse who specialises in the care of older people requires advanced assessment skills that are quite different and less obvious than those of other nurse specialists. Ageing and illness may make it difficult to communicate effectively with the older person, so the nurse specialist needs to have expert communication skills. However, the nurse who specialises in the care of older people might not appear to other specialists to be a specialist at all. Some writers actually consider that the idea of a

The nurse who specialises in the care of older people requires advanced assessment skills

gerontological nurse specialist is not consistent with care outside hospitals (Oberski et al., 1999).

If a nurse wishes to specialise in an area such as intensive care, it is fairly easy to work out what skills are required. The nurse will require experience of working in an intensive care unit. When the National Boards were responsible for accrediting courses, the nurse who was developing his or her skills would require an ENB 199 or equivalent course: specialist education was the route to recognition and promotion.

However, if a nurse wished to specialise in gerontology it was more difficult to work out what experience was required. There were fewer ENB courses and the courses that were available were generally shorter and less demanding than those for other specialities. As gerontological nursing was often considered to be 'basic', specialist education did not guarantee recognition and promotion in the same way that other courses did.

- The ability to understand that the older person is a unique human being with a wealth of experience and views and expectations about what care is required and why.

- The ability to work effectively in a mutidisciplinary team.

- The ability to relate to the older person and to work in partnership to provide care and support.

- Knowledge of the ageing process and how this affects a person.

- Knowledge of healthy ageing.

- Knowledge of the illnesses that can affect the older person.

- Knowledge of rehabilitation.

- Knowledge of palliative care.

- Advanced communication skills.

- Advanced skills in diagnosis.

- Advanced skills in planning care that is centred on the needs, hopes and aspirations of the older person.

- Ability to deliver effective research-based care.

- Change management skills.

- Education skills.

- Political awareness and the ability to influence.

Figure 6.5 A skills and knowledge framework for gerontological nurses

Despite all the changes in nurse education in recent years, the gerontological nurse specialist requires skills that are not normally required of other specialists. He or she requires a breadth of knowledge and also a depth of knowledge. This knowledge is not solely related to a curative or palliative model of nursing. Such nurses require a unique understanding of the older person as an individual human being as this is, perhaps, the most demanding of all specialist roles. Figure 6.5 outlines the knowledge and skills considered necessary for such a role.

Nurses working with older people will begin their careers as novices and will develop their skills and expertise as they gain experience and knowledge. The challenge now is to identify the skills and level required as nurses progress from novice to effective practitioner to expert.

The Royal College of Nursing recently developed a programme that identifies and accredits nurses working in accident and emergency departments. The programme identifies three levels of practitioner.

Associate Members

The first level is for people who have been working in emergency nursing for less than two years. They will possess foundation knowledge regarding emergency nursing, which they use in their clinical practice. They will require the indirect supervision of an expert nurse.

Members

Members will have over two years' emergency nursing experience, enabling them to use their knowledge in practice to deliver emergency care without direct supervision. They will require support from an expert emergency nurse in relation to some aspects of care.

Fellows

Fellows will be expert emergency nurses – people who are able to take responsibility for the delivery of emergency care without supervision. They will draw upon a broad knowledge base to lead an inter-disciplinary team and to organise the delivery of emergency care to a group of patients with diverse problems.

The Royal College of Nursing plans to launch a series of faculties. The next planned faculty will be on nursing older people. It is expected that, once again, there will be three levels of nursing expertise (Ford, 2004).

6.8 Do specialist skills make a difference?

Although older people occupy around 60 per cent of all NHS beds it is important to realise that they need high-quality care in community and care home settings. Hospital care is only a small part of an older person's life. All services should be centred on the needs of the older person (see Figure 6.6).

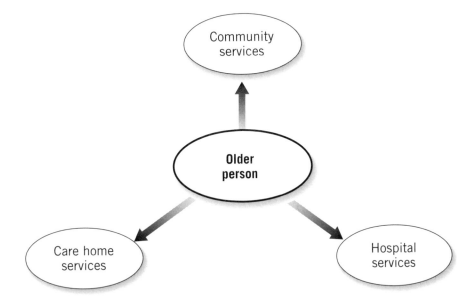

Figure 6.6 Services and the older person

CASE STUDY — Specialist skills

One of Veronica Gibb's priorities is to reduce the number of unnecessary admissions to the older people's wards. The wards are full to bursting and on any one day there are 40 older people placed inappropriately in other hospital wards. Older people with acute medical problems are placed on the ear, nose and throat ward and on other non-specialist wards. On these wards nurses do not have the specialist skills required to care for older people.

Veronica finds that the wards have levels of readmission. Many older people discharged home and to care homes are readmitted to the wards. Veronica discussed her findings with the deputy director of nursing:

'I need to find out why patients are being readmitted.'

'Perhaps, Veronica, we are discharging patients too early.'

'No, it's not that our average length of stay is higher than other hospitals in London. I need to find out why people are returning.'

Reflect on practice

If you were Veronica, what aspects of discharge and readmission might you concentrate on? Can you think of some reasons for high readmission rates? What strategies do you think could be introduced to reduce readmission rates?

The older person living at home should be enabled to remain well. This involves encouraging the person to remain active, encouraging the person to eat a balanced diet and preventing preventable diseases such as diabetes and stroke. The person who has a chronic disease (such as hypertension) requires good chronic-disease management to prevent complications such as stroke.

The older person who has been admitted to hospital requires effective treatment that prevents the person becoming more disabled during the hospital stay. The person may require rehabilitation. All older people require effective discharge planning.

The older person who has been admitted to a care home may require active treatment or effective palliative care. The person will require good chronic-disease management and high-quality care to prevent excessive disability.

Nurses with specialist skills can make a difference to the quality of care in all care settings. In general practice, the management of chronic disease is now often undertaken by nurse practitioners. Nurse practitioners are generalists in the same way that general practitioners are. However, research from the USA indicates that nurse practitioners who have specialist knowledge and expertise in older people can improve the quality of primary care (Kane and Huck, 2000). Older people who receive high-quality primary care are less likely to require hospital treatment. One nurse-led programme in primary care provided older people who had chronic diseases with a programme of education, physical activity and information and support to keep well. A year later the people who had taken part in the programme demonstrated an improvement in their ability to carry out the activities of daily living, were in better health, used fewer psychotropic drugs and had fewer hospital admissions than those who had not participated (Leville et al., 1998).

In hospital settings older people who do not benefit from high-quality care can rapidly lose ability. The older person might loose the ability to remain continent and might become malnourished. Nursing staff – in their efforts to prevent accidents – might use restraints (such as bedrails) inappropriately and thus contribute to the older person becoming fearful and losing mobility (Evans et al., 2002). The older person may suffer pressure damage and infection. If an older person loses ability within a hospital, discharge can become difficult, and the older person may be at risk of readmission on return home. Alternatively, he or she might be admitted to a care home. Nurses who have specialist skills and expertise in the care of older people can plan discharge effectively; this leads to improved patient outcomes and reduced readmission rates (Shaw, 1999).

The use of nurses with specialist skills in gerontology in nursing homes has been researched more extensively than in hospitals. There is evidence that nurses who have degrees in gerontology make a real difference to the quality of care in nursing homes. They move the focus of the homes from a custodial one – where care is delivered – to a rehabilitative one – where nurses work in partnership with the older people. Older people in such homes are less likely to develop pressure sores, continence problems, wound infections and other problems (Kane et al., 1980). In nursing homes, nurses with specialist skills not only improve care but they also reduce the costs of care by introducing specialist programmes, such as continence promotion and wound care (Knapp, 1994; Nazarko, 2003).

Falls are a major issue in hospitals and nursing homes. Nurses use bedrails in an effort to reduce falls but this strategy can backfire, leading to the older person becoming less able and more dependent. Researchers have worked hard to reduce restraint without increasing the risk of falls or injury. Efforts to reduce restraint in hospitals have not always been successful and, sometimes, have actually led to an increase in restraint in the long term (Evans et al., 2002). One successful restraint-reduction programme was carried out in nursing homes (Evans et al., 1997). This programme differed from the unsuccessful ones because it involved a nurse specialist. This programme showed a 56 per cent reduction in the use of bedrails. Further research found no increase in falls, fall-related injuries or falls at night. There was also no increase in night sedation or use of psychotropic drugs (Siegler et al., 1997; Capezuti et al., 1998; 1999).

In the UK older people living in care homes are cared for by general practitioners and nurses. However, extended practice roles are rarely used within nursing homes. Older people living in nursing homes usually have chronic diseases, and general practitioners may not always manage these diseases appropriately. When chronic diseases (such as heart failure) are poorly managed, older people are more likely to deteriorate and to require hospital admission. Hence this inappropriate management can contribute to unnecessary admissions (Bowman et al., 2001). The presence of an advanced practice nurse within a nursing home can make a huge difference to the quality of care. Researchers have found that it leads to a reduction in visits to accident and emergency departments, a reduction in hospital admissions, a reduced use of psychotropic medications and a reduction in restraint and incontinence (Mezey, 1994).

6.9 The place of specialist skills

There is an African saying: 'A tree cannot be a forest.' This applies to the care of older people. Nurses with advanced skills can make a huge difference to the quality of care older people receive but they are not a panacea. Older people who have nursing needs require nursing care, so hospitals and care homes that provide nursing care need to provide sufficient nurses to deliver that care. There is a danger that nurses with specialist skills will be considered an easy way to plug the gap between need and provision.

Researchers have found that many people living in care homes that do not employ nurses have significant nursing needs and require nursing care (Waters, 1996). Nurse specialists may be parachuted into such settings to improve care. There is evidence that such strategies are ineffective (Gosney and Tallis, 1991). The solution to unmet nursing needs is to ensure that older people are appropriately placed in care settings where there are sufficient staff with the necessary expertise to meet their needs. Nurses who are employed in the care of older people need to lead from the front. They need to be directly involved in providing care and guiding staff. Nurse leaders need to be doing more than completing paperwork. Greater numbers of registered nurses working in such settings lead to significant improvements in an older person's functional ability and to lower mortality rates (Bleisemer, 1994).

If we are to improve the quality of care older people receive, we need to do more than develop specialists' skills. It is important that nurse education includes the fundamental skills required to care for older people effectively and humanely (Lekan-Rutledge, 2000). Degree programmes aimed at groups of nurses (such as nurse practitioners and district nurses who will provide significant amounts of care for older people) *must* have core components in gerontology.

The nurse with advanced skills can educate and enable staff to move practice forward. June Worby (1999) provides some words of wisdom for nurse specialists:

> *Ensure that the word nurse is in your job title and on your name badge. Be sure that you practise advanced nursing not second-rate medicine. Always carry out fundamental nursing care when necessary – it is just as important as your advanced skills. If you work in a clinical setting where uniforms are worn ensure that you wear a nursing uniform. Please do not wear a white coat ('she thinks she's a doctor') or a business suit ('she thinks she's a manager'). And finally above all gain respect by excellent clinical practice.*

Reflect on practice

How have you moved practice forward in your workplace over the last two years? What skills and knowledge did you acquire in order to do this? If you work with specialist nurses, how have they help you move practice forward?

6.10 Conclusion

The care of older people is changing, and it's changing quickly because policy-makers have realised that it is not a gentle backwater. The way we care for older people matters. If we do not provide effective care to the older person at home, he or she becomes unwell and might require care in a hospital or a care home. If the older person in hospital does not receive effective care, he or she could become less healthy and more dependent, discharge could be delayed and more intensive ongoing care might be required at home or in a care home. If the older person in a care home does not receive effective care, he or she might need to visit the accident and emergency department and might require hospital admission. Now policy-makers have realised that the care we provide for older people is not so basic after all. There is a growing recognition that older people are more vulnerable to the effects of poor-quality care and have special needs that require nurses who have different levels of specialist knowledge. In Chapter 7 we look at how you can enable and develop staff to meet these needs.

Key Points

○ Traditionally, the care of older people has been viewed as unskilled.

○ Caring for older people requires a wider range of skills than other specialities.

○ This breadth of skill can make it difficult for others to recognise those skills.

○ Effective care requires nurses to combine both the highly regarded science of nursing and the less visible art of nursing.

○ Nurses who have specialist skills make a huge difference to the quality of care.

○ Skilled nursing improves the lives of older people and reduces costs.

○ Policy-makers are now aware of the difference advanced skills make to healthcare and are driving forward change.

References and further reading

SECTION 6.1

Goffman, E. (1961) *Asylums*. Penguin Books, London (reprinted 1998).

Butler, R.N. (1969) *Testimony: Subcommittee on Retirement and the Individual*. The US Senate Special Committee on Aging, 15 July. US Senate, Washington, DC.

SECTION 6.2

Butler, R.N. (1969) *Testimony: Subcommittee on Retirement and the Individual*. The US Senate Special Committee on Aging, 15 July. US Senate, Washington, DC.

Harding, T. (1997) *A Life Worth Living*. Help the Aged, London.

Nazarko, L. (2000) 'Rehabilitation. Part one. The evidence base', *Nursing Management*, 8: 14–18.

Phillipson, C. (1999) *Reconstructing Old Age*. Sage, London.

Royal Commission on Long Term Care, chaired by Professor Sir Stewart Sutherland (1999) *With Respect to Old Age: Long Term Care Rights and Responsibilities*. Stationery Office, London.

SECTION 6.3

Audit Commission (1995) *United They Stand: Co-ordinating Care for Elderly Patients with Hip Fractures*. Stationery Office, London.

Birchall, R. and Waters, K. (1996) 'What do elderly people do in hospital?', *Journal of Clinical Nursing*, 5: 171–6.

Collier, M. (2003) 'Wound bed preparation: theory to practice', *Nursing Standard*, 17: 45–52.

Nazarko, L. (1993) 'Out of the darkness', *Elderly Care*, 5: 8.

SECTION 6.4

Benner, P. (1984) *From Novice to Expert*. Addison-Wesley, Menlo Park, CA.

McKinley, A. and Cowan, S. (2003) 'Student nurses' attitudes towards working with older people', *Journal of Advanced Nursing*, 43: 298–309.

Stevens, J. and Crouch, M. (1995) 'Who cares about care in nursing education?', *Journal of Nursing Studies*, 32: 233–347.

Wade, S. (1999) 'Promoting quality of care; developing positive attitudes to working with older people', *Journal of Nursing Management*, 7: 339–47.

SECTION 6.5

Clark, J. and Lang, N.M. (1994) 'Nursing the next advance: an international classification for nursing practice', *International Nursing Review*, 39: 109–12.

Stevens, J. and Crouch, M. (1995) 'Who cares about care in nursing education?', *Journal of Nursing Studies*, 32: 233–347.

Section 6.6

Association of Community Health Councils in England and Wales (ACHEW) (1997) *Hungry in Hospital*. ACHEW, London.

Covinsky, K.E., Palmer, R.M., Fortinsky, R.H. et al. (2003) 'Loss of independence in activities of daily living in older adults hospitalised with medical illness: increased vulnerability with age', *Journal of the American Geriatrics Society*, 51: 451–8.

Department of Health (2000) *Shaping the Future NHS: Long Term Planning for Hospitals and Related Services* (consultation document on the findings of the National Beds Inquiry). Department of Health, London (available at **http://www.doh.gov.uk/pub/ docs/doh/nationalbeds.pdf**).

Nazarko, L. (2003) 'Guard against conveyor belt care', *Nursing Times*, 99: 17.

Section 6.7

Ford, F. (2004) 'Building the future', *Nursing Older People*, 15: 7.

Oberski, I.M., Carter, D., Gray, M. and Ross, J. (1999) 'The community gerontological nurse; themes from a needs analysis', *Journal of Advanced Nursing*, 29: 454–62.

Section 6.8

Bowman, C.E., Elforda, J., Doveya, S., Campbell, S. and Barrowclough, H. (2001) 'Acute hospital admissions from nursing homes: some may be avoidable', *Postgraduate Medical Journal*, 77: 40–2.

Capezuti, E., Strumpf, N.E., Evans, L.K., Grisso, J.A. and Maislin, G. (1998) 'The relationship between physical restraint removal and falls and injuries among nursing home residents', *Journals of Gerontology Series A: Biological Sciences and Medical Sciences*, 53a: M47–M52.

Capezuti, E., Strumpf, N., Evans, L. and Maislin, G. (1999) 'Outcomes of nighttime physical restraint removal for severely impaired nursing home residents', *American Journal of Alzheimer's Disease*, 14: 157–64.

Evans, D., Wood, J. and Lambert, L. (2002) 'A review of physical restraint minimization in the acute and residential care settings', *Journal of Advanced Nursing*, 40: 616–25.

Evans, L.K., Strumpf, N.E., Allen Taylor, S.L., Capezuti, E., Maislin, G. and Jacobsen, B. (1997) 'A clinical trial to reduce restraints in nursing homes', *Journal of the American Geriatrics Society*, 45: 675–81.

Kane, R.A., Kane, R.L. and Arnold, S. (1988) 'Geriatric nurse practitioners as nursing home employees: implementing the role', *The Gerontologist*, 28: 469–77.

Kane, R.L. and Huck, S. (2000) 'The implementation of the EverCare demonstration project', *Journal of the American Geriatrics Society*, 48: 218–23.

Knapp, M. (1994) 'Nurse practitioners: expanded role in long term care', *The Brown University Long Term Care Quality Letter*, 6: 1–2.

Leville, S.G., Wagner, E.H., David, C. et al. (1998) 'A nurse led programme improved physical function in older adults with chronic disease', *Journal of the American Medical Association*, 45: 1191–8.

Mezey, M.D. (1994) Presentation at a special session on staffing and the quality of care in nursing homes. Annual general meeting of the Gerontological Society of America, Atlanta, GA, November.

Nazarko, L. (2003) 'Rehabilitation and continence promotion following a stroke', *Nursing Times*, 99: 52–5.

Shaw, M.C. (1999) 'Discharge planning and home follow up by advanced practice nurses reduced hospital readmissions of elderly patients', *Evidence-based Nursing*, 2: 125.

Siegler, E.L., Capezuti, E., Maislin, G., Baumgarten, M., Evans, L. and Strumpf, N. (1997) 'Effects of a restraint reduction intervention and OBRA '87 regulations on psychoactive drug use in nursing homes', *Journal of the American Geriatrics Society*, 45: 791–6.

SECTION 6.9

Bleisemer, M. (1994) 'Outcomes of the Minnesota nursing home residents and their relationships to structural and process related attributes.' Unpublished PhD dissertation, Rush University, Michigan.

Gosney, M. and Tallis, R. (1991) 'The burden of chronic illness in local authority residential homes for the elderly', *Health Trends*, 22: 153–7.

Lekan-Rutledge, D. (2000) 'Diffusion of innovation: a model for implementation of prompted voiding in long-term care settings', *Journal of Gerontological Nursing*, 26: 25–33.

Waters, J. (1996) 'How care in the community has affected older people', *Nursing Times*, 92: 29–31.

Worby, J. (1999) 'Always remember who you are (letter)', *Nursing Standard*, 14: 30.

CHAPTER 7

Enabling and developing staff

Introduction

Most of us will have worked in different environments during our careers. We have worked in organisations where we were controlled and had to watch our backs. In such organisations you had to be careful not to take risks because, if things went wrong, you would be blamed. You will also have worked in organisations where you felt valued and you were encouraged to try new things, to learn and to develop. Most of us, if we're honest, know that we'd rather work in an enabling organisation rather than one that seeks to control and is unsupportive. The difference between the disabling organisation (where you feel like unimportant cogs in a wheel) and the organisation where you feel that you can make a difference are the people and the way they manage and lead.

All of us are influenced by the culture of the organisation that we work for. Sometimes we work in places where we feel that we are in tune with the organisation and the people in it. In such environments it's easier to take risks because we feel safe and supported.

In other organisations we have the sense that it's risky to be noticed and to try to make changes. In such organisations the feeling is that it's better to keep your head down. The management styles in organisations influence not only our willingness to take risks but also to our willingness go the extra mile.

Sometimes, when a problem seems to be insoluble, reframing the problem can lead to innovative solutions. Education is a lifelong process, and developing a culture where learning is valued enables all staff to meet older people's needs for safety and care effectively.

In a learning organisation, managers identify skills that the organisation requires and also the skills that staff would like to attain. The skilled manager must balance those needs to ensure that education and training meet the organisation's requirements and individual desires.

Nursing is changing and the constraints that once bound nurses are being released. As nurses develop new ways of working, their educational requirements will also change.

This chapter examines these issues and aims to help you develop a culture that supports and nurtures excellence.

Aims

7.1 The learning organisation	7.8 Identifying the gap
7.2 Building a shared vision	7.9 Identifying individual training and development needs
7.3 Motivating your team	
7.4 Learning what demotivates people	7.10 How adults learn
	7.11 Barriers to learning
7.5 Be fair	7.12 Career pathways
7.6 Being open and honest	7.13 Defining higher-level practice
7.7 Identifying training and development needs	7.14 Expanding roles
	7.15 Conclusion

7.1 The learning organisation

In some organisations many staff feel disengaged and disempowered: they do what they have to do but no more. In such organisations staff are unwilling to go the extra mile. This feeling of disempowerment is often a product of a command-and-control culture. In cultures where staff are considered to be untrustworthy and of lesser value than senior staff, a blame culture often exists. In a blame culture when something goes wrong, staff at all levels look for someone to blame, preferably someone who has left or a temporary member of staff such as an agency nurse. Blame cultures may be effective at fixing blame but they do not learn from their mistakes because everyone is too busy fixing the blame and covering his or her back to work out what really happened. Blame cultures teach people that errors will be punished, and people learn what they have to do to avoid punishment (Skinner, 1971). Learning organisations aim to do things differently. They aim to find out what happened: they examine the systems, processes and people involved so that they can act to prevent problems from recurring. The NHS, like many organisations, is moving from being a blame culture to becoming a learning culture.

The Department of Health report, *An Organisation with a Memory* (2000), acknowledges that adverse events occur in around 10 per cent of admissions and that service failures can have serious consequences for individual patients. It is now known that 5 per cent of medications given in hospitals are the wrong ones. The error may be a transcribing error or a dispensing error. This report draws on work in the airline industry and shows that many errors are the result not of 'bad' staff but of bad systems that can be corrected. This report proposes not merely that individuals are held to account for their actions but also that organisations should put in place systems that reduce the likelihood of service failures. The report states that the NHS has a body of knowledge relating to adverse incidents in hospital settings but lacks detailed information about primary care where greater numbers of patients are treated. The report sets out strategies for primary care trusts and acute trusts but does not mention the independent sector.

Peter Senge's book, *The Fifth Discipline* (1990), examines the way organisations work. This is known as 'systems theory'. Senge considers that there are core disciplines crucial to building a learning organisation.

Systems thinking

Although the world is often thought of as being made up of unrelated and uncontrollable forces, this is not necessarily the case. There is a pattern, but people have difficulty seeing this because they are caught up in the day-to-day workings of this pattern. Systems thinking employs a framework and a set of tools to help us see the whole pattern clearly. If you can see the pattern clearly, you can identify leverage points in the system. This will help you to make significant changes with the least possible amount of effort.

Personal mastery

The discipline of personal mastery starts by identifying the things that really matter and then tries to work out ways of those achieving those things. When you develop a vision of how things could be, this is often unclear and lacking in detail. Personal mastery clarifies and deepens these visions. When you want to change things, it's all too easy to be everywhere at once and, hence, to make little impact on anything. Senge advises us to focus our energies. Anyone who sees how things are and how they could be can easily become inpatient with the here and now and attempt to push forward. Senge, however, argues for the value of patience. Sometimes in your efforts to improve practice, you can overstate current problems or oversell possible improvements. Senge encourages us to develop skills so that we can view reality objectively.

Mental models

Everyone has thoughts, assumptions and generalisations about him or herself, about other people and about world he or she lives in. These influence how people understand the world and how they act when they encounter problems. Sometimes models like these hold people back from developing innovative solutions to problems; at other times they make people do things the hard way.

CASE STUDY — Reframing a mental model

When the USA and the USSR launched their space programmes, the astronauts in both programmes had difficulty recording information. In a weightless environment the ink from ballpoint, fountain and felt-tip pens leaked into the atmosphere, but the astronauts needed pens to write with. The Americans spent millions of dollars developing a ballpoint pen that could write upside down and in zero gravity.

The Russians reframed their mental model. They asked: what is the problem? The problem was not that they needed a pen. The problem was that they needed something to write with. Once they had reframed the problem they worked out a simple solution (see Figure 7.1).

Figure 7.1 Reframing a mental model

Reframing works. It took the Americans three years and millions of dollars to develop a ballpoint pen that wrote in zero gravity. It took the Russians less than three minutes to put a pencil on the spacecraft.

Reflect on practice •••

If you are to do things differently, you need to think of things in different ways. Think of a problem that your organisation is investing a lot of effort in. Have they defined the problem properly or do they think they need a revolutionary new pen? Can you think of any ways of reframing the problem? If so, can you think of any simple solutions to solve this problem? If you can, perhaps you should share them with the organisation.

Senge advises that people should examine their mental models carefully – they should hold up a mirror to them so that they can view them differently and scrutinise them carefully.

CASE STUDY – Reframing a problem

A hospital was concerned about the level of drug errors. It was clear that the people who dispensed drugs from the medicine trolley were nurses, so the problem was that the nurses were not skilled in giving out medicines. The deputy director worked day and night and finally presented the board with a solution. All the nurse were to be educated in, and assessed on, their skills in dispensing medication. Every nurse would have two days' training in giving oral medication. The nurse would then be examined and, if successful, would be allowed to give oral medicines. There would be an additional two days' training for controlled drugs and a further two days' training for intravenous drugs. Agency staff would not be allowed to dispense medicines unless they had been certified competent at drug administration.

The board approved this expensive and time-consuming strategy. Nursing staff felt demoralised because they thought they were being asked to prove what they considered a fundamental competency for registered nurses. Senior management were unperturbed; if the troops were restless so be it – it was a price worth paying if drug errors could be eliminated.

A strange thing happened: the rate of drug errors remained unchanged. A consultant was appointed to investigate. The consultant found that the hospital had made a number of errors in defining the problem. The first was that the hospital had not defined what drug errors were or why they occurred. One definition of a drug error the hospital used was 'the failure to dispense a prescribed medication'.

There were a number of reasons why staff did not dispense prescribed medication. Sometimes patients experienced adverse reactions, so staff withheld the medicine until the prescriber saw these patients. This is good practice but was counted as an error. Sometimes medication was not dispensed from the pharmacy, so staff were unable to give out medicines. Sometimes patients decided that they no longer needed such medicines as analgesics because pain was no longer a problem. This was considered to be an error until the medicine was discontinued.

Patients were often transferred to the ward from the medical assessment unit. Ward staff were not allowed to give medicines prescribed on the medical assessment unit chart, which was different from the ward chart. They had to have a ward chart written up. In the mean time medicines on a 'live' chart that were not given were recorded as errors. The rate of errors in the administration of controlled and intravenous drugs was negligible.

The deputy director of nursing had defined and framed the problem according to her mental model. This narrow mental model did not look beyond the nurses and nursing in relation to medication errors. The consultant used a whole systems approach to examine the issue across boundaries and to reframe the problem before suggesting solutions.

Reflect on practice

Nursing is part of a wider workforce: nurses' work impacts on others and the work of others impacts on nursing. Can you think of a situation in your organisation where senior management were limited because of their mental models? Can you think of a situation where you were limited because of your mental models? What can you learn from these situations?

7.2 Building a shared vision

In a command culture, people comply with managers because managers have the power. However, no one wants to work for a tyrant. No one wants to be pushed and shoved in a direction that someone else thinks he or she should be going in. Senge believes that people work more effectively if they can see the direction the organisation is going in and can contribute to the vision and the direction of the organisation.

Team learning

Senge believes that teams, not individuals, are the fundamental learning units of modern organisations: 'Unless teams can learn, the organisation cannot learn.' Team learning starts with team members taking the brave step of putting aside their assumptions. They then brainstorm and bounce ideas off each other in a non-competitive way. This requires trust and good, open relationships. Team learning is about building the team's confidence and capacity to see things differently, to do things differently and to discuss differently.

Learning organisations

No organisation is perfect; even if it were perfect it would still have to change because needs and expectations change. Healthcare organisations are changing rapidly because of changes in the population, changes in healthcare and changing expectations.

Learning organisations aim to nurture people and to set them free from the old ways of thinking and working so that they can be an important part of the organisation.

7.3 Motivating your team

When you become a nurse, it is your technical and people skills that are most prized. You are encouraged to go on courses to enable you to cannulate safely, to perform Doppler ultrasounds and to develop your skills for when you return to the workplace. As a nurse you quickly learn that you cannot function alone. Even the most junior nurse must work with and motivate healthcare assistants and student nurses. As you become more senior you have to learn how to get the best from the team, yet little in your education and training prepares you for this. You learn by doing and by being sensitive to the feedback you receive from those you aim to motivate.

Management literature can help you to understand some of the features of teamwork and how to get the best from staff.

A clear sense of purpose

Successful teams have a clear sense of purpose (Deeprose, 2003). If you are to manage your team well, you need a common purpose. The organisation may have a mission statement but this is often not specific to your workplace. If you work in a large corporate nursing home group with 200 homes, there will be a variety of different types of home within the organisation. If you work in a ward in a large acute NHS trust, the trust will be providing all sorts of services – from cardiac surgery to outpatients. It's important to have a values statement or philosophy for your workplace. This should reflect the aims and values of your workplace and the team vision for the future.

Reflect on practice

Ask the staff in your workplace what the team's aims are. If there are many different visions, it's time to review or develop a philosophy of care. How might you get the team to contribute to this philosophy?

Knowing and understanding the people you are working with

When a new manager is appointed, that person does not start off with a clean slate: the organisation he or she will work in and its people have a history. The manager who understands the history of the organisation and the motivations, concerns and aspirations of the people working within it will be more able to plan the future.

CASE STUDY – Getting to know the people and the organisation

When Veronica Gibbs was appointed as modern matron for the older people's wards, she found staff unmotivated and suspicious of any new ideas to move the wards forward. Veronica got to know the ward managers and asked them to help her plan the future by telling her about the past.

The staff were suspicious of change because of their experiences of the previous two modern matrons. The first had encouraged staff to develop and to work differently but left because of promotion. The next matron was authoritarian. She found the staff who had been empowered by the previous matron too challenging. She discouraged innovation and new ways of doing things. She then left. The staff now felt powerless. They wanted to change and improve things but it didn't seem to matter what they did: nothing appeared to make any difference.

The staff were holding back to see what Veronica was like and to find out if they could trust her before they put their heads back up over the parapet.

Reflect on practice

The staff in this case study eventually opened up to Veronica and confided their fears in her. In her situation, how would you build on this to develop good relationships and to foster teamwork?

Understanding the big picture

If you are to enable teams to function, you need to understand organisational and national priorities. If the organisation is focused on one or two big issues, you need to understand not just the team's aspirations but also the organisation's. You can then identify potential sources of conflict and also areas where you can align team objectives with organisational objectives. As you become more skilled, you can also begin to align organisational objectives with team objectives. If the team is developing ways to look at the quality of care within your ward or home, you can outline how this fits in with the organisation's quality strategy.

Developing a leadership style that is open and involving

It is important to develop a style that enables staff to come forward and discuss their concerns and aspirations openly. If you put people off by being unapproachable or autocratic, people will feel that they are not valued. In such situations staff turnover rises, gossip flourishes and people do not give of their best. If you are approachable, staff tell you about the little problems and what they did to try to solve them. They ask when they need help and you are better informed about what is going on. This 'stitch in time' approach can be very effective.

CASE STUDY — An open and involving leadership style

When Laura Edwards was appointed matron/manager of the Haven, a fifty-bed nursing home, she held a staff meeting. It was first staff meeting that had been held in the home for five years. The previous matron didn't believe in them and said that she talked to staff on a day-to-day basis.

Laura introduced monthly meetings. She invited staff to raise any issues that they wished to discuss and provided coffee and doughnuts. For six months she updated staff on improvements, and in this time the staff did not make a single suggestion or comment. At the December staff meeting she was delighted to find that the staff had raised seven issues they wished to discuss. At the January meeting they established a dialogue and ways of examining and solving issues. In February another member of staff agreed to take responsibility for co-ordinating the meetings.

It had taken six months before staff felt able to open up and signal their readiness to work with Laura as a team.

Reflect on practice ··

Why do you think Laura faced such barriers in her efforts to engage staff? Think of a similar situation in your workplace and identify some of the issues that lead the staff to hold back from engaging with their manager. Do you feel that this process could have been speeded up?

7.4 Learning what demotivates people

People do not appreciate being treated like mushrooms: being kept in the dark. Communication is an important aspect of developing a team. Let your team know what is happening in the organisation and how it might affect them. If you have had a complaint and have had to interview staff, let them know the outcome of the investigation.

Working in a healthcare setting means you live with constantly changing goalposts. In care homes, the introduction of National Minimum Standards is leading to huge changes. In the NHS, the introduction of the National Service Framework for Older People and centrally imposed targets are leading to huge changes. Staff may be unaware of the detail of these changes but they can see the moving goalposts. So take time to explain why the goalposts are moving and how these changes will impact on day-to-day practice. Stress the positive aspects of the changes and the team's ability to move forward.

One of the greatest demotivators is failure to notice. Sometimes staff put in special effort, work really hard and deliver brilliant results. How many of us take time to say: 'Thank you. I know how much effort you've put into that and I really appreciate it.' Often we have noticed but we just haven't bothered to say anything. Praise should be delivered as closely as possible to the time the act was carried out if it is to mean anything. So praise loudly and publicly, and criticise softly and privately.

The most serious management sin is to say one thing but to do another. If you tell staff that is it important to be punctual and that it is disrespectful to the team to roll in half an hour late, preventing the registered nurse in charge of night duty from going home, you must provide a positive example. If you say one thing and do another staff will not respect you.

7.5 Be fair

Teamwork is about people working together and contributing to the team. Nothing splits a team and makes people feel angry and upset so much as a team leader who has favourites. It is important to treat all members in the same way, to have the same standards for all team members and to be seen to be fair.

Schein (1985) describes five mechanisms that managers use to foster effective working and healthy workplace cultures (see Figure 7.2).

1 What they pay attention to in order to manage and control.

2 Their reactions to critical incidents and organisational crises.

3 Deliberate role modelling, teaching and coaching.

4 Their criteria for the allocation of rewards and status.

5 Their criteria for recruitment, selection, promotion, retirement and excommunication.

Figure 7.2 Fostering effective working and healthy workplace cultures

7.6 Being open and honest

There are limits to the power a manager has within an organisation. If there are things that the team would like you to do and you do not have the power or resources to deliver, be open and honest about this. Don't make promises that you cannot keep. If you do make promises and you can keep them, deliver on those promises. Imagine how you would feel if your manager promised to do something and then 'forgot' or was 'too busy'. You'd feel demotivated and so would your staff.

Reflect on practice

Can you identify any ways that you may have inadvertently demotivated people? What can you learn from this? Can you identify any demotivated people in your team? How could you work with an individual to enable that person to contribute fully as a team member?

7.7 Identifying training and development needs

Some senior managers believe that identifying training and development needs is a rational, well organised process in their organisations. This is often a mistaken belief. In reality, training and development needs might or might not be identified at an annual appraisal. Vanessa Fowler's research (2003) found that only 51 per cent of healthcare assistants working in the NHS had an appraisal and a personal development plan. This means that almost half the healthcare assistants did *not* have a personal development plan. There is no reason to believe this is untypical.

Appraisals vary: some are conducted effectively whilst harried managers conduct them in a rushed fashion. Some appraisals specify individuals' learning needs and are referred to throughout the year; others are filed and not referred to again. Sometimes

---

KINGFISHER

a better place for living

STAFF APPRAISAL SCHEME

1. **Introduction**

1.1 Given that staff are the most important resource that Kingfisher has in delivering quality services to residents, relatives, carers and other users of our service, Kingfisher believes that it is necessary to put in place a formal Staff Appraisal Scheme

2 **Scheme Objectives**

2.1 Kingfisher believes that the following objectives can be met from the application of a formal Staff Appraisal Scheme:
   - assessment of past performance by an employee
   - objective setting for individuals and individuals as team members and clear communication of these objectives to employees so that they are fully aware of work requirements placed on them and standards expected of them
   - improvement in future performance
   - assessment of future potential/promotability
   - assessment of training and development needs, as well as other needs not related to training and development
   - monitoring the performance of employees to ensure the maintenance of an appropriate level and quality of service to residents, relatives, carers and other service users

3. **Prerequisites for the Success of the Staff Appraisal Scheme**

3.1 Both the Head or Deputy Head of Department or manager (*the appraiser*) and the employee (or *the appraisee*) should prepare for the appraisal process and the appraisal meeting should be a genuine dialogue with agreed action for both parties to implement.

3.2 Appraisal should be a supportive process, giving recognition and positive feedback.

3.3 The professional growth and development of the employee should be identified and planned

3.4 As the Appraisal Scheme deals with issues of performance and training and development both the appraisee and appraiser and others in possession of the information generated should treat it with confidentiality. Information must only be shared on a "need to know" rather than a "wish to know" basis.

Staff appraisal scheme

successive appraisals identify the same learning needs because everyone has been too busy to address the issues identified.

It's vital that you identify training and development needs effectively so that education and training can be planned to fit in with the needs of the workplace. The first step is to identify what care is provided in your workplace. If you are running a care home for people with dementia, staff will require a completely different set of clinical skills from staff on an acute stroke ward.

Staff working on a particular ward or in a care home will require a range of skills – everyone does not need to be an expert in everything. You need to enable staff to develop a range of skills and different depths of knowledge. Table 7.1 shows how you can identify the skills required for caring for people with dementia.

Table 7.1 Some of the skills required to care for people with dementia

ACTIVITY/PROBLEM	SKILLS REQUIRED
Caring for people with dementia	Understanding of dementia
Communication difficulties	Advanced communication skills
Continence problems	Skills in promoting continence and in managing incontinence
Nutritional problems	Understanding of nutrition and the problems experienced by people with dementia

There are dangers in concentrating all the skills in one area, as the following case study shows.

CASE STUDY — The dangers of concentrating skills in one area

Lawton War Memorial Hospital had changed a great deal over the years. It had once provided continuing care but was now caring for a range of patients in the local area. One of Gloria Lennox's first actions was to identify the categories of patients cared for and to work with staff to draw up an admissions policy.

Patients who required subacute care were now being admitted to the hospital. A typical such patient might be an older woman with a chest infection who had become confused because of illness and who required antibiotic therapy, nursing care and perhaps intravenous fluids. Patients who required palliative care were also admitted – for example, when the local hospice was full or when medium-term palliative care was required. Increasing numbers of patients who required rehabilitation were similarly being admitted – typically, patients from the nearby elective orthopaedic centre following joint replacement or from the district general hospital when acute care was no longer required.

Gloria's analysis showed that 77 per cent of patients were admitted because of rehabilitation needs, 17 per cent because of their need for subacute care and 6 per cent for palliative care and symptom control. Gloria spent time speaking with the staff to discover what they thought the core purpose of the hospital was. Staff were very clear about their purpose and wondered why Gloria was asking about this. Their purpose was to provide palliative and continuing care to people who lived in the village and the neighbourhood. When Gloria examined the skills profiles of the registered nurses, she wasn't surprised to find that they had all taken courses in palliative care and pain control. No one had any further training in rehabilitation or subacute care.

Reflect on practice

Gloria believes that the staff at Lawton War Memorial need to develop different skills to enable them to care for patients who require rehabilitation and subacute care. She suspects that it's going to be difficult to convince the staff of this. What barriers might Gloria face? How might she overcome these?

7.8 Identifying the gap

When you have identified the purpose of your workplace and the clinical skills required, you can then work out what skills the staff actually have. In many cases these are not identified accurately on appraisals, and the best way to find out is to talk to individual staff. Sometimes appraisals can give you misleading information and, if you do not clarify with the people concerned, you can get a completely wrong impression of what the issues are. The case study below illustrates this.

CASE STUDY — Misleading information

At Lawton War Memorial, local general practitioners provide medical cover. If there are problems with a patient, the general practitioner visits. A few weeks after her appointment, Gloria was invited to the general practitioners' weekly development meeting where she met all the local GPs. They welcomed her warmly and said that they were looking forward to her sorting out the problems with intravenous infusions and with taking blood.

Ted Ramsey, the senior partner in the local practice, explained: 'The nurses at Lawton War Memorial can't take blood or cannulate. The bloods aren't a problem in the week because my practice nurse, Susie, is more than happy to visit – in fact, she takes blood for all the patients when she visits. But we have a few patients now on IV fluids and, if a drip tissues at the weekend, whoever is on call through the local GP out-of-hours co-operative has to come in and we're often very busy.'

If Gloria had jumped to conclusions she would have decided that the staff needed training in venepuncture. Gloria wisely went back to ask the staff why they didn't cannulate. She found that all the staff had been on the IV cannulation course and that Susie was supervising them as they gained the skills required in taking blood, but cannulation was a different matter. One member of staff commented: 'None of us have had any practice since we did the course and none of us can support anyone else because no one is confident.'

Reflect on practice ....

If you were Gloria, how would you resolve this situation? Can you think of a similar situation in your workplace? Who was responsible for dealing with it? Do you feel that the situation was dealt with sensitively?

When you have identified the gap, you can begin to map the skills the unit requires with the skills the people on the unit already possess (see Table 7.2).

Table 7.2 Identifying organisational skills gaps

SKILLS AND COMPETENCIES	STAFF WHO POSSESS	STAFF WHO REQUIRE DEVELOPMENT
Ability to perform Doppler ultrasound	Robert Flood Mary Lake	Sherry Pearce, Princess Odige, Margaret Walters
Compression bandaging		
Ability to choose appropriate dressings		
Ability to carry out level 2 continence assessment	Margaret Walters	

An organisational skills gap analysis will enable you to get the whole picture regarding the educational needs of the unit (Gould et al., 2004). You then need to identify individual competencies. The skills gap analysis will enable you to help staff prioritise their learning needs. If, for example, a member of staff identifies a learning need in relation to a skill that many staff in the workplace possess (such as palliative care and one that is less common, such as rehabilitation), you can discuss prioritising the rehabilitation course because it fits in with the overall needs of the unit.

7.9 Identifying individual training and development needs

No one has all the skills required to do a job when first appointed. Everyone has development needs, and sometimes these needs evolve as the client group changes. At other times a complaint or critical incident suddenly throws up the need to develop practice further. Everyone should be encouraged and enabled to develop the skills required to enable him or her to develop practice, but it's important not to leave it to 'them' but to take responsibility for identifying his or her learning needs. If you find that staff need help to identify their learning needs, where do you begin?

Looking at a person's job description is a good place to start. A well written job description sets out the skills and competencies required to carry out a role. You can draw up a table that outlines the competencies required (and any gaps in these) and the strategies you can use to fill those gaps (see Table 7.3 on page 172).

Table 7.3 Skills and competencies analysis

SKILLS/ COMPETENCY	CURRENT ACHIEVEMENT	GAPS	STRATEGY TO MEET
Managing staffing budget for 20-bed ward	Some understanding of principles	Unable to understand monthly finance reports	Education in budgetary control. Work-based learning with experienced ward manager who is able to use financial information
Teach ward staff	Some understanding about how people learn	Ability to present information at the right level for healthcare assistants, students and registered nurses. Ability to plan teaching session	One-to-one teaching from nurse consultant. Help in planning teaching sessions. Support in teaching ward staff

There's normally no shortage of courses available on clinical issues, but staff often lack change management skills to enable them to put newfound skills into practice. The case study below illustrates this problem.

CASE STUDY — The need for change management skills

Sherry Pearce has been qualified for two years. Sister Evans, her ward manager, identified that Sherry needed to improve her knowledge of wound care. Sherry spent six months on a part-time, degree-level tissue viability course. Now, when patients with leg ulcers are admitted to Lawton War Memorial Hospital, they have Doppler ultrasounds of their legs and, if appropriate, compression bandaging. When Gloria Lennox met Sherry to evaluate the course, Sherry told her that she hoped to become a tissue-viability nurse specialist one day.

Two weeks later, when Gloria met Sherry on the ward, Gloria asked her how she was. Sherry burst into tears. She confided over tea: 'I think it would be best if I left. They are so stuck in their ways here. Sister Evans wants one particular dressing on all the wounds and it's not appropriate, but I'm just a staff nurse and I can't change anything, so maybe it would be better if I left.'

Reflect on practice

Sherry's problem is that she has developed the clinical skills to improve practice but lacks the skills and knowledge in change management to move practice forward. How would you deal with this situation? Have you encountered this type of problem in your workplace? How was it dealt with? Do you feel that it could have been managed more effectively?

It is important that education and development consist of more than technical competencies. As nurses become more senior they need to develop a range of competencies that encompass clinical managerial, teaching and research, and audit skills. Some organisations have drawn up professional development plans for groups of staff to enable them to develop a range of skills.

7.10 How adults learn

People learn from the moment of their birth and throughout their lives. Adults are accustomed to learning, so why do they sometimes find it difficult to learn? Sometimes they are not taught in ways that they can readily understand; sometimes it's not the right time for them to learn because they have other concerns. Learning theory helps us to understand how we learn and how we react to learning at certain times and in certain circumstances.

Kolb's work on learning styles (1984) identifies three different types of learning:

1 *Rationalist* learning focuses on the acquisition, manipulation and recall of abstract symbols. This is the traditional type of education.
2 *Behavioural* learning aims to change behaviour. There is no place for conscious, subjective experience in this learning process. Behavioural learning helps people to make the sort of adaptations that are made unconsciously when they encounter a problem or happen upon a better way of doing things. A few months ago the handle on a cupboard in my kitchen broke, so I hooked my hand over the door and opened it from the top. When it was eventually fixed, I still found myself hooking my hand over the door.
3 *Experiential, integrative* learning is a combination of experience, perception, cognition and behaviour.

The case study opposite shows how you can use experiential learning to improve practice.

CASE STUDY — Experiential learning

When Laura Edwards was appointed as matron/manager at the Haven she noticed that many of the residents required assistance to eat. Staff all pitched in to help but their practice was poor. The priority, it seemed, was to feed people as much as possible and as quickly as possible.

Laura organised a series of teaching sessions away from the workplace. The first covered good practice in nutrition and enabling older people to eat. The staff nodded in agreement. Then came the session that showed staff the gap between the theory and their practice. Juan Fernandez, the Haven's chef, brought in the food, and the staff were divided into pairs. One of each pair was to be fed and the other was to feed. Then they switched roles and discussed their experiences with each other.

Laura grinned as she saw the carefully prepared food being mixed together into a grey mush and being spooned rapidly into people's mouths. She listened to staff telling each other:

- 'I didn't like the way you stood over me as if you were in a rush. It was horrible.'
- 'You put too much on the spoon. It was going down the back of my throat.'
- 'The metal from the spoon touched my filling.'

Staff discussed what it was like to be feed and how they could improve their practice. Over the coming months Laura noticed staff practice improve. When the staff sat down to feed the residents, they took their time. Small spoons were used, and pureed food was not mixed together into a grey mush.

Reflect on practice

Can you think of any practice in your work situation that would lend itself to experiential learning? How do you think experiential learning can help move practice forward? Would you consider using experiential learning as a tool to improve practice?

Everyone learns best in a supportive environment

It is important to understand the nature of change because people in learning situations change, and change is a process, not an event. Introducing people to new ways of doing things does not mean they will immediately begin to do them. Change is a process that must unfold over time.

Change happens to individuals, and there are individual responses to the change process. Change involves personal growth and development. This growth and development are slow to start but gain momentum. Change takes time, and there is no one 'right' way to teach adults.

Different methods are suitable for different types of knowledge. Sometimes mixing theory and practical work can help people link theory to practice. The adult is an adult; he or she has many different roles and responsibilities in life. It is important to treat the adult as an adult and to respect him or her. And, finally, everyone learns best in a supportive environment.

7.11 Barriers to learning

Organisations that are developing as learning cultures are going through a process of change. In the past, staff might have been encouraged to project an image of competence at all times. However, it takes courage to admit that you do not know all that there is to know, and some people might not want to acknowledge that they need further development. You can help by providing a positive role model and by acknowledging that you are not infallible. Staff will respect you for this and might find it easier to acknowledge their own learning needs as a result.

Some staff, especially healthcare assistants, might have left school at sixteen and now, twenty or thirty years later, you are suggesting that they consider studying for an NVQ. This can be scary. The care assistant might worry that she will fail, and she might worry that her colleagues will think she's getting above herself. She might also worry about how she's going to combine NVQ studies with a full-time job and running her home and looking after her children. In such situations you can offer support and explain that these fears are natural. If you have staff who have successfully completed an NVQ, you can ask one of them to 'buddy' the student and to support her formally and informally.

Some registered nurses have not undertaken a period of formal study for years and might also feel unsure. You can share your experiences with them and explain how you felt before doing a course.

7.12 Career pathways

Once nurses who wanted to advance their careers found that the only way forward led them further away from patients into management or teaching. This is changing; it is now possible to progress your career in the care of older people in care homes, acute NHS trusts and community settings whilst, at the same time, continuing to deliver patient care.

Making a Difference (Department of Health, 1999) outlines the NHS strategy for nursing and it identifies four levels of expertise within healthcare (see Figure 7.3).

Level 1

Healthcare assistants working at Level 1 can gain NVQ qualifications. By 2005, in care homes, 50 per cent of healthcare assistants will be required to have NVQ Level 2

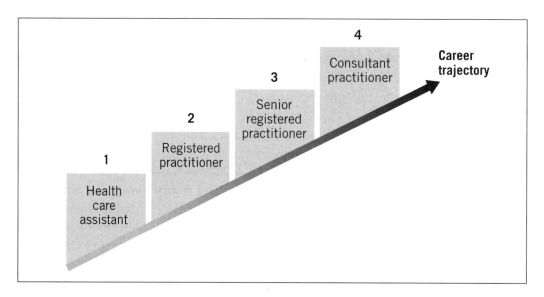

Figure 7.3 The four levels of expertise within healthcare

qualifications (Department of Health, 2001). There are no similar requirements in the NHS, but the role of the healthcare is expanding. NVQ Level 3-qualified care assistants have the qualifications required to enter nurse education programmes and to become registered nurses. Some universities are now offering NVQ Level 3 healthcare assistants shortened courses.

In NHS settings, healthcare assistants who do not wish to become registered nurses might want to develop their role further by becoming an STR (support time recovery) worker (Nursing Times, 2004). Other healthcare assistants working in such areas as accident and emergency and elective orthopaedic centres are learning about physiotherapy and nutrition so that they can expand their roles to offer a more holistic service. In many NHS settings, healthcare assistants perform tasks (such as taking blood or performing ECGs) that were once considered to the preserve of the registered nurse (Fowler, 2003).

In care home settings, healthcare assistants who care for people requiring residential care (but not nursing care) can obtain further qualifications, such as that of registered manager, and can go on to become a deputy or manager of a care home that cares for people with residential needs. There has, as yet, been no expansion of clinical roles within care homes.

Level 2

Newly qualified and experienced registered nurses working at Level 1 will increasingly be required to demonstrate specialist knowledge of older people in order to gain promotion.

Newly registered diploma and degree-prepared nurses often feel stressed and anxious (Runciman et al., 2000). Staff shortages and lack of support from experienced registered nurses can often make newly registered nurses feel inadequate and ill-prepared for their roles (Charnley, 1999). Sometimes mentoring is more of a myth than a reality. Some organisations have well developed mentorship schemes and staff development programmes. The best programmes provide rotation to enable nurses to gain experience in different clinical area and also to gain additional qualifications.

Nurses who do not have a diploma in nursing require 120 Level 2 credits to gain a diploma. Nurses who do not have a degree require a diploma and a further 120 credits at Level 3 to gain a degree. Universities and further education colleges have developed systems for measuring that experience so that you can gain academic credit for it. There are two systems for gaining credit: APEL and APL.

APL is 'accreditation of prior learning'. This means that, if you studied management as part of a course or even attended several high-quality study days on management, this learning is valued and awarded academic credit. In universities a unit is normally 15 credits. These credits can be at Level 2 (diploma), Level 3 (degree) or Level M (masters).

APEL is 'accreditation of prior experiential learning'. As you progressed through your management career, you may have introduced different methods of working or managing people. You learnt as a result of these experiences and you gain credit for this work.

If you want to gain APL and APEL credit, you need to find a university or college of further education and discuss the course you plan to do. Education providers have APL/APEL units and will help you prepare the paperwork to make a claim. The maximum credit you can have towards a course is 50 per cent. Some universities have a 25 per cent maximum. If you consider that you have a lot of appropriate experience, it's important to check the university's policy before applying and making a claim for credit. It's best to have the level of credit agreed in writing before enrolling for a course as, otherwise, credit claims can drag on or be disputed later.

There are a number of suitable courses at Levels 2 and 3 for nurses wishing to improve their skills in caring for older people. These courses are often based on the old National Board courses and include the following:

● Care of Older People (ENB 941).
● Continence Promotion (ENB 978).
● Palliative Care.
● Rehabilitation.

These courses usually have 15 credits at Level 2 (for nurses who do not have a diploma) or Level 3 for nurses who want to build towards a degree. There are other courses available (such as the N11 in Dementia Care) which have 30 credits. Students gain 90 credits from taught courses and gain the additional 30 credits required for a degree or diploma by completing an integrating study.

Currently, NHS nurses are working to a clinical grading structure and progress from D grade to I grade. Nurses who have six or more months' experience might be successful in gaining an E grade post. Evidence of studies in the care of older people can give nurses the edge at short listing and interview.

For F grade posts, it is important that nurses demonstrate not only academic qualifications but also a range of experience and growing clinical and managerial skills. Nurses gain these skills through mentoring, through becoming link nurses and through undertaking projects to improve care.

In the NHS, the introduction of the *Agenda for Change* means that nurses will be graded according to their responsibilities. This complex job-evaluation package will lead to all NHS staff (other than doctors and senior managers) being placed on one of eight pay bands. Registered nurses will be paid on band five, specialist nurses on band six, highly specialist nurses on band seven and nurse consultants on band eight (Department of Health, 2003) (see Figure 7.4).

Level 1 Understanding of a small number of routine work procedures which could be gained through a short introduction period or on-the-job training.

Level 2 Understanding of a range of routine work procedures possibly outside immediate work area, which would require job training and a period of induction.

Level 3 Understanding of a range of work procedures and practices, some of which are non-routine, which requires a base level of theoretical knowledge. This is normally acquired through formal training or equivalent experience.

Level 4 Understanding of a range of work procedures and practices, the majority of which are non-routine, which requires intermediate-level theoretical knowledge. This knowledge is normally acquired through formal training or equivalent experience.

Level 5 Understanding of a range of work procedures and practices which requires expertise within a specialism or discipline, underpinned by theoretical knowledge or relevant practical experience.

Level 6 Specialist knowledge across the range of work procedures and practices underpinned by theoretical knowledge or relevant practical experience.

Level 7 Highly developed specialist knowledge across the range of work procedures and practices underpinned by theoretical knowledge and relevant practical experience.

Level 8 Advanced theoretical and practical knowledge of a range of work procedures and practices or specialist knowledge over more than one discipline/function acquired over a significant period.

Figure 7.4 The *Agenda for Change* banding levels

Most care homes have not officially adopted the NHS clinical grading structure. Roles and salaries within care homes are influenced by NHS grades and salaries because both the NHS and care homes must attract staff if they are to deliver high-quality patient care. Most registered nurses working in homes are Level 2 practitioners. Matrons, deputy matrons and sisters in some homes are working as Level 3 or even Level 4 practitioners.

Level 3

It is important that Level 3 practitioners gain solid nursing experience. *Making a Difference* defines Level 3 practitioners as ward managers and clinical nurse specialists. Modern matrons, lecturer practitioners, nurse lecturers and most nursing home matron managers could be added to this list. Table 7.4 (see page 181) sets out the required education and experience for such roles. In the real world, many nurses who are working at Level 3 do not have the specified level of education. This may change as newly registered nurses now have either a diploma or a degree on registration. Nurses who do not have degrees may, in the future, find it more difficult to obtain promotion.

In care homes, all registered managers are required to have an NVQ Level 4 or equivalent in management. Many nurses who are currently working as care home managers are studying for this qualification or an equivalent. In the future nurses who want to work as care home managers may find that they are unable to obtain promotion until they have gained this qualification.

In the NHS, nurses who work as ward managers are not required to have any management qualifications. Clinical nurse specialists working in the NHS are currently paid on a range of grades. Some are graded at G whilst others are graded at I.

The grade awarded is sometimes, but not always, dependent on the person's role, expertise and qualifications. The qualifications currently required vary enormously. Some nurse specialists are required to have a degree, and there may be an expectation that they are working towards a master's degree. Some nurse specialists do not have degrees and, sometimes, they do not have any post-registration qualifications in their specialist area of practice. This situation is changing rapidly and, in the future, nurse specialists will be required to have degree-level qualifications and/or qualifications and expertise in their area of practice.

In care homes, many matron/managers have gained qualifications and developed a level of expertise that is at nurse-specialist level. At present there is little recognition of this role within care homes but some homes, especially larger homes and those run by charities, have developed nurse specialist roles.

CASE STUDY — The nurse specialist

Tizy Staines was employed by the Royal Star and Garter Home in Richmond, a care home for ex-servicemen, as a clinical nurse specialist in continence care. Tizy's role included assessing patients with continence problems, carrying out a range of investigations and working with staff in the home to promote continence or to manage incontinence effectively. Her role included teaching staff and working with staff to develop practice. Tizy left to work as a continence adviser with a primary care trust, and the home employed a practice development nurse to continue developing staff and improve practice.

Lecturer-practitioner posts within the NHS enable nurses to develop both practice and teaching skills. Lecturer practitioners normally spend part of their time working with nurses in clinical practice and part of their time teaching at the local university. Posts are normally at H grade, though some trusts grade these posts at G or I. A first degree is normally required, and many lecturer practitioners are studying for MSc qualifications. Lecturer practitioners may aim to become nurse consultants or nurse teachers.

Nurse practitioner roles are developing rapidly. The nurse practitioner might be employed by a general practitioner, a primary care trust, an NHS hospital or a private walk-in centre. Nurse practitioners can be qualified to degree or MSc level. The nurse practitioner often sees a patient, diagnoses a problem and provides treatment and follow-up. Nurse practitioners also have an important role to play in chronic disease management. Nurse practitioners are one of the groups of nurses developing expanded nursing roles. Some nurse practitioners might be practising at Level 4.

The modern matron's role is a new one and is not yet well defined. The aim is to provide visible managers who have the authority to enable and empower staff and to improve the quality of care. The educational requirements and the experience demanded of this role vary. Normally, modern matrons are required to have clinical expertise and to be developing managerial expertise. Nurses who are already qualified to degree level may wish to study management at postgraduate certificate or diploma level or at MSc level.

When the matron's role was discontinued in the NHS it persisted within independent sector hospitals and care homes. Matron/managers of nursing homes have a much wider role than that in the NHS. The typical matron is responsible for all aspects of care, including domestic and catering staff, recruitment, retention and clinical care. Salaries for matrons vary according to the size of the home, the scope of the role and the part of the UK the home is in. Some salaries are equivalent to NHS G grade whilst others are higher than NHS I grade. As matrons are now required to have significant experience in caring for older people and also management qualifications, it is less easy to recruit suitable matrons and so salaries are rising.

Nurse lecturers are based in universities. Their roles are varied: they spend time teaching, supporting students in clinical practice and planning lectures. Many universities prefer lecturers to have MSc-level qualifications and to have published papers in nursing journals (Hardacre, 2003). Newly appointed lecturers are usually required to obtain postgraduate qualifications in teaching, such as the postgraduate certificate or diploma in education.

Level 4

The nurse consultant role was introduced in 2000. There are now 50 nurse consultants for older people in the NHS in England. Nurse consultants are employed by primary care trusts and NHS hospitals. Some nurse consultants work for both a primary care trust and an NHS hospital. The nurse consultant spends half of the time working with patients in clinical practice. This may include working with patients within care homes and in community settings. The nurse consultant spends around 25 per cent of the time on education and 25 per cent of the time working strategically to develop systems and processes to improve care. In many areas the nurse consultant is the person who has formal responsibility for implementing the National Service Framework for Older People. Most nurse consultants have over 20 years' experience in their speciality and have a master's degree. Some are continuing their studies to doctoral level. Many employers have found it difficult to recruit suitably qualified nurse consultants and some have appointed nurse consultants who are qualified to degree level. Degree-qualified nurse consultants are usually required to continue their studies to MSc level.

7.13 Defining higher-level practice

At the moment there no agreed qualifications for roles such as clinical nurse specialist, nurse practitioner or other roles where the title implies that the nurse is practising at a higher level. Some nurses have acquired the competencies and education associated with such roles but others have not. The Nursing and Midwifery Council announced in September 2003 that they had begun to develop a framework to protect the title of some advanced and specialist practice roles by setting up agreed competencies. The NMC intends to create competencies and titles that are meaningful to nurses, employers and the public (NMC, 2003) (see Table 7.4).

Table 7.4 The NMC competencies and titles

	Typically people here will, at a minimum, be competent ...	Typically posts will include ...	Typically people here will have been educated and trained to ...
I	... to provide basic and routine personal care to patients/clients and a limited range of clinical interventions routine to the care setting under the supervision of a registered nurse, midwife or health visitor	... cadets and healthcare assistants and other clinical support workers	... National Vocational Qualification levels 1, 2 or 3

II	... to do the above and exercise clinical judgement and assume professional responsibility and account-ability for the assessment of health needs, planning, delivery and evaluation of routine direct care, for both individuals and groups of patients/clients; direct and supervise the work of support workers and mentor students	... both newly registered nurses and midwives and established registered practitioners in a variety of jobs and specialities in both hospital and community and primary care settings	... higher education diploma or first-degree level, hold professional registration and in some cases additional specialist specific professional qualifications
III	... to do the above and assume significant clinical or public health leadership of registered practitioners and others and/or clinical management and/or specialist care	... experienced senior registered practitioners in a diverse range of posts including ward sisters/charge nurses, community nurses, midwives, health visitors and clinical nurse specialists	... first or masters-degree level, hold professional registration and in many cases additional specialist specific professional qualifications
IV	... to do above and provide expert care, to provide clinical or public health leadership and consultancy to senior registered practitioners and others and initiate and lead significant practice, education and service development	... experienced and expert practitioners holding nurse, midwife or health visitor consultant posts	... masters or doctorate level, hold professional registration and additional specialist specific professional qualifications commensurate with standards proposed for recognition of a 'higher level of practice'

7.14 Expanding roles

Nursing is changing rapidly, and nurses are now beginning to undertake roles that were unthinkable 20 years ago. *Making a Difference* outlines 10 key roles for nurses:

1 Ordering diagnostic investigations, such as pathology tests and X-rays.
2 Making and receiving referrals directly.
3 Admitting and discharging patients with specific conditions within agreed protocols.
4 Managing patient caseloads.
5 Running clinics.
6 Prescribing medications and treatments.
7 Carrying out a wide range of resuscitation procedures, including defibrillation.
8 Performing minor surgery and outpatient procedures.
9 Triaging patients.
10 Taking the lead in the way local health services are organised and the way they are run.

Liberating the Talents (Department of Health, 2002) provides details of how different organisations are developing these roles. The development of expanded roles will affect all nurses at all stages of their careers. Nurses who have experience at E grade and above can complete the nurse prescribing course. This course enables nurses to examine patients, to diagnose and to treat illness. Nurses at all levels are increasingly ordering diagnostic investigations and referring patients directly. Nurse practitioners and specialists are managing chronic diseases, running clinics and changing treatments, using patient management plans if they are prescribers.

7.15 Conclusion

If you are to provide quality services you need to provide an environment that encourages staff to give of their best. Healthcare is changing rapidly, and those of you who work with older people are now looking after people with much more complex needs than ever before. If you are to meet those needs, you must develop your own practice by gaining expertise and educational qualifications, and by encouraging and enabling staff to develop practice.

Key Points

○ People are influenced by the culture of the organisation they are working for.

○ A learning organisation encourages people to develop practice.

○ Management style influences staff motivation.

○ It is important to identify the skills required within a ward or care home.

○ Staff who have a range of skills can effectively meet older people's needs for safe and effective care.

○ Identifying individual learning needs enables you to help staff develop.

○ Managers may need to balance organisational and individual learning needs to ensure that staff have a range of skills.

○ Nursing roles are expanding as healthcare is changing.

References and further reading

SECTION 7.1

Department of Health (2000) *An Organisation with a Memory. Report of an Expert Group on Learning from Adverse Events in the NHS Chaired by the Chief Medical Officer.* Stationery Office, London.

Senge, P. (1990) *The Fifth Discipline. The Art and Practice of the Learning Organisation.* Doubleday, New York.

Skinner, B.F. (1971) *Beyond Freedom and Dignity.* Alfred Knopf, New York.

SECTION 7.3

Deeprose, D. (2003) *Smart Things to Know about Motivation.* Capstone Publishing, London.

SECTION 7.5

Schein, E.H. (1985) *Organisational Culture and Leadership.* Jossey-Bass, San Francisco.

SECTION 7.7

Fowler, V. (2003) 'Health care assistants: developing their role to include nursing tasks', *Nursing Times,* 99: 36.

SECTION 7.8

Gould, D., Kelly, D. and White, I. (2004) 'Training needs analysis: an evaluation framework', *Nursing Standard,* 18: 33–6.

SECTION 7.10

Kolb, D.A. (1984) *Experiential Learning Experience as the Source of Learning and Development.* Prentice-Hall, Englewood Cliffs, NJ.

SECTION 7.12

Charnley, E. (1999) 'Occupational stress in newly qualified nurses', *Nursing Standard,* 13: 33–7.

Department of Health (1999) *Making a Difference. Strengthening the Nursing, Midwifery and Health Visiting Contribution to Health and Healthcare.* Department of Health, London.

Department of Health (2001) *National Minimum Standards for Care Homes for Older People.* Stationery Office, London (also available at **http://www.doh.gov.uk/ncsc**).

Department of Health (2003) *Job Evaluation Handbook* (1st edn). Department of Health, London.

Fowler, V. (2003) 'Health care assistants: developing their role to include nursing tasks', *Nursing Times,* 99: 36.

Hardacre, J. (2003) 'Meeting the requirements for becoming a nurse lecturer', *Nursing Times*, 99: 31.

Nursing Times (2004) 'Nurses to take the lead in the future NHS (editorial)', *Nursing Times*, 100: 11.

Runciman, P. et al. (2000) *The Work of Newly Qualified Nurses: Core Skills and Competencies*. National Board for Nursing, Midwifery and Health Visiting for Scotland, Edinburgh.

SECTION 7.13

NMC (2003) 'Higher level practice standards', *NMC Newsletter*, December: 8 (also available at **www.nmc-uk.org/nmc/main/pressStatements/ NMCbeginsworkonhigherlevelpracticestandards**).

SECTION 7.14

Department of Health (2002) *Liberating the Talents. Helping Primary Care Trusts and Nurses to Develop the NHS Plan*. Department of Health, London.

CHAPTER 8

Enabling older people

Introduction

When the National Health Service was introduced, politicians thought that costs would fall within a few years as ill-health was reduced. The body was considered to be like a car, and healthcare was provided to fix the body when it broke down. No responsible driver would consider this a sensible way to run a car. You need to top up the screen wash so that you can wash your windscreen. You need to top up the oil in the engine. No driver would consider letting his or her car run short of oil so that the engine seized and had to be replaced. Drivers would not think of putting themselves in danger of a crash by driving with bald tires or defective brakes. Cars also need regular servicing if they to run reliably.

If older people were thought of as the owners of cars, the cars that they are running need ongoing and expert attention because they are vintage cars with many miles on the clock. No reputable garage would consider carrying out work on someone's car without discussing the options and implications with the car owner. Older people sometimes receive a poorer service than car drivers in this respect. This chapter examines ways to work with older people so that they can enjoy the best possible quality of life.

Healthcare services that care predominately for older people are less well resourced than those that are aimed at younger people. It is considered acceptable in many settings that care for older people should have fewer nurses and less well educated nurses. The myths that 'justify' these actions are that older people do not need well educated nurses because they only require 'basic' care and that older people are less likely to complain than younger people.

Research has exploded these myths and proves that older people are as critical of poor services as younger people. Research also indicates that older people are especially vulnerable to the effects of poor-quality healthcare. Poor staffing levels and poor management of health care have a huge impact on recovery.

In healthcare (as in all services) there is little point in service providers working hard to produce a high-quality product if the product does not meet the needs of the people it is designed for. This chapter explores research that indicates what older people's health priorities are. It also examines how the way care is delivered and managed affects the older person's ability to recover as fully as possible from illness and injury.

People in junior and middle management posts, and those whom they manage, often suffer from myopia. Their view of the world begins and ends in their particular department, ward or care home. They see the leaves but not the trees or the forest. The patient's experience of healthcare is wider than that of the staff. The patient must journey through a system that should be, but often is not, seamless. This chapter aims to give you some insight into the patient's perspective of healthcare and how the way each part of the system is important and affects the person's health and wellbeing.

This chapter aims to enable you to understand that the way services are delivered at all parts of the patient's journey can enable or disable the older person. Ultimately, this chapter aims to enable you to make connections, to see your part in the healthcare chain and to empower you to make a difference.

Aims

8.1 Older people's priorities in healthcare	8.6 Cultural differences
8.2 Communication	8.7 Services that disable
8.3 Staffing	8.8 Learned helplessness
8.4 The patient's journey	8.9 Services that enable
8.5 Managing the patient's journey	8.10 As others see us
	8.11 Conclusion

8.1 Older people's priorities in healthcare

Older people are often presumed to be grateful and uncritical of the services they receive. This view (as noted in Chapter 1) is mistaken. Older people are more critical and less satisfied with the services they receive than younger people. This may be because the quality of care older people receive is critical to their quality of life, and because older people are much more vulnerable to adverse outcomes than younger people.

Older people's expectations of healthcare can be grouped under three main headings: communication, staffing, and attitude and approach. Although each of these issues is woven with the others, it is probably simpler to examine them separately.

8.2 Communication

When adults are ill they expect to be provided with information about their illness and the treatments available. They expect to be involved in decisions about treatment and transfer of care. Effective communication is vital to this process. However, there are often barriers when communicating with older people, and it is important that managers are aware of these barriers, take action to minimise them and work with staff to enable them to adapt communication styles to enable older people.

Everyone has a place where he or she feels secure and safe. Most people feel secure and safe in their homes and regard them as their territory. However, it is much easier to be assertive and to call the shots when you are in your own home. Community nurses regard themselves as nursing in a person's home (Howkins and Ewens, 1997). In hospital settings and, to a slightly lesser extent, in care homes, the older person is in foreign territory. In hospitals and care homes the people who make decisions about when breakfast is served, what time the lights go out and so many other aspects are usually nursing staff. It is much more difficult to be assertive in such circumstances (Marsh, 1988): the older person is a strange environment and may be unsure of what is happening and what is planned.

If you are to develop an equal partnership with the older person, you need to be able to communicate effectively. Communication involves transmitting an idea to another person using an appropriate channel, checking that the message has been understood and receiving a message back from the person you are communicating with. Research from older people and from nurses suggests that, when nurses communicate with older people, there is often a lack of meaningful interaction; communication is often superficial ('How are you, Mr Jones?') or task orientated ('I'm just going to do your dressing') (Davies, 2001; Miller, 2002).

Reflect on practice

Consider what positive and negative attitudes you and your colleagues may have about older people and their ability to communicate. How might these attitudes affect the way you communicate with older people? How could you improve your communication style and that of your colleagues?

Barriers to communication

Older people are not a homogeneous group. The people you care for may be aged from 60 years to over 100. These people will come from a range of cultures and social classes and will have had different experiences. All these issues will affect the person's ability to communicate effectively. They may also affect your attitude and willingness to communicate. There are, however, many other barriers to communication (see Table 8.1).

Table 8.1 Barriers to communication

BARRIER	CAUSES
Sensory	Hearing problems, visual problems, difficulty understanding speech because of stroke or other neurological problem
Language	Inability to understand English, strong regional accent, rapid speech, complex speech, use of jargon (e.g. 'TIA'), patronising, oversimplified speech
Environmental	Lack of privacy, noisy environment with lots of background hum
Cultural	The older person might consider it inappropriate to discuss some topics (such intimate body functions) with a younger person or a person of a different gender. The subject might be in conflict with the older person's deeply held beliefs
Attitudinal	The nurse might not want to discuss an issue in depth with the older person because of a fear of upsetting the older person or because the nurse feels that the older person might have difficulty understanding
Physical	Nurse towering over seated patient, conversation conducted over high nursing station
Negative body language	Nurse looking busy or harassed, patient looking to end of ward for visitors, closed body language

Overcoming barriers to communication

The most effective way to overcome barriers to communication is to audit current practice in your workplace to identify the barriers to communication. You can then adopt a problem-solving approach to enable you to develop strategies to overcome these barriers.

CASE STUDY – Overcoming barriers to communication

In care homes, staff are required to draw up an individualised care plan with the older person, and the older person is required to sign the plan to signify that he or she has been consulted and agrees with the plan. Homes are required to produce detailed care plans. At Rectory House Nursing Home, Hilary Marsden (the matron/manager) and a colleague discovered that the older people in the home found the detailed care plans difficult to understand. Hilary and her colleague drew up a second simplified care plan they called 'Care at a glance' (see opposite). Residents found this easier to understand, and signed and kept a copy of it. A copy of 'Care at a glance' is kept in each resident's room so that staff can refer to it and give residents the individualised care they require.

This simple way of meeting an older person's needs and providing continuity of care has been welcomed by inspectors responsible for inspecting the home.

Reflect on practice

Can you identify any barriers to communication within your workplace? Can any of these be solved simply? Consider involving other staff within your workplace in a project to identify some barriers to communication and introducing one change to reduce these barriers.

8.3 Staffing

Older people are concerned about shortages of staff in healthcare settings (Health Advisory Service 2000, 1998). They are also concerned that staff do not meet their fundamental care needs and do not preserve their dignity (Help the Aged, 2000). They are concerned that staff lack expertise in caring for older people (Help the Aged, 2002).

There are no agreed staffing levels for different types of hospital wards. Staffing levels in such wards vary enormously in different NHS trusts. The skills mix also varies – some wards have higher levels of registered nurses than others. Traditionally, staffing levels have been lower in wards considered to be for older people than in such wards as surgical, which are considered more acute. In 1962 (2nd edn 1975) Doreen Norton wrote that:

CARE AT A GLANCE

Elimination: *Stress incontinence. Wears Gamanil pants.*	**Name:** *Mrs Edith Norman* **Address/Ward No./Room No.** 7 .... **Additional comments:**	**Skin:** 1. Dehydrated (Note tongue) 2. Oedematous–mark areas as: 3. Broken areas: *Small red area on buttocks* Sensation 1. Pain – describe & mark areas as: 2. Lacks sensation mark as:

Speech: *Clear no communication problems*	**Reason for Assessment:**	**Date:** *7.8.04*	**Signature:** *M Wilson*	**Remarks:**

Vision: *Wears reading glasses*	**Sleep:** *Sleeps well, no problems*	**Emotion/Mental:** *Now settling into home well and making friends*	**Respiration:** *No problems*

Oral Hygiene: *Wears dentures, remove, brush and soak in Steradent overnight.* *Use polygrip in top denture*	**Movement:** *Walks with frame*	**Diet:** *High fibre, tends to constipation*	**Hearing:** *Wears hearing aid left ear. Check batteries and replace as needed, needs help to put aid in ear*

Staff in care homes are required to draw up individualised care plans *geriatric nursing had long been recognized as being largely routine work of a particularly heavy nature, [and that] the result of this was an emphasis on a task-based work system designed to 'get the work done'.*

This perception unfortunately persists to this day, despite a revolution in medical and surgical care and increasing longevity. In hospitals, the staffing and skills mix may vary from shift to shift, with the high levels of RN staff on some shifts and minimal levels on others. In English care homes, the National Minimum Standards do not set minimal staffing levels. Before the introduction of National Minimum Standards, many inspectors stated that the minimum staffing ratios for an early shift should be 1:4 or 1:5, 1:6 or 1:7 for a late shift and 1:10 for a night shift. Registered nurses were required to make up between 25 and 50 per cent of those numbers.

Are older people right to be concerned about staffing levels? Do higher levels of staffing make a difference to the quality of care? Research suggests that higher levels of registered nurses lead to improved outcomes for older people in hospitals. Person and colleagues (2004) found that higher levels of registered nurses reduced mortality levels in cardiac patients. McCloskey (1998) found that the wards with the lowest levels of registered nurses had higher rates of falls and a higher incidence of pressure sores. The only difference between the wards was the level of registered nurse staffing. Needleman and colleagues (2002) found improved outcomes and lower rates of urinary tract infections when higher levels of registered nurses were employed.

In nursing homes there are also clear indications that higher levels of registered nurses lead to improved outcomes. Older people living in nursing homes are less likely to require hospital treatment if there are high levels of registered nurses within the home (Zimmerman et al., 2002). In the USA, experts are now calling for the introduction of minimum staffing levels within nursing homes to improve the quality of care (Harrington et al., 2000).

Older people are right to be concerned about staffing levels, but it is doubtful if older people make the distinction between registered nurses and healthcare assistants. The research outlined above clearly shows that increasing the numbers of healthcare assistants does not affect outcomes but that increasing the numbers of registered nurses does. Most of the studies have taken place in the USA, and there may be differences between the way that registered nurses work in the USA and the UK. In some workplaces within the UK, registered nurses do not engage in the practice of nursing but, instead, confine themselves to tasks such as dispensing medications or dressing wounds. This may be because some nurses have had poor role models and have been taught that fundamental care (such as enabling a person to wash or dress) is not part of the registered nurse's role, or the nurses may simply be suffering from burnout. Nurses in all care settings can 'burn out' and disengage from their work. Burnout can lead to the nurse leaving the workplace and sometimes even leaving nursing. Research carried out in the UK, USA and Canada suggests that improved staffing and supportive management cut the levels of burnout and registered nurse turnover (Aiken et al., 2002). It could be that registered nurses make a difference only when they care for a patient in a holistic manner.

Reflect on practice

It has been suggested that managers can reduce levels of registered nurse turnover and reduce burnout by supporting nurses in their efforts to improve care. How much support do you receive from your manager? What further support would help you? How much support do you provide to more junior staff? Do you feel that you offer an appropriate level of support? If not, how can you provide improved levels of support in the future?

Expertise of staff

Older people are concerned that staff lack expertise in the care of older people. Increasingly, employers are requiring that nurses who have senior positions in areas where older people are cared for have qualifications and expertise in caring for older people. Some employers continue to have differing expectations for different areas of practice and demand high skill levels from nurses in popular specialities and lower levels from nurses in such specialities as caring for older people. In some workplaces, long-serving staff who were recruited years ago may have either a greater or lesser range of skills than newly recruited staff. A skills audit, ongoing education programmes and benchmarking will enable you to determine what skills are required within your workplace and what skills staff possess. You can then develop a programme to enable staff to develop or extend their skills.

Reflect on practice

Do you consider that there should be mandatory minimum staffing levels in hospitals and nursing homes? Why do you hold this view? What do you consider the advantages of introducing these might be? What problems might they bring? Do you believe that people working with older people should be required to have certain qualifications and expertise? What would the benefits of this be? What are the disadvantages of this?

Attitude and approach

Older people encounter negative attitudes from some staff. These range from staff being rude and abrupt to neglect and failure to meet fundamental care needs. Sometimes older people are not consulted about their illness or the range of possible treatments available. Research indicates that higher levels of registered nurses do not lead to huge increases in patient satisfaction (Bolton et al., 2003). Clearly there is more to providing a quality service than just keeping up the numbers of registered nurses: 'it's not what you do, it's the way that you do it.'

I remember once as a ward sister observing two student nurses giving bed baths. Annie – a large, untidy girl with a beaming smile – slopped the water over the bed table. The soap slipped out of her hand and she dropped the talcum powder. There were clouds of dust everywhere. She made up for this clumsiness in her approach to the patient, which was sensitive and positive. It was a wonderful bed bath that made the patient feel worth while and human. Maura's bed bath was technically perfect and accomplished exactly what she wanted it to do. It despatched another task on the list of jobs to do for the morning. It was mechanistic; there was no love and no sharing of herself with the patient, and no meaningful interaction. It was a soulless and rather chilling bed bath.

In some care settings the culture is such that a negative attitude and approach to older people would be unthinkable. In others it is a part of everyday life. The difference between high-quality care settings and impoverished care environments, where people are viewed simply as units of work to be gotten through as quickly as possible, is leadership. Leadership at all levels of clinical practice, from staff nurse to nurse consultant, makes a huge difference to the attitude and approach of staff. It requires passion, commitment and courage to challenge negative attitudes and approaches constructively when caring for older people. Education and practice development can help move practice forward, but education on its own is not enough, as the following case study illustrates.

CASE STUDY — Education and practice development are not enough

Gloria Lennox was pleased with the changes at Lawton War Memorial Hospital. The F and G grade-nurses had attended a course in rehabilitation nursing at the local university. Gloria could see the difference: the average length of stay had gone down and patients were more able on discharge than before. Now, when a patient was admitted, a multidisciplinary team consisting of the ward physiotherapist, the occupational therapist, the ward manager and the primary nurse worked a discharge date. Everyone then worked towards rehabilitating the patient and discharging on the set date.

Gloria was very surprised to receive a complaint from Mrs Edwards about how her mother's discharge had been poorly planned: 'I am disgusted. It's been freezing for days and today I've been told my mother is going home this afternoon. I'm supposed to drop everything, leave work and drive 20 miles to my mother's house to put on the heating. Then I'm supposed to get some shopping in for her so everything is ready this afternoon. This is ridiculous. My mother has been in your hospital for three weeks. If someone had just given me some notice I wouldn't be in such a panic.'

Gloria went to see Dora Evans, the ward sister, and expressed her surprise that Mrs Bessie Simpson's daughter, Mrs Edwards, was unaware of her mother's discharge now that discharge dates were planned on admission. The sister explained: 'Yes, we should have told her yesterday'.

'Don't you inform patients and relatives of planned discharge on admission?' asked Gloria.

'No, we usually tell them the day before. It's best if they don't have too much notice. Old people can get very worried about this sort of thing, you know.'

In 1983, Wade identified four different models of care in nursing homes and NHS long-stay geriatric wards. She called these models supportive, protective, controlled and restrained (see Figure 8.1).

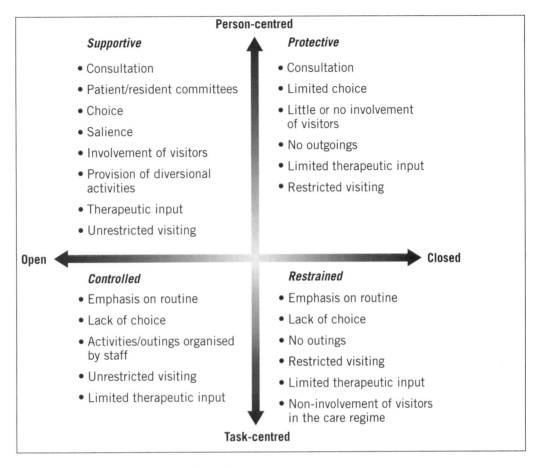

Figure 8.1 Wade's models of nursing care

Although Wade's models apply to long-stay settings, they can be used to examine practice in other settings where older people receive care. For example, Dora Evans, if she were honest, might admit that she sees older people not as adults but as children who ought to be protected from worries, such as discharge. It is unlikely that anyone holding such views would consider it appropriate to develop a partnership with the older person and to discuss the costs and benefits of various treatments.

Wade suggests that the supportive model, which involves the older people as well as their families in the care, is the most appropriate.

Reflect on practice

Gloria Lennox's reliance on education alone to change the culture and deeply held views of the long-serving staff at Lawton War Memorial was unrealistic. Dora Evans is in a powerful position to influence practice for better or worse in her ward. How would you work with Dora to help her to develop a more positive and enabling attitude to older people?

8.4 The patient's journey

As a professional you are always busy. There is never enough time and always lots to do. Everyone works hard to do his or her utmost to offer patients the best possible quality of care. The trouble with busy professionals is that they can be very short-sighted: they can only see part of the picture. So when you concentrate on providing high-quality care you tend only to consider that in relation to your workplace. The ward-based nurse often thinks that patient care begins and ends in the ward. The nurse in a care home might consider the person only in relation to care needs. Nurses in all areas of practice can easily fall into the trap of being unaware of how what has gone before affects the person's perceptions of care and ability to enjoy the best possible quality of life. This section looks at one theoretical patient's journey to illustrate this process.

CASE STUDY — A patient's journey

Mrs Phyllis Warburton has lived alone in a large detached house since her husband, George, died several years ago. Mrs Warburton loves her home. Her children were born and grew up there, and her grandchildren played there and visit now with their own children. Mrs Warburton slipped in her drive when getting out of the car one frosty afternoon. She was unable to get up and lay there for hours because her neighbours were out at work and no one heard her calls for help.

Mrs Warburton's journey started when the ambulance crew arrived and began to treat her (1). This was the first link in the chain of her journey. She was cold, shocked and in considerable pain. When she fell and fractured, she damaged blood vessels and haemorrhaged into her thigh muscles. The paramedics checked her temperature, pulse, blood pressure and oxygen saturation levels. They began to warm her up on her journey to hospital, gave her oxygen and began to stabilise her condition.

The next link in the chain was admission to accident and emergency (2). If Mrs Warburton were not to be seen quickly and further stabilised, she would suffer more extensive damage and her recovery would be prolonged. She was transferred to a trolley but had already suffered from pressure damage to her skin because she had lain on an icy tarmaced drive for four hours. The effects of this damage were not yet visible but, if the trolley did not have a pressure-relieving surface, she would suffer further pressure damage.

Mrs Warburton was in shock and required intravenous fluids and blood to combat this. If there were to be a delay in providing this, she would be at risk of further pressure damage and, if she were in severe shock, renal damage. She required analgesia because she was in severe pain (analgesia should be given to patients who have suspected hip fracture before the fracture is confirmed by X-ray – Hallstrom et al., 2000). Mrs Warburton was frightened, shocked and in pain. She needed to be informed of what the staff intended to do and to be assured that her needs will be met promptly and sensitively.

The next link in the chain is usually the transfer to a ward (3). Mrs Warburton would be cared for until she had surgery to repair her fracture. She would be more likely to experience a full and uncomplicated recovery if her fracture were to be repaired within 24 hours of fracture. If her operation were delayed, she would be at increased risk of complications, such as deep-vein thrombosis, chest infection and pressure damage (Audit Commission, 1996). If her operation were to be delayed, it would be vital that her nutritional needs were met. Malnutrition increases the risks of poor recovery, pressure damage, poor wound healing and readmission (Porter and Johnson, 1998).

The next link in the chain is the surgical repair of Mrs Warburton's fracture (4). However, if the earlier links in the chain were flawed, even the most perfect operation might not lead to an uneventful recovery.

The next link is effective post-operative care (5). The importance of adequate pain relieve and early mobilisation is well known. If the early links in the chain are flawed, these will effect Mrs Warburton's recovery. If Mrs Warburton's earlier care was not of the highest quality, she might develop a pressure sore or post-operative complications, such as infection or poor wound healing. She is terrified that she will not make a full recovery and will be forced to leave her home and to move into sheltered accommodation. Effective post-operative care should take into account Mrs Warburton's fears and hopes for the future.

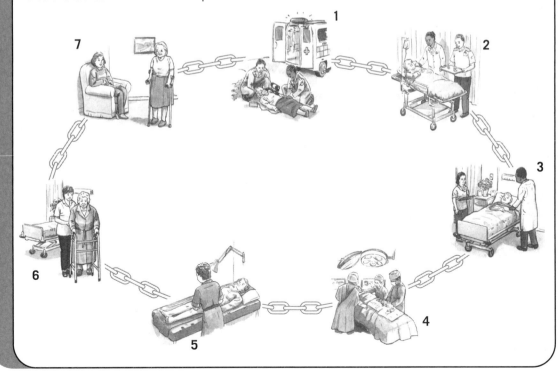

> **Reflect on practice** •
>
> Can you think of an example of how one aspect of a patient's journey affected that person's ability to recover from illness or injury? How could that break in the chain be corrected? How do you think looking at the whole patient journey will affect the quality of care an individual receives? What other benefits of examining a patient's journey can you think of?

As can be seen, Mrs Warburton's journey through the healthcare system consists not of separate unrelated periods of treatment but of links in a chain. Actions or inactions in any part of this chain affect her potential to recover quickly. They also affect her psychological state. If Mrs Warburton was in pain in accident and emergency and this was not promptly treated, she might be reluctant to mobilise post-operatively because she fears untreated pain.

If you are to offer quality services you need to begin to look at the patient experience in totality. This is a paradigm shift and enables you to look at care and the outcomes of care with new eyes. In the past, if a problem was identified on a particular ward or department, there was a tendency to look at that ward or department to see what had gone wrong and to try to fix the problem. If you look at the patient's journey, this will allow you to take a *whole systems* approach and to look at how different parts of the journey actually impact on patient care. The case study below illustrates this.

CASE STUDY — A whole systems approach

There are major problems with discharges in a trust. This has led to a shortage of beds, and patients are forced to wait a long time in accident and emergency until beds are available. Maureen O'Callaghan has been appointed to discover why discharges are delayed and to work with staff to reduce delays. Maureen spends a great deal of time visiting other hospitals and analysing the average length of patient stay within the trust and within other hospitals with comparable patients. She discovers that the average length of stay for patients who have fractured a femur is longer than in a nearby three-star trust.

Maureen spoke to the discharge co-ordinators to find out the reasons that patients' stays are longer in the trust. The discharge co-ordinators explained that they work with ward staff to discharge patients promptly, but that many of the patients have complications post-operatively. The major complications delaying discharge are pressure sores and chest infections. These complications lead to hospital stays being extended by 50 per cent. This is leading to lengthening waiting lists, prolonged stays in accident and emergency and many other problems.

Maureen arranged to meet Veronica Gibbs to discover why there are high rates of infection and pressure sores in orthopaedic patients. They worked together to audit care within the wards and noticed that staff are careful to assess pressure sore risk and to take action to minimise this. Despite this, there are high rates of pressure sores. Veronica commented: 'I think we're starting too late. The place to start is in accident and emergency. There is no pressure-relieving equipment down there and I'm sure that's where half of the problems begin.'

Maureen arranged to meet Robin Clarridge, the clinical nurse specialist in accident and emergency, to find out if practice in accident and emergency is contributing to post-operative problems. They worked together to audit care and discovered that patients with fractures are being cared for on trolleys for an average of six hours. There are no pressure-relieving mattresses on the trolleys, and nurses are reluctant to reposition patients because of pain. Robin explained: 'It's not fair to lay all of this at our door. We're very busy and, anyhow, these orthopaedic patients spend ages in theatre flat on their backs and there's no pressure-relieving equipment on the operating table.'

Reflect on practice

Maureen has identified most of the chain of causation that increases an older person's risk of pressure sores developing. If you were Maureen, how might you begin to untangle the problems and influence practice in accident and emergency, in theatre and in the wards to reduce the risks of pressure sores? What problems do you think you might encounter in attempting to change practice? How might you begin to overcome these barriers?

8.5 Managing the patient's journey

In the past, managers were taught how to manage within their area of practice. The ward manager responsible for the acute care of older people was taught how to manage services within the ward, including some rudimentary education on discharge. This was often confined to the simple management of discharge and consisted of how to organise medication, transport and ongoing care, such as district nursing. It seldom included education on how other parts of the system worked, what their problems were and how to work with other parts of the system to provide continuity of care. This is now changing, and nurses and other professionals are being encouraged to manage in ways that enable a smooth transfer of care. The case study below illustrates some of the problems that can occur when transferring an older person from one care setting to another.

CASE STUDY – Managing transfers

Laura Edwards and the staff at the Haven were thrilled when they received a contract to provide rehabilitation to older people who had undergone elective orthopaedic surgery at the local hospital. The contract was funded as part of a waiting-list initiative. Patients were to be assessed prior to admission. Individuals were to be admitted to the hospital for five days using a patient care pathway. On the fifth day patients were either to be discharged home with support or to have up to 14 days' rehabilitation in the Haven if further rehabilitation was required. Jeanette Hamilton was appointed to co-ordinate care from home, to hospital, to rehabilitation (if needed) and to home.

It soon became clear that there were a few problems with transfers of care. Laura and her team found that, although they received a transfer letter, this did not help them provide continuity of care. The transfer letter provided information about medication, mobility and wound care but not about other important aspects of care. Laura and her team wanted to know when the individual had last eaten, when analgesia was last given and other more detailed information. She arranged to meet the co-ordinator and found that, if the hospital was transferring a patient from an acute surgical ward to another ward within the hospital, this sort of information was handed over verbally on transfer. Patients admitted to the Haven did not normally have a nurse escort and so this information was being lost.

Reflect on practice

If you were Jeanette, how would you improve communication between nursing staff on the orthopaedic ward and nurses at the Haven? What strategies might you use? What are the main advantages and disadvantages of each method? Could better planning have avoided this problem?

8.6 Cultural differences

Culture is an intangible thing; we work within a culture and often fail to consider how the culture of our organisation affects the way we work or how we work with others. The culture within acute hospitals is very different from that of nursing homes. The culture in hospitals and nursing homes is very different from normal life. In hospitals, for example, adults are expected to wear nightclothes or hospital gowns all the time.

Hospitals have visiting hours. In many hospitals these are from 2 pm to 8 pm, although some hospitals have introduced 'open visiting'. In late 2003, King's College Hospital London closed wards to visitors in an effort to improve the patients' nutritional status. The Department of Health was considering compelling all hospitals to shut wards at lunchtime to allow patients to eat without being disturbed

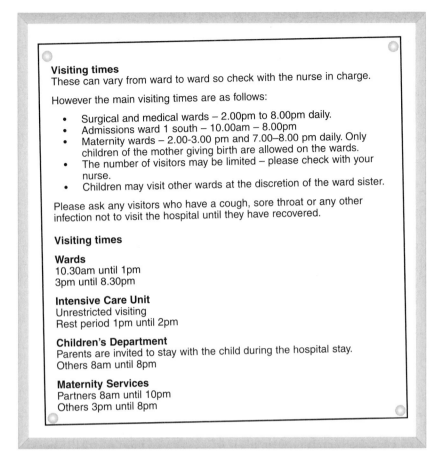

Visiting times
These can vary from ward to ward so check with the nurse in charge.

However the main visiting times are as follows:

- Surgical and medical wards – 2.00pm to 8.00pm daily.
- Admissions ward 1 south – 10.00am – 8.00pm
- Maternity wards – 2.00-3.00 pm and 7.00–8.00 pm daily. Only children of the mother giving birth are allowed on the wards.
- The number of visitors may be limited – please check with your nurse.
- Children may visit other wards at the discretion of the ward sister.

Please ask any visitors who have a cough, sore throat or any other infection not to visit the hospital until they have recovered.

Visiting times

Wards
10.30am until 1pm
3pm until 8.30pm

Intensive Care Unit
Unrestricted visiting
Rest period 1pm until 2pm

Children's Department
Parents are invited to stay with the child during the hospital stay.
Others 8am until 8pm

Maternity Services
Partners 8am until 10pm
Others 3pm until 8pm

Hospitals have visiting hours, whereas care homes usually have a policy of open visiting

by visitors. In early 2004, the Department of Health stated that this policy would not be compulsory. They chose instead to offer NHS trusts that wanted to support this policy a training pack to enable them to do so (Nursing Times, 2004).

This policy of closing wards to enable patients to eat lunch undisturbed is strange. It sends a number of odd messages. The first is that it is important to have lunch without being disturbed by visitors, but it's not important to have supper undisturbed. Most adults have their main meal in the evening. This policy seems at odds with much of government policy about developing partnerships with patients and about giving them a choice. Would the patient prefer to eat lunch undisturbed or would he or she prefer to have a visit from a friend? Restricting visiting may deprive a patient of visits from friends and family who find it difficult to visit in those limited times. The older person's friend may also be old and, if he or she is unable to visit until 2 pm, he or she will have to leave early or go home in the dark on a winter's night. The older person's daughter may have young children and may find it difficult to visit if she has to pick up her children from school. The hospital may also prohibit children under 12 from visiting, so the older person may not be able to see his or her grandchildren or great grandchildren. If you examine this policy using Wade's model, you'll see that it is part of a closed, task-centred model of care.

In nursing homes older people normally get up and dress in normal clothes. There is usually a policy of open visiting and family and friends often pop in to visit. There are seldom problems because most people are sensible and courteous and will wait if the older person needs assistance or treatment. In the community, nurses are providing care in the person's own home and are guests in that person's home.

Sometimes these cultural differences affect the ability to offer continuity of care because each nurse working in a particular setting sees care through the prism of the culture he or she works in.

CASE STUDY – Cultural differences and the continuity of care

Jeanette Hamilton has spent a lot of time at the Haven working with Laura Edwards and the staff to develop a patient care pathway. The pathway states what care each person receiving intermediate care will receive on each of the 14 days in the Haven. Each person has a number of goals to meet in a set period. These include washing, dressing and increasing mobility.

When Jeanette arrived at the Haven she was disappointed to find that some of the people on the programme had not met their goals: 'What's the problem? Are they not having enough therapy? I was concerned that there might not be enough physiotherapy time to help us meet these goals.'

Laura explained that this was not the problem. The problem was that the people participating in the rehabilitation programme did not always seem clear about why they had been transferred to the Haven: 'Some of them think that they are here to be looked after and don't realise that this is about recovery, not ongoing care. It can take a day or two to get the message across. The other problem we have is getting clothes in. No one arrives with clothes and shoes and it's difficult to get the programme started when people don't have suitable clothes and shoes. It can take three or four days to get relatives to bring in clothes.'

The problem here is one of communication. Staff in the acute orthopaedic wards are focused on care for people pre- and post-operatively. They are not communicating the aims of the rehabilitation programme to patients and relatives. In the acute ward, patients are not dressed. The staff are busy organising discharge and do not think of what patients will need on the next stage of their journey.

Reflect on practice

If Jeanette is not able to help staff at the Haven discharge patients promptly, the orthopaedic ward will not have the beds required to operate and get the waiting list down. If you were Jeanette, how would you tackle this problem? What strategies might you use to improve communication between the orthopaedic ward and staff at the Haven?

8.7 Services that disable

Older people can, unless care is of the highest quality, lose ability in hospitals and care homes. Research suggests that the older a person is, the more likely he or she is to loose the ability to carry out the activities of daily living for reasons completely unrelated to those that lead to admission (Covinsky et al., 2003). The case study below illustrates this problem.

CASE STUDY – Disabling care

Veronica Gibbs checked on the wards before she set off on holiday for two weeks. When she arrived at Annie Zunz Ward, Mrs Harrington was being admitted. Mrs Harrington walked slowly down the ward with her stick.

When Veronica came back on duty two weeks later, she barely recognised Mrs Harrington, who was being hoisted. 'What has happened?' Veronica asked.

Sister James replied: 'Well, there's nothing physical wrong, the medics have checked her out. She's just given up. It often happens with older people.'

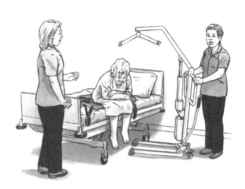

8.8 Learned helplessness

The theory of learned helplessness can help to explain what has happened in Mrs Harrington's case. Seligman accidentally discovered an unexpected phenomenon whilst doing experiments on dogs. In a series of well-known experiments, Pavlov discovered that if a ringing bell or tone is repeatedly accompanied with the presentation of food, a dog salivates. Conditioning dogs in this way means that when you ring a bell the dog salivates. In Seligman's experiment, Seligman restrained a dog in a hammock and applied a harmless electric shock. The aim was to teach the dog to associate the bell with a shock so that the dog would run away when the bell sounded.

In the next phase of the experiment, the dog was put into a box with two compartments. A low fence divided these compartments. The dog could see the way out and jump over the fence to avoid the shock. The experimenters rang the bell expecting the dog to jump over the fence but nothing happened; the dog just lay there. Then they put a unconditioned dog in the box, rang the bell and the dog jumped out. The conditioned dog had learnt that trying to escape from the shocks is futile. This dog learnt to be helpless (Seligman, 1972).

The theory of learned helplessness was then extended to human behaviour, providing a model for explaining depression and passivity (Seligman, 1969). Depressed people learnt that whatever they do is futile. During the course of their lives, depressed people apparently learn that they have no control. Learned helplessness (Seligman, 1992) affects people in the following ways:

- **Motivation** – reduced; no incentive to try new coping responses.
- **Cognition** – inability to learn new responses to overcome prior learning that trauma is uncontrollable.
- **Emotion** – the helpless state resembles depression.

Learned helplessness might explain why some people feel trapped in situations and feel that they have little control over their lives. Researchers began to find that not everyone was affected by negative experiences in the same way. Some people did not get depressed, even after many bad life experiences. These people dusted themselves off and started all over again. They were able to put bad experiences behind them and to get on with life. Seligman discovered that a depressed person thought about the bad event in more pessimistic ways than a non-depressed person. He called this thinking 'explanatory style'.

Gilbert (1984) expanded on Seligman's work and states that individuals are vulnerable to learned helplessness if the individual:

- is aware of uncontrollable factors in his or her environment;
- views the situation as unchangeable; or
- blames him or herself for his or her helplessness – 'internal attribution'.

Reflect on practice

Do you feel that staff attitudes have contributed to Mrs Harrington loosing ability during her hospital stay? If you were Veronica, what actions might you take to enable Mrs Harrington to begin recovering? What actions might you take to reduce the risks of this type of problem in the future?

8.9 Services that enable

Virginia Henderson (1966) defined the nurse's role as follows:

The unique function of the nurse is to assist the individual, sick or well, in the performance of those activities contributing to health or its recovery (or to peaceful death) that he would perform unaided if he had the necessary strength, will, or knowledge. And to do this in such a way as to help him gain independence as rapidly as possible.

If you are to offer enabling services, you need to work out what type of care is appropriate for an individual. A report by the Audit Commission (2000) identified three different types of care. The care of those:

- who will recover quickly and who do not need more that a limited amount of help with rehabilitation;
- who will take much more time and will need a lot of help; and
- whose recovery may be limited and who need palliative or continuing care.

The aim of enabling services should be to offer the right care in the right place at the right time using the right staff. How do you know you are doing this? How do you know what it feels like to receive particular services from particular staff in a particular workplace? How do you know what you do well and what you need to improve on? It's terribly difficult to evaluate your colleagues, your services and yourself but, if you do not develop these skills, you will be unable to move services forward.

8.10 As others see us

If you are to get a real idea of what your services are like for the patients, you need to ask the people who use your services. There are many methods that you can use to find out what it's like to experience your services. No one method provides a full picture, but you can use different methods and combine the findings to help develop a fuller picture of care from a patient perspective.

Questionnaires

Questionnaires are of limited value in evaluating your services. However, they can provide some important information about services if they are well designed and patients are encouraged to use them. They are best used to examine one aspect of care or general levels of satisfaction. It is important to keep questionnaires short as most people will compete a short questionnaire but will be reluctant to answer page upon page of questions. It's also important to ask open and closed questions. You can combine 'yes' and 'no' questions with a few questions that provide spaces for the older person to add his or her comments. Many older people find it difficult to read small type, even when wearing glasses, so questionnaires should be printed in a type size that can be easily read. If you are caring for a diverse range of people, questionnaires should be available in the appropriate languages.

Focus groups

Sometimes, even when invited to give their comments and provided with customer comments forms, people fail to tell organisations of their negative experiences. This is often because people feel that their comments will not be taken seriously and will not make any difference. Focus groups can sometimes provide information that people are reluctant to complain about or write about in questionnaires. It's important to plan focus groups well, to have a limited number of people and to use an experienced facilitator.

Survey of In-Patients at Bridgetown Memorial Hospital

Thank you for taking the time to complete this form. Please answer by placing a cross in the box that best represents your answer ☒ or by writing clearly in the comments boxes.

ABOUT COMMUNICATING WITH HOSPITAL STAFF

A1. When you reached the ward, did you get enough information about ward routines (e.g. times of meals and visiting rules)?

☐ Yes definitely ☐ No

☐ Yes to some extent ☐ Not sure/can't remember

A2. Do staff new to you tend to introduce themselves?

☐ Always ☐ Sometimes ☐ Never

A3. How much information about your <u>condition</u> has been given to you?

☐ Not enough ☐ Right amount ☐ Too much ☐ Not sure

A4. How much information about your <u>treatment</u> has been given to you?

☐ Not enough ☐ Right amount ☐ Too much ☐ Not sure

A5. Was your consent given before information about your treatment and care was given to family/friends?

☐ Yes ☐ No ☐ Not sure ☐ Not applicable

A6. Do staff have discussions in front of you as if you aren't there?

☐ Always ☐ Sometimes ☐ Never ☐ Not applicable

A7. Please add any comments you would like to make about how hospital staff have communicated with you:

Questionnaires can provide useful information about services if they are well designed

Service groups

All of us work with other groups of staff and we all pick up on different aspects of care. Sometimes, employing a service group to map a patient's journey can be useful because it helps you to get a fuller picture of patient care within a particular area or throughout a patient's journey. Gloria Lennox used a service group to help obtain a full picture of rehabilitation services at Lawton Memorial Hospital.

CASE STUDY – Using a service group to obtain a fuller picture

Charles Wheeler, the director of clinical services at the primary care trust, has just had an uncomfortable conversation with the chief executive. The chief executive has been asked to speed up patient turnover at Lawton War Memorial to help ease the pressure on the local hospital. The hospital needs to discharge people more rapidly and free up beds if it is to meet its accident and emergency waiting targets: 'I'm sure, Charles, that we could help if we could speed up rehabilitation in Lawton War Memorial. Can you find out what the blockages are and let me know how we can clear them?'

Charles asks Gloria Lennox if she can map the patient journey and identify any factors that are slowing rehabilitation. Gloria decides to organise a multidisciplinary team to map the patient journey and to work out ways to improve care. Dora Evans (one of the ward sisters), Anne Blake (the physiotherapist) and Jane Lewis (the senior occupational therapist) attend. They begin by mapping the patient's day. Gloria is astounded to discover that it can take four days before the physiotherapist sees a patient. Anne explained: 'I'm the only physiotherapist employed for the wards and we have 48 patients. Some of the patients have had dense stokes and require a lot of physiotherapy. There's only so much I can do. The nurses on Balleter Ward do help a lot. They encourage everyone to go to the dining room for meals so they are walking around. On Lancaster Ward it's a different story – meals are served at the bedside so I have to work harder on those patients.'

Jane Lewis explained how this affects the ability of the occupational therapists to carry out their role: 'There's little point in assessing patients and working out what aids and adaptations they need at home until they've had some physiotherapy and have begun to recover. In my last job there weren't these delays because there was more physiotherapy and the nurses worked more as part of a team. Dora's staff are reasonable, though they could improve, but it's just hopeless on Lancaster. Everyone seems to think that therapists and nurses work on different planets. Last week when my junior was off sick I asked the nurses to help me with a reminiscence group. They weren't busy but I had to push really hard to get help.'

Dora Evans replied: 'I know that there is more that we could do on the ward to help patients recover but it's very difficult for us. There's no physiotherapy at weekends and we'd like to do more to make up for this but we can't. Our ward clerk has been off sick for four months and at the weekend we clear a mountain of paperwork. During the week we have to run around answering the phone and ordering transport and doing lots of other things that get in the way of rehabilitation.'

Imagine that you are Gloria Lennox. What problems have you identified in the service group? Develop an action plan to tackle these problems. What resources will you require to provide faster and more effective rehabilitation within the wards at Lawton War Memorial? How might you make a case for increased resources? Can you identify the forces for change in this situation? What might the restraining forces be? Can you think of any other action that you might take in this situation?

Service groups can, if well managed, help not only to identify problems within current services but also to find solutions to these problems.

Advocacy groups

Sometimes advocacy groups are a rich source of expertise, and members of advocacy groups, such as Age Concern, often have a large national network that you can tap into. Members of advocacy groups are well aware of the problems with your services and also of solutions that have been successfully used in other parts of the country. Advocacy groups can provide a different perspective on your services and can help you to work out solutions.

Patient diaries

Patient diaries can be used to capture the whole patient journey through healthcare or one part of that journey, such as inpatient treatment. Diaries can be used to record facts and feelings. The facts that the patient may record are events in his or her day, the times of treatment and the actions of staff. The feelings that the patient may record are his or her feelings about being ill, receiving treatment and the attitude and approach of staff.

If you want to collect information using patient diaries, it is important to provide clear instructions to the person who will be recording the dairy. This can be done by providing a pre-printed diary with some headings that prompt the person to record his or her experiences of particular aspects of care. If you are providing a pre-printed diary, it is important to stress that this is a guide. If you ask a person to keep a patient diary you are asking a person who is unwell to make an extra effort. People are more likely to help if their efforts in collecting such information are acknowledged and they have a clear idea of how the information will be used to improve care.

People who are recording a patient diary will need support whilst recording information

People who are recording a patient diary will need ongoing support whilst they are recording information. You need to be clear about how the information will be used so that confidentiality is not breached. When the project is over you should provide feedback to patients on how the information was used to improve practice.

Individual interviews

Individual interviews can be used to obtain information about your services from the perspective of an individual patient. Normally this type of interview is semi-structured. The interviewer develops a series of key questions, and the discussion is centred around these key questions. The interviews are normally carried out in the person's own home and are recorded. Individual interviews are time-consuming – the average interview takes 45 minutes to an hour and the interviewer must travel to the person's home. After the interview the tape is normally transcribed. Usually a number of individual interviews are carried out, and the researcher analyses the interviews for key themes. These key themes can be used to move services forward.

CASE STUDY – Using feedback from interviews

Veronica Gibbs was happy to support Cecilia Adejeboye's work for her degree in gerontology nursing. Cecilia aimed to interview patients who had been admitted to Annie Zunz Ward as emergency admissions to identify the best and worst aspects of care. Veronica explained: 'I hope that you'll share your findings with me, Cecilia, so that we can use this work to feed back to staff and to improve practice further.'

When Cecilia had completed her research she produced a report and gave Veronica a copy. They agreed to met to discuss it over coffee. Cecilia found that patients admitted as emergencies were relieved to get to the ward after treatment in accident and emergency. They found the nurses helpful and hard working. They also found the nurses were always willing to listen to their concerns and to explain about medical treatments. Many of the patients who were admitted in the evening commented that they were hungry and would have appreciated a meal. The worst aspect of care was having to wait up to 18 hours from being admitted to the hospital to having a meal.

Veronica was surprised by this finding and decided to investigate. She found that staff in accident and emergency did not routinely offer patients meals: 'Our priority is to get them seen and off to the wards.'

The wards did not have any food. Meals were delivered to the ward and any food not eaten was thrown away. If a patient was admitted in the evening, staff could obtain a snack box. This involved staff going to the kitchen some distance away and using a smart card to open a store of snack boxes. Individual snack boxes contained a sandwich, a yoghurt, crisps and fruit. Veronica found that, when the ward was accepting emergency admissions, staff felt that their first priority was to admit the patient; providing a snack was low on the nurses' priorities but high on the list of patient priorities.

Reflect on practice

Nutrition is an extremely important aspect of patient care. Older people who are malnourished are less likely to make an effective recovery. Cecilia's research uncovered a problem in Annie Zunz Ward. If you were Veronica, what actions might you take to ensure that older people admitted in the evening had something to eat? Do you feel that the hospital's snack system is appropriate? What alternatives can you suggest?

8.11 Conclusion

Older people are adults. Ageing and chronic disease can affect their ability to recover as fully as possible following illness. The quality of care provided by a range of staff at all stages in the care process affects the ability to maximise physical and psychological wellbeing. If you are to do things well, you need to do things differently by viewing the care process as a flow and not as a series of unrelated events. This requires you to develop new skills so that you can see linkages between inputs at different stages of the person's journey and how these affect outputs.

Adults are individuals. Adults come from a range of backgrounds and cultures. If you are to offer care that meets an adult's needs, you must offer care that is appropriate to the person's culture and background. Adults have different fears, hopes, needs and aspirations. Some adults are more affected by illness and loss of ability than others. If you are to enable the person to recover as fully as possible, you need to be aware of the person's reaction to illness and to work with the person to address fears and to fulfil hopes.

Older people are vulnerable to the effects of poor-quality care in all parts of the care process. If you are to reduce the risks of adverse outcomes that impede recovery, you must work together to ensure that care appears to be seamless at the point of delivery, even when it is provided by different staff in different places.

Key Points

- Older people are as critical of services as younger people.
- Older people have concerns about the level of staffing in wards and about the expertise of staff.
- Research indicates that staffing levels and the way care is managed have a huge impact on recovery.
- If you are to manage effectively, you need to manage differently and to take a whole systems approach to care.
- Services can enable older people to recover as fully as possible.
- Poorly planned services can impede recovery, and the effects of this impact throughout the whole service.
- Nurses can identify problems and work with patients to improve services and to maximise recovery.

References and further reading

FURTHER READING

Christopher, J. (2000) *Becoming a Reflective Practitioner*. Blackwell Science, Oxford. This excellent practice-based book combines theory with practice to enable you to reflect on and develop your practice.

NHS Modernisation Agency (2002) *Improvement: Leader's Guide to Involving Patients and Carers*. NHS Modernisation Agency, London. This and a series of other useful guides on improving practice can be downloaded from **www.modern.nhs.uk**. These guides can be used by nurses working in the NHS and care homes.

Websites

Cardiff Business School. *Speciality*: innovative quality development programmes (**www.cf.ac.uk/carbs/**).

Commission for Health Improvement (CHI). *Speciality*: quality of patient care (**www.chi.nhs.uk**).

Institute of Healthcare Improvement. *Speciality*: healthcare improvement (**www.ihi.org**).

National Institute for Clinical Excellence (NICE). *Speciality*: NHS frameworks/protocols/guidance (**www.nice.org.uk**).

National Primary Care Research and Development Centre. *Speciality*: clinical governance in primary care (**www.npcrdc.man.ac.uk**).

References

SECTION 8.2

Davies, S. (2001) 'The care needs of older people and family caregivers in continuing care settings', in M. Nolan et al. (eds) *Working with Older People and their Families*. Buckingham, Open University Press.

Howkins, E. and Ewens, A. (1997) 'Community nurses' perceptions of self in role', in P. Denicolo and M. Pope (eds) *Sharing Understanding and Practice*. EPCA Publications, Farnborough.

Marsh, P. (1988) *Eye to Eye: How People Interact*. Andromeda, Oxford.

Miller, L. (2002) 'Effective communication with older people', *Nursing Standard*, 17: 45–55.

SECTION 8.3

Aiken, L.H., Clarke, S.P., Sloane, D.M. and the International Hospital Outcomes Research Consortium (2002) 'Hospital staffing, organization, and quality of care: cross-national findings', *International Journal of Quality Health Care*, 14: 5–13.

Bolton, L.B., Aydin, C.E., Donaldson, N., Brown, D.S., Nelson, M.S. and Harms, D. (2003) 'Nurse staffing and patient perceptions of nursing care', *Journal of Nursing Administration*, 33: 607–14.

Harrington, C., Kovner, C., Mezey, M. et al. (2000) 'Experts recommend minimum nurse staffing standards for nursing facilities in the United States', *The Gerontologist*, 40: 5–16.

Health Advisory Service 2000 (1998) *Not Because They are Old. An Independent Inquiry into the Care of Older People on Acute Wards in General Hospitals*. Health Advisory Service 2000, London.

Help the Aged (2000) *Our Future Health. Older People's Priorities for Health and Social Care*. Help the Aged, London.

Help the Aged (2002) *Hospital Care Problems in Hospital Care*. Help the Aged policy statement, June. Help the Aged, London.

McCloskey, J.M. (1998) 'Nurse staffing and patient outcomes', *Nursing Outlook*, 46: 199–200.

Needleman, J., Buerhaus, P., Mattke, S., Stewart, M. and Zelevinsky, K. (2002) 'Nurse-staffing levels and the quality of care in hospitals', *New England Journal of Medicine*, 346: 1715–22.

Norton, D. and Exton-Smith, N. (1975) An *Investigation of Geriatric Nursing Problems in Hospital* (2nd edn). Churchill-Livingstone, London.

Person, S.D., Allison, J.J., Kiefe, C.I. et al. (2004) 'Nurse staffing and mortality for Medicare patients with acute myocardial infarction', *Medical Care*, 42: 1–3.

Wade, B. (1983) 'Different models of care for the elderly', *Nursing Times*, 79: 33–6.

Zimmerman, S., Gruber-Baldini, A.L., Hebel, J.R., Sloane, P.D. and Magaziner, J. (2002) 'Nursing home facility risk factors for infection and hospitalization: importance of registered nurse turnover, administration, and social factors', *Journal of the American Geriatric Society*, 50: 1987–9.

SECTION 8.4

Audit Commission (1996) *United they Stand. Co-ordinating Care for Elderly Patients with Hip Fractures*. Audit Commission, London.

Hallstrom, I., Elander, G. and Rooke, L. (2000) 'Pain and nutrition as experienced by patients with hip fracture', *Journal of Advanced Nursing*, 9: 639–46.

Porter, K.H. and Johnson, M.A. (1998) 'Dietary protein supplementation and recovery from femoral fracture', *Nutrition Reviews*, 56: 337–40.

SECTION 8.6

Nursing Times (2004) 'Lunchtime closures to stay optional', *Nursing Times*, 100: 2.

SECTION 8.7

Covinsky, K.E., Palmer, R.M., Fortinsky, R.H. et al. (2003) 'Loss of independence in activities of daily living in older adults hospitalised with medical illness increased vulnerability with age', *Journal of the American Geriatrics Society*, 51: 451–8.

SECTION 8.8

Gilbert, P.E. (1984) *Depression: From Psychology to Brain State*. Lawrence Erlbaum Associates, London.

Seligman, M.E.P. (1969) 'For helplessness: can we immunize the weak?', *Psychology Today*, 42–5.

Seligman, M.E.P. (1972) 'Learned helplessness', *Annual Review of Medicine*, 23: 407–12.

Seligman, M.E.P. (1992) *Helplessness: On Depression, Development, and Death*. W.H. Freeman, New York.

SECTION 8.9

Audit Commission (2000) *The Way To Go Home: Audit Commission Report of Rehabilitation and Remedial Services for Older People*. Audit Commission Publications, London.

Henderson, V. (1966) *The Nature of Nursing*. Macmillan, New York.

CHAPTER 9

Partners in care

Introduction

An adult's life does not start or end when he or she enters a hospital or a care home. The adult in hospital remains part of his or her community and retains bonds with relatives, friends, supporters and colleagues. The older person retains these bonds when he or she enters hospital or a care home. The aim of care in hospital is to enable the person to return home whenever possible or to move to an environment where care needs can be met if a return home is not possible. The aim of care in a care home may be to enable the person to return home following intermediate or respite care or to provide continuing care. In all care settings the continued involvement of family and friends enriches an adult's life and improves the quality of care.

Adults in all care settings have the right to privacy, and it is important to ensure that the older person consents to you sharing information about his or her condition with people who inquire. The older person, like everyone else, might want to share different levels of information with different people. The older person might want you to provide full details of his or her condition to his or her best friend but only general information about progress with a relative whom this person merely exchanges Christmas cards.

Hospitals provide episodic care when accident or illness make it impossible for an older person to be cared for safely at home. The aim of hospital care (or any other healthcare intervention) is to enable the older person to recover as fully as possible and to return home. Many older people who live at home rely on help and friendship from carers who support the older person voluntarily. There are thought to be seven million carers in the UK. Yet, when an older person is admitted to hospital for acute care or to a care home for intermediate or continuing care, the carer's role is often overlooked. Carers have a great deal to offer and can work with the older person and staff to plan and manage care and, where appropriate, discharge home.

In healthcare settings nurses and other professionals often focus on the older person, and research suggests that staff seldom seek the views of relatives and carers. At policy level there is a growing recognition of the important role relatives and carers can play in working with staff to plan care and to transfer care and plan discharge. This chapter explores ways in which you can improve communication with older people, their relatives and carers.

In healthcare settings an older person moves from department to ward and increasingly from ward to community or care home settings. These transfers aim to offer the older person the right care in the right place at the right time, with the right level of support. Older people, like all of us, can become anxious when they have settled and change is planned. They ask questions about what they can expect on the next part of the healthcare journey. If we are to provide them with accurate information and provide care that appears seamless, we need to have the ability to communicate effectively with professionals working in other settings. We also need to understand how the whole healthcare system works. This chapter aims to enable you to develop a greater understanding of whole systems and to work with older people and their families when transferring a person from one care setting to another.

Aims

9.1 Relative involvement in the drivers for change

9.2 The value of relatives

9.3 Relatives' views of discharge

9.4 What involvement means to relatives

9.5 Good practice in discharge planning

9.6 How to involve relatives

9.7 Department of Health guidance on discharge

9.8 Working together for effective transfer of care

9.9 Conclusion

9.1 Relative involvement in the drivers for change

People are now living longer. There are now unprecedented numbers of people living into their eighties and nineties. Most people enjoy a healthy old age, but increasing numbers of older people are frail and unable to perform all the activities of daily living without support. Some older people require help with shopping, laundry, cooking, cleaning, gardening and household maintenance. Some of the tasks that older people require help with are often carried out by social services.

However, social services would be unable to cope if an army of unpaid and often unrecognised carers did not support them. There are estimated to be 7 million carers in the UK. One adult in six provides care and support to other people in the community. This support may be informal and low level, such as a neighbour asking the frail older person if she needs something each time she goes shopping. Sometimes informal support grows over the years. Around 60 per cent of the adults who provide care and informal support spend 20 hours a week on supporting a person; around 20 per cent of carers provide 50 or more hours of care in a week (Rowlands, 1998). The current value of support given by carers is about £57 billion. However, many carers are not in the best of health – an estimated 40 per cent have an illness or disability (Iles, 2003). Sometimes the older person is admitted to hospital because the carer is unwell and temporarily or permanently unable to continue caring.

Many of the services provided by social services and independent home care organisations are based on a traditionally female-dominated care model. It is fairly easy to get help to shop, wash or dress from social services but difficult to get a light bulb in a stairwell replaced or a leaky downpipe repaired. Many household maintenance tasks are vital in enabling frail older people to remain at home, but these tasks are largely invisible. The common stereotype of a carer is a middle-aged female. Research suggests that this stereotype is outdated. Older people often care for their spouses and men and women both share caring work. Some writers (e.g. Wenger, 1990) have commented that services are more geared to the stereotype of the middle-aged daughter, and that older people and men providing care are ill-served by such services.

Government policy is changing, and there is a growing recognition of the fact that the older person is part of the community and receives informal support and help from family and friends. The NHS plan (Department of Health, 2002) pledges to shape the NHS around the needs and preferences of individuals, families and carers. The National Service Framework for Older People (Department of Health, 2001) places carers at the centre of services. Standard 2 states that older people should have their confidentiality respected and that staff will work with older people and carers. Staff will provide older people and carers with information on the services and options available. The NSF standards on stroke, falls and mental health also emphasise the importance of working with carers and families.

In recent years, there have been reports of older people being inappropriately kept in hospital because the services to support them at home were not available. An estimated 4,100 people have their discharges delayed in England each year because of such problems (National Audit Office, 2003). In January 2004, the Delayed Discharges Act was introduced. This Act aims to improve efficient discharge by encouraging social services departments to increase efficiency; social services are fined £150 for each day a discharge is delayed. One of the ways that social services can minimise discharge delays is to work with hospitals and to consult with relatives at an early stage about discharge and the support required.

NHS hospitals are required to meet certain targets. These include a maximum wait of four hours in accident and emergency before being admitted to a hospital bed. If hospitals are to meet these targets, they must be able to discharge people when they are well enough to go home and ensure that the person has appropriate support to prevent unnecessary readmissions. There is now an increased emphasis on working with relatives and carers and preventing discharge delays. Many hospitals have now introduced discharge co-ordinators who work with families, carers and other care providers to ensure appropriate transfers of care. Many, however, still have no plans to introduce discharge co-ordinators, as the case study below illustrates.

CASE STUDY — Discharge co-ordinators

The trust is in crisis and in danger of failing to meet its targets. The hospital is on red alert and searching for beds to admit patients. The additional beds opened in the emergency medical assessment unit are full. The additional beds in the step-down units are full. The board has decided to appoint discharge co-ordinators to help reduce the number of delayed discharges within the trust.

Veronica Gibbs has been appointed to the working group to determine the role of the discharge co-ordinator and how this co-ordinator will work with staff to reduce delayed discharges. Veronica told the staff about this and sought their views before the meeting. She told them that the average length of stay in the trust is four days longer than in neighbouring trusts.

May Murphy, an experienced ward sister, commented: 'Well, that's all very well, Veronica, but there's more to it than average length of stay. They have an arrangement with the local nursing homes in the other trust. When patients are discharged from hospital they get up to two weeks' rehabilitation; our patients have to be fitter on discharge.'

At the meeting senior management were keen to gain managers' commitment to reducing the average length of stay by appointing discharge co-ordinators, but no mention was made of additional resources.

Reflect on practice

Imagine that you are Veronica Gibbs. What are the advantages of appointing discharge co-ordinators? What are the possible disadvantages? What other methods might you use to reduce discharge delays?

Well managed care homes have appreciated the contribution of family and friends for many years. It is, of course, much easier to work with family and friends when older people remain in a care setting for a relatively long time. The introduction of National Minimum Standards has formalised that relationship. Staff in care homes are required to share the older person's care plan with a representative, who must agree and sign the care plan if the older person is unable to sign and/or understand the plan. (An estimated two thirds of older people living in care homes are cognitively impaired; most have dementia.)

The introduction of the Registered Nursing Care Contribution has also increased relatives' awareness of the type and level of care required. The NHS now pays a contribution towards an older person's care costs if the person requires care from registered nurses (under the provisions of the Health and Social Care Act 2001). In England, patients are paid on one of three levels depending on the level of care required. Many relatives are now becoming involved in finding out what type and level of care are required because of these changes. In Scotland and Wales the legislation is different: older people receive a flat-rate allowance for care.

9.2 The value of relatives

Relatives, like older people, are not all the same. Some relatives have a distant relationship with the older person; some have a close relationship but live some distance away. Some are willing and able to take on a caring role and to offer support and assistance to the older person. Some are willing to take on a caring role but are unable to because of ill-health or work or family commitments. Sometimes relatives feel that they have caring responsibilities thrust upon them because nurses assume that they are willing and able to offer care and support. A study of carers in England, Wales and Scotland was carried out in 2001, related to carers' experiences of discharge in 2000 and 2001. Almost 70 per cent of carers felt that they had no choice about taking on caring responsibilities when a person was discharged from hospital. One carer commented:

No doctor or any staff asked me if I would cope with the discharge and whether any help was needed. They may have spoken to my husband who is more than capable for speaking for himself, but even he forgets to ask if I am coping. I feel strongly the carer should have input (cited in Holzhausen, 2001).

Some carers are not relatives: sometimes an older person's friend or neighbour adopts the caring role.

One of the difficulties of caring for older people is that illness, accident and chronic disease can cause confusion. When the older person is unwell and unable to communicate effectively, relatives are a godsend. The relative has known the person for many years and is able to tell you how the person normally is and what the person's care preferences are. Relatives can enable you to provide sensitive care to individual older people when the older person is unable to tell you what he or she would want to tell you.

It can be very difficult to pick up subtle changes in a person's behaviour if you are working on a busy acute ward and the person has been recently admitted. Relatives and others who know the person well are much better at this than busy nurses who do not know a person well. Sometimes a relative will say: 'My husband isn't quite himself today. The last time he was like this he turned out to have a kidney infection.' A sensible nurse will listen to relatives, act on their subtle perceptions and check the older person out. In my experience relatives who are concerned are usually right to be concerned. Relatives can – if you listen to them and encourage them to voice their concerns – provide an important early warning system.

9.3 Relatives' views of discharge

Older people's care needs at the point of hospital discharge vary. The person who had had an elective hip replacement might well make a full recovery and require little follow-up and support. The person who has suffered a major stroke and has made only a partial recovery will require ongoing care, treatment and support. The relative's view of discharge is influenced by these factors. Some relatives have adopted the role of carers. This role might be a new one because the older person has recently become unwell, or it may be a role that the relative adopted some time ago. The relative's experience of the caring role also affects perception of discharge. People who have been a carer for some time might understand the system well and be aware of how to access services and support. People who are new to the caring role might be unaware of what help is available and how to obtain it.

Research by the Carers National Association (Henwood, 1998) found that only 28 per cent of carers reported that discharge was well organised and that they were consulted throughout the process. The survey found that older carers were more likely to be consulted about discharge. Younger carers and people from ethnic minorities were less likely to be consulted about discharge. Most carers (82 per cent) found that discharge was poorly planned. Although carers are involved in delivering day-to-day care, only 50 per cent were informed about what care was required after discharge. Only 20 per cent of carers were provided with a copy of the person's care plan. Many carers (43 per cent) felt that they were not given sufficient help when the older person was discharged home. Many felt that the older person was being discharged from hospital too early (43 per cent of those discharged were readmitted

- Listen to the carer.
- Ensure the carer has information on the illness, about available support services and where to find out about benefits.
- Ensure there are sufficient support services in place on discharge.
- Give sufficient notice of discharge and be flexible about timing.
- Ensure the patient is not discharged too soon.
- Improve co-ordination within NHS services and with social services.
- Ensure vital equipment is available on discharge.
- Give the carer a choice – don't assume the carer can cope.
- Ensure there is one point of contact.
- Improve transport arrangements.

Figure 9.1 Carers' recommendations for effective discharge

within two months of discharge). The report recommends that hospital staff change their practice to improve hospital discharge (see Figure 9.1).

9.4 What involvement means to relatives

Nurses and relatives have different perspectives, pressures and priorities. In 2003, 9 per cent of hospital discharges were delayed and, each week, 4,100 patients were inappropriately delayed in hospital (National Audit Office, 2003). Acute hospitals are under pressure to minimise delayed discharges so that they can reduce unnecessary delays in accident and emergency and cut waiting lists. Hospitals are busy, and most nurses consider that wards are understaffed (Royal College of Nursing, 2004). In busy wards, staff may fail to recognise the contribution that relatives make to care. This lack of recognition may lead to staff not asking what level of care relatives provide and to not recording information about the relatives' contribution to caring for the older person (Jewel, 1994). If nurses are unaware of the relatives' contribution to care, it is not surprising that they do not always involve relatives in care.

CASE STUDY – Involving relatives in care

When Gloria Lennox received a complaint about Mrs Bessie Simpson's discharge from Lawton War Memorial Hospital and found that Dora Evans (the ward sister) did not normally inform patients and relatives of planned discharge until 24 hours before discharge, she decided to investigate. She found that almost half the complaints received in the last two years related to discharge. Many of the complaints related to relatives not being given sufficient notice of discharge.

Gloria felt that it would be a good idea to audit current practice in order to work out what staff at Lawton Memorial did well and what they needed to improve on. She worked with staff to form a group, and they decided to use the communication standard in *Essence of Care* to audit practice. This standard has 11 factors. Gloria and the team chose to concentrate on factors 1, 4, 6 and 10:

1   Staff demonstrating effective interpersonal skills to communicate effectively.
4   Assessment to identify principal carer.
6   Providing accessible, acceptable up-to-date information and sharing it actively with patients and carers.
10 Ensuring that the patient's and carer's expert contribution to care is valued, recorded and informs care and discharge.

The team used a variety of methods to obtain this information. These included observation, checking documentation questionnaires and one-to-one interviews. Staff from one ward also observed care and interaction on another ward in an effort to reduce bias.

The audit found that staff needed to improve their communication skills, in particular their interpersonal skills. There was no process in place to identify if the older person had a principal carer and no space on the documentation to record this information. Information sharing with relatives was ad hoc. Relatives who visit and inquire are provided with appropriate information, but those who do not visit find it difficult to obtain such information. Some patients and carers felt that staff value their contribution and that it informs care and discharge, but other patients and carers do not feel valued.

Sherry Pearce, a staff nurse at Lawton War Memorial who had been involved in the audit, asked: 'I had no idea that we had so much to do to improve communication. Where do we start?'

Reflect on practice

If you were Gloria, how would you guide your team in prioritising areas for improvement? Why have you prioritised in the way that you have?

Look back to the issues identified in Figure 9.1. Do you think that the expectations outlined are realistic? What barriers might you face in meeting these expectations? How well do you think you meet carers' expectations? Can you think of any simple things that you could change to enable you to meet some of those expectations? Which expectations might be the most difficult to meet and why?

Research suggests that nurses rarely reach out to relatives and that, if relatives want to be involved in care, they must establish contact with nurses (Collier and Schirm, 1992; Duncan and Morgan, 1994). Research carried out in 2001 by Walker and Dewar identified relatives' needs for involvement:

- Feeling that information is shared.
- Feeling included in the decision-making process.
- Feeling that there is a contact person available.
- Feeling that the service is responsive to their needs.

9.5 Good practice in discharge planning

Effective discharge planning involves effective communication not only with older people and their relatives but also with others involved in the care of the older person. If the older person is returning home, he or she will receive medical care from a general practitioner. It is important that general practitioners are aware of what investigations have been carried out in hospital, what treatment was given and what medication the person is discharged on.

If the older person requires care in a care home, it is important to contact social workers who will work with the patient, staff and family to determine the level of care required and who will provide information on funding. If a person is to be admitted to a care home, the older person and family must chose a suitable home. Normally, a senior member of staff from the home visits the older person to assess the person's care needs and to determine if these can be met within the home. It is important to develop good relationships with care home staff and to be open and honest. The case study below illustrates how poor communication can damage relationships.

CASE STUDY — Poor communications

When Laura Edwards and her team secured a contract to provide intermediate care, the team were enthusiastic and easily solved the initial problems with communication. Now there is a new manager at the elective orthopaedic centre. Patients who do not meet the admission criteria for intermediate care are now transferred to the Haven. Laura returned on duty after a few days off to find that Mrs O'Flynn (a lady who was expected to stay for two weeks) had been transferred as an emergency to the acute hospital.

Janet Warren, the deputy matron, explained: 'I was worried about her when she was transferred. She didn't look well but we thought she might be worn out by the journey. I became even more worried when I checked her temperature, pulse and blood pressure and listened to her chest. So I called Dr Khan. He said she had bronchopneumonia and felt she needed intravenous antibiotics.'

Laura and her team wanted to maintain good relations with the staff at the elective orthopaedic centre but needed to raise this issue so that they can prevent inappropriate transfers of patients who are acutely ill.

Reflect on practice ....

Why do you think this problem has arisen? How do you think Laura can ensure that people are not transferred inappropriately to the Haven? In your own workplace, what checks are made to ensure that people are not discharged too early? Do you feel that these checks are effective? What more could be done to prevent inappropriate discharge?

9.6 How to involve relatives

The way care is organised and the way staff work can either help or hinder relative involvement. This section looks at some simple ways to help relatives contribute to care.

Develop vision, strategy and an operating policy

Older people's services are delivered in different environments and in different ways. The vision that you develop should be appropriate to the services you deliver, the client group you are delivering them to and also the level of involvement of relatives and carers in the older person's care. A vision for involving relatives in an acute medical ward or a geriatric ward in an acute hospital would be different from that of a nursing home or an NHS continuing care ward.

In the nursing home or continuing care unit, staff, patients and residents will stay for months or even years. Staff have more time to build a relationship with the older person and the family. In the acute ward, patients will stay for days or, at most, a few weeks, so there is less time to develop relationships. Older people and their relatives may also have different expectations of different care services. The acute ward might be judged successful if the stay resolves an acute problem. The nursing home might be judged successful if staff are kind and caring and the person enjoys the best possible quality of life.

The vision is a broad outline of what relatives' involvement looks and feels like within your service. In a rehabilitation service it might be something like:

We will involve relatives in admission, planning of rehabilitation and transfer of care.

The strategy is more detailed. When formulating a strategy, you need to ask: 'How will we do this? How will we translate the vision into a strategy? How will we involve relatives in the admission process? How will we involve them in planning rehabilitation? How will we involve them in transfer of care? How will we know if we have succeeded in this? How will we measure our success?'

In the strategy for a rehabilitation unit, for example, you might decide to find out which relatives are closest to the older person and offer the main support. You might ask their views on how the older person was coping before an accident or illness. The strategy is more detailed than the vision and involves practical aspects of how you will make the vision a reality.

The operating policy is the nuts and bolts of making the vision a reality. If you decide to involve relatives and the strategy outlines how you will involve them, you need to look at what you do now and how you must change that to deliver the vision. The case study below illustrates this.

CASE STUDY – Improving communication with relatives and carers

Gloria Lennox and the team at Lawton War Memorial Hospital decided that they would work to improve communication and involve relatives and carers more fully. They decided to identify the relatives who provided most support to the patients and to involve them in admission, care planning and transfer of care. The group gathered together to identify what they do now and what they must do differently. Gloria asked the group to look at the barriers to improving the involvement of relatives. They came up with the following list:

- When a patient is transferred from an acute hospital the relative who is closest is not identified.
- Documentation at Lawton War Memorial does not have space to identify more than one relative, so it can be difficult to identify a main carer or supporter and other relatives.
- The documentation is not designed to identify or use input from relatives.
- The multidisciplinary team meetings take place on Wednesday mornings. Relatives cannot attend because the team discusses all the patients and it would be a breach of confidentiality.
- Older people and their relatives receive little formal feedback from the multidisciplinary team meetings.
- Most relatives seem to visit in the evenings and at weekends and often there are no senior staff on duty who can speak to them.
- Discharge checklists have spaces for writing about discussions, referrals and consultations with GPs, district nurses, therapists and specialists but none for relatives.

Reflect on practice

As you can see, a simple vision to involve relatives involves a great deal of work to turn it into a reality. In your workplace, do you feel that relatives are sufficiently involved in admission, ongoing care and discharge or transfer of care? What could you do to involve relatives more? What do you think has prevented these strategies from being adopted? If you wanted to change practice, what barriers might you face?

Primary nursing

The way care is organised can help nurses to provide individualised care that is appropriate to the older person's cultural background and to work in partnership with the older person and his or her family. There are many barriers to providing individualised care in hospitals and homes. A hospital ward many have as many as 30 beds. Nursing homes have grown larger, and the average nursing home now has 45 beds. In wards, staff often divide the wards into sections in order to allocate staff. In nursing homes staff are often allocated to a floor within the home. Sometimes, when there are staff shortages or the duty roster is poorly planned, staff are required to look after patients or residents with whom they unfamiliar.

The way you organise care can make it difficult for nurses really to get to know patients. If nurses are allocated to care for patients on a day-to-day basis, it can be difficult to do more than deliver care on a shift-by-shift basis. When patient turnover is high in acute settings, it is even more difficult to get to know the older person and to deliver appropriate care. Sometimes older people can get lost in the system, and staff may have little idea of the aims of care and whether the person is progressing or not.

Primary nursing enables nurses to care for a small group of patients whom they get to know really well

Primary nursing aims to reduce such problems and to enable nurses to care for a small group of patients whom they get to know really well. The registered nurse is allocated a small group of patients and is responsible for planning and managing their care. The registered nurse might also work with care assistants who are sometimes known as key workers. The key worker works with the registered nurse and helps to ensure that the older person receives consistent care that meets the person's changing needs and aspirations.

One of the problems that relatives have when they try to work with staff is that they do not know whom to approach and how to build up relationships with staff. Primary nursing means that the older person and the relative know who is responsible for care and is up to date with all aspects of the person's care.

Primary nursing originated in the USA in the 1970s and was an integral part of care planning. It has been adopted by some hospitals and care homes in the UK (Bowers, 1989). Primary nursing aims to empower nurses because the nurse is responsible for the older person's care throughout the whole episode of care. It aims to empower patients because the older person, like everyone else, is able to relate more easily to one person than a large and possibly changing team of nurses. Primary nursing enables nurses to work together more effectively. Effective teamwork improves nursing morale, and this leads to better patient care and a reduction in complaints and problems (Rafferty et al., 2001).

In your workplace, do you consider that the way care is organised makes it easier or more difficult for you to identify and meet the needs of an individual older person? Why do you think that care has been organised in this way? Do you feel that doing things differently would improve the quality of care in your workplace? What barriers might you face if you wished to introduce primary care within your workplace?

Open visiting

If you are to involve relatives and carers in admission, in informing care within healthcare settings and in discharge and transfer of care, you need to ensure that they can visit when it is convenient to them. Some wards and most nursing homes have open visiting policies but some have restricted visiting hours. When visiting hours are restricted, these are usually between 2 pm and 8 pm weekdays. Some wards and homes have less restrictive visiting hours at weekends and on bank holidays.

Many younger relatives and carers of older people work. If a person is working, the only time that person can visit is in the evening after work. The older person who has been up early might not be at his or her best in the evening. He or she may be tired or even worn out. Some of the older person's friends and relatives are themselves old and retired. If visiting hours are restricted, these relatives might have to make the choice between cutting short a visit or returning home in the dark on a winter's night.

Open visiting enables visitors to pop in more often and to visit when it is convenient for them as well as staff. Staff who have worked in wards or homes with restrictive visiting hours might resist efforts to introduce open visiting, as the case study below illustrates.

CASE STUDY — Open visiting

Cecilia Adejeboye has completed her degree in gerontology and has been appointed as a junior sister on one of the wards at the trust. Cecilia is keen to improve practice and asked to see Veronica Gibbs, the modern matron for the wards: 'Veronica, I'm really enjoying my new post and I want to involve relatives in care planning and discharge. I feel that our visiting hours are more of a hindrance than a help. If we could introduce an open visiting policy it would make things easier. Relatives would have more opportunity to talk to nursing staff, doctors and therapists. I've discussed it informally with staff and there's a lot of resistance. Some staff are convinced that it will lead to chaos, with relatives coming in and disrupting the ward and making it impossible to deliver care. I've tried to tell them that we manage to deliver care during visiting hours but that hasn't worked. I need your advice and support. How can I move this forward?'

Veronica suggested that they call a staff meeting to discuss piloting a change in visiting hours. She promised Cecilia that she would attend and support her.

Reflect on practice

Imagine that you are Veronica Gibbs. How will you prepare for this meeting? Why do you think that some of the staff are so unhappy with the idea of open visiting? What are the possible disadvantages of open visiting from a staff perspective? Make a list of their possible arguments to keep visiting as it is. What are the advantages of open visiting from a staff perspective? How might you persuade staff to try adopting an open visiting policy?

In your workplace, how are visiting hours organised? Does the way that visiting hours are organised enable relatives to visit and contribute to care? What changes could you make to enable relatives to participate?

Patient/relatives' information letter

If you look through the relatives' eyes, healthcare settings can be confusing and it takes time to understand what staff require and how relatives can meet these requirements. If the older person is admitted to hospital following a fall and fracture, the relative may bring in pyjamas and toiletries but finds that the person is wearing a hospital gown or nightclothes. It can be difficult for relatives to work out if staff do not want a supply of clean nightclothes or if they will want them later.

If a person is transferred from one ward or care setting to another, is this normal practice or is it because staff are concerned that the person is not doing well? Many nursing homes have traditionally provided information leaflets and brochures giving older people and their families information about such things as what to bring, what is required and what is provided. All homes are now required to do this under National Minimum Standards.

In hospital settings, practice varies. Some hospitals provide information to patients and families when care is planned. The older person who is to be admitted for cataract surgery will usually receive a letter telling him or her when he or she is to be admitted, how to prepare, what to bring and how long he or she is expected to remain in hospital.

Many older people are admitted to hospital as emergency admissions (Department of Health, 2000). The older person might be admitted to an emergency medical centre within the hospital and might be transferred from this centre to a ward within a specified period of time, usually no more than 48 hours. If the hospital is short of beds, a patient may be admitted to a ward that has a bed and then be transferred to a more suitable ward when a bed is available.

Patients who have certain conditions such as stroke may be admitted to a specialist unit for a specified period and then transferred to a general ward and on to a rehabilitation unit. This might be entirely normal, and staff might be very familiar with this process but it could be bewildering to patients and relatives. The patient

Welcome to the Haven Care Home. You are being treated on **Hyacinth rehabilitation unit.** The phone number is: **0161 207 8240**

You have been admitted to the Haven so that we can help you to recover and return home. Our team of nurses, physiotherapists and occupational therapists will work with you to help you to recover as fully as possible. The senior physiotherapist is **Sheila Walters** and the senior occupational therapist is **Janet Wilson**.

Patients are normally admitted for a maximum of six weeks, many return home sooner. We are aiming to discharge you on:

During your stay a team of nurses will look you after. One Registered Nurse known as a primary nurse, will care for you, supervise your care and manage your discharge. Your primary nurse's name is:
. . . .

What if I have any questions or concerns?

If you or your family have any questions or concerns please ask to speak to **Anne Morris** who is the senior sister in charge of the unit. She is supported by two sisters: Rosemary Webb and Juliet Dominguez, they can help you if the senior sister is unavailable.

If you have further concerns or are unable to resolve your concerns please ask to speak to **Laura Edwards** who is matron manager of the Haven.

We hope that you enjoy your stay in Hyacinth rehabilitation unit and welcome your comments and suggestions. If you have any concerns please do not hesitate to let us know. We're here to help.

Patient information sheet

and relatives might, if communication is not excellent, have to try to work out what is going on, who is responsible for care in each different care setting and what staff expectations are.

A patient information sheet can help improve communication. This is usually a single sheet of A4 paper with information written in a typeface that older people can easily read. It gives details of the primary nurse or person responsible for the individual's care. It might also give the names of therapists. It will also give the names of the ward manager and the doctor responsible for medical care. Information sheets provide practical information such as how to buy a newspaper or toiletries or how to make a phone call.

A relatives' information sheet provides details of whom to contact if the relative wishes to discuss care. When primary nursing is practised, this is usually the primary nurse. It might also give details of key workers involved in care. It will also give the names and contact details of senior ward-based nursing staff. Some information sheets also provide details of how to contact the modern matron.

Information sheets usually explain what the ward or unit aims to do, how this will be done and what is required to help achieve this aim. The case study below illustrates how information sheets can be used to improve care.

CASE STUDY — Information sheets

The Haven is part of a group of nursing homes. The group now provides intermediate care to enable older people to return home following surgery and illness. Laura Edwards, the manager of the Haven, has been asked by the group's regional manager if the manager of another home in the group can visit as she is also providing intermediate care.

When Laura met Jack Martin, the manager of the Pines, he explained the difficulties he had been having in providing rehabilitation: 'It's terribly difficult. As you know, we have patients admitted five days post-operatively and we have two weeks to get patients well enough to return home. We've had two major problems. We need to mobilise patients quickly and make progress every day. Often we cannot start this process for days because patients arrive without clothes and suitable shoes. We can lose two or three days waiting for these. The other problem is that patients admitted for rehabilitation sometimes think that they've come to a nursing home to be cared for. They think of it as a sort of convalescence but need an awful lot of persuasion to do things for themselves with support. This is also slowing down the rehabilitation process.'

Laura realised that the problems stemmed from poor communication. Patients and relatives were not aware of what to bring, and patients' expectations of care were different from those of staff and purchasers. She asked Jack what information was provided before people were admitted to the elective orthopaedic centre: 'The elective orthopaedic centre provides a lot of information about the care they provide and community care but, come to think of it, there isn't anything about our services. I expect it's because only a minority of the patients they treat require residential rehabilitation.'

Laura explained that she worked with the elective orthopaedic centre to produce a booklet that provides information about residential rehabilitation after surgery. She told Jack that staff identify most of the people who will require residential rehabilitation preoperatively, and that most people are aware that they will need a period of rehabilitation post-operatively. They come to the Haven with suitable clothing and shoes and are aware of the purpose of their stay.

Reflect on practice

How much written information do you provide to older people and their families? What do you think the advantages of providing written information are? Can you think of any disadvantages? If you do not provide written information, what are your reasons for this? If you provide written information, is it relevant and up to date? How could you improve written communication within your workplace?

Newsletters

You can use newsletters to communicate easily with large numbers of people. Relatives who live some distance away might welcome newsletters and find that they are a good way to keep up to date with changes but, remember, people who visit frequently might be more up to date than the newsletter.

Newsletters are probably of limited use in acute care settings because large numbers of people are being treated for short periods. In acute care settings, newsletters can be used to explain general changes (such as building new wards or changing practice) if they are displayed on noticeboards and in wards. They are of little use to relatives who want specific information.

In care homes and NHS continuing care units where older people are cared for for long periods, newsletters can be useful ways to provide more specific information. Newsletters can give details of planned outings and activities and can inform relatives of new staff appointments.

Noticeboards

A relatives' noticeboard can provide relatives with important information. Noticeboards can give information about:

● life on the ward
● where to get coffee or a snack

- the location of a relative's room
- the location of the nearest payphone
- the use of mobile phones
- how care is planned and managed
- how relatives can work with staff
- visiting times
- support groups.

Relatives' noticeboards can be used in acute and non-acute setting, and information on boards can be tailored to different care setting. Noticeboards can help relatives to obtain information that is important to them easily and without having to bother busy staff.

Drop-in sessions

Relatives, like everyone else, have different personalities. Some relatives do not hesitate to ask questions or to seek out the person who can answer their questions about care or other concerns. Some people are quieter and hesitate to bother staff. Sometimes, relatives find it difficult to find the person who can answer their questions. Staff working shifts and relatives with busy lives might miss each other. Drop-in sessions can help relatives and carers to obtain information about care and plans at a time when staff are available and unhurried.

Drop-in sessions can be invaluable in all care settings, though they may need to be more frequent in acute settings where change is more rapid. Drop-in sessions can be formal or informal. In a small nursing home, the manager might have an informal drop-in session on the first Sunday of every month. Relatives could be encouraged to visit and chat with the manager over a tea or coffee. In an acute setting, the ward manager might hold a drop-in session one evening a week to update relatives on ward rounds or multidisciplinary team meetings and progress.

If you plan drop-in sessions it is important to explain to relatives that they do not have to wait for these sessions and that they can ask questions or raise concerns at other times.

Reflect on practice

Do you feel that drop-in sessions would improve communication and help you to engage with relatives in your workplace? What do think the barriers to drop-in sessions might be? How could you overcome these barriers if you wished to introduce drop-in sessions?

Relatives' meetings

In care homes and NHS continuing care settings, relatives' meetings are often used. These can be informal one-to-one meetings and might be more accurately described as drop-in sessions. However, they could be more formal. In long-term care settings, relatives' meetings may be held every two or three months. These can be used to update relatives on planned changes within the home or hospital and on planned activities and outings. Managers can use relatives' meetings to take the temperature of the organisation and to obtain a relatives' perspective of care.

In some long-stay care settings, there is a well established relatives' association and relatives themselves run the meetings. Staff may be invited to attend part of the meeting.

Relatives' meetings can also be used to educate and support relatives. If an older person has developed a certain condition such as dementia or Parkinson's disease, relatives will require information about the disease, treatment and common problems if they are to provide effective care and support. The relatives might also want to know about support groups (such as the Alzheimer's Disease Society or the Parkinson's Disease Society) so that they can obtain further information and support.

In acute and non-acute settings, relatives' groups can be used to provide this type of information and support. Staff could do a short presentation on a particular disease or illness and follow this up with a question-and-answer session. Some charities can provide a speaker for such sessions.

Communication books

Some older people are well informed about their care and treatment and can update relatives when they visit. Some are also very good at passing messages from staff to relatives and vice versa. Some older people, however, especially when they are unwell, are not so good at passing messages and sometimes relatives might get muddled information. Communication books can be helpful in such circumstances. The communication book is left with the older person, and staff and relatives explain what they are writing and why they are writing it. Relatives might also use the book to communicate with each other as well as with staff.

Communication books can record who visited and when they plan to visit again. If the older person is forgetful, staff can refer to the book to remind the older person when a relative has visited and when he or she plans to visit again.

Communication books can be used to help improve communications in acute and non-acute settings with some older people. However, they are not suitable for all older people.

Reflect on practice

When do you think communication books might be most useful? Do you feel that they might be a useful communication tool in some circumstances in your workplace? What do think the dangers of communication books might be? If you were to use a communication book, how would you safeguard the person's privacy whilst sharing information?

Summary care plans

Relatives and carers often want to know how the older person is getting on. If the person is going home, relatives and carers might require information about what the older person can do independently, what he or she requires help with and what help will be provided at home. You can talk to relatives and carers about this but relatives – like everyone else – can forget important details. Written information is often more useful because it can be used to refresh memories and check out details. Sometimes staff provide carers with copies of care plans.

Date	Identified problem or need	Aim of care	Care required	Evaluation and outcomes of care	Date of evaluation
1.7.04	Immobile following repair of fractured femur.	To enable Mrs Jones to regain previous level of mobility.	Currently unable to transfer unaided from bed to chair. Assessed by physiotherapist, requires one person to help transfer. Requires regular analgesia as fear of pain may impede transfers. To walk five metres with physiotherapist and one member of staff three times a day.	Now transferring with minimal assistance of one person. Mobility improving, to walk with physiotherapist with one member of staff available to help if needed.	5th July 2004
1.7.04	At risk of developing pressure sores, Braden scale = 14, sacrum red.	To prevent pressure sores. To enable red sacrum to heal.	Pressure relieving overlay on bed. Cushion supplied for chair. Encourage to change position in bed and chair. Assist to change position if unable. Observe skin for deterioration and report if this occurs.	Now moving freely in bed and able to change position in chair. Condition of skin on sacrum improved, now pink.	7th July 2004
1.7.04	Appetite poor, weight 45kg. Encourage to eat normal diet and snacks to regain weight.	To regain weight, normally weighs 50kg and has lost weight whilst in hospital.	Encourage to eat meals, ensure that Mrs Jones is able to chose meals that she likes. Encourage her to eat snacks between meals.	Appetite improving now eating $3/4$ of meals provided and some snacks.	8th July 2004
1.7.04	To control pain post operatively.	To prevent Mrs Jones experiencing severe pain post operatively.	Give Tramadol six hourly as prescribed. Observe Mrs Jones to ensure that this effectively controlling pain.	Pain well controlled. Seen by doctor. Paracetamol prescribed regularly for pain. Tramadol now to be given only on an as required basis if paracetamol ineffective. Please observe and report on pain control.	9th July 2004.

Care plan

Care plans can be long, detailed, technical and difficult for older people and their relatives to understand. Care plans might also be out of date so that carers could worry about something that has already been resolved. However, summary care plans can be used to meet the needs of most carers and can be easily updated to meet changing needs.

Written discharge plans

Older people and carers can be anxious about discharge. They might worry that services promised will not be delivered, about when the discharge is to take place and

---

PATIENT DISCHARGE/TRANSFER SUMMARY SECTION

Name of nurse completing this section...Dora Evans............Contact no. ....

Patient being discharged / transferred from: ...Lawton War Memorial Hospital

Date of this admission 1/7/2004   Date of discharge / transfer 9./8./2004

Name ...Mrs Susan Young   Likes to be called......Sue.........................

Date of Birth......25/6/ 1924..... Telephone Number..

Home Address......23, Grange Gardens, Lawton, Bucks,

Destination Address......As above...

Next of kin & relationship...Mr George Young (husband) Contact tel. no...As above...............

Involvement in care......Will help with household tasks and shopping

Significant others...Daughter Mrs Laura Hays Contact tel. no...............................

Involvement in care......Will support Mrs Young and her husband with household tasks and shopping

Hospital Nurse completing discharge.........Dora Evans ....

Community service contacted........Yes 3rd August ....

Name of person contacted (If known)...Jane Jardine district nurse......

Other people / services involved	Name	Tel.No.	Contacted re discharge or transfer? yes/no	Date	Signature	Arrangements made & documented? yes/no
G.P.						
District Nurse						
Social Worker						
Case Co-ordinator						
Consultant						
Occupational Therapist						
Physiotherapist						
Macmillan Nurse						
Day Hospital/ Day Centre						
Other						

Patient Name..   CR Number.............................

SUMMARY OF CARE-NURSING

Summary of recent problems, treatments and therapy including describing those found to be ineffective or causing a problem (e.g.allergic reaction to a wound product)

Discharge plan

about what care will provided after discharge. A written discharge plan can provide details of care and services and when these will start, as well as giving details of relevant services so that the older person or carer knows how to contact these if there are problems or concerns.

Auditing

Older people and their relatives differ. Sometimes services that work well in a particular area with a particular set of people and a particular set of relatives are ineffective in a different area with a different group of older people and relatives. Staff can bring ideas with them from different areas, and these might be introduced into the workplace. It is important with all services to check that any changes have made a difference and meet the needs of the local population. A change that works well in rural Yorkshire might not meet the needs of a diverse population in inner London.

If you have introduced changes it is important that you audit practice to find out if the changes have indeed been introduced or if there are still barriers in practice. The case study below illustrates how things might appear to have changed but, in reality, they have not.

CASE STUDY – Auditing practice

Cecilia Adejeboye's pilot of open visiting was so successful that it has been implemented on all the elderly care wards in the trust. Veronica Gibbs was pleased that this had been successful in the wards and planned to work with the ward managers to evaluate this, but she had been busy and didn't have the time.

One morning she went to Nelson Ward and met a visitor outside. As she keyed in the code to open the door the visitor asked: 'Do you think I could possibly see my father just for a few minutes? I know it's not visiting time but I have to drop some pyjamas and fruit off. If I could just say hello to him…'

Veronica assured the visitor that she could visit and let her in. She noticed that some of the staff look displeased to have a visitor at 11 am and so she asked the nurse in charge about visiting. The nurse said: 'I don't think Mark, our charge nurse, is going to be very pleased if he finds out. He wasn't very keen on open visiting. To be honest, we've discouraged it except in special cases.'

Veronica had found Mark Collins difficult to manage since she took up the post of modern matron. Mark had applied for this post himself unsuccessfully and had initially opposed every proposed change Veronica or any of the ward managers suggested. Veronica has spent a great deal of time with Mark securing his agreement to changes and working with him. She had thought that Mark was working with her but has now found that he has quietly blocked changes. Veronica asked to see Mark to discuss visiting times.

Reflect on practice

Why do you think Mark discourages people from visiting the ward in the mornings? Imagine that you are Veronica Gibbs – how will you prepare for this meeting with Mark? If Veronica allows Mark to continue discouraging visitors in the morning, what message will this send out to the ward managers? What levers of power can Veronica use to ensure that Mark allows open visiting? How might Veronica's use of power affect her relationship with Mark and her standing with the ward managers?

9.7 Department of Health guidance on discharge

In 2003, the Department of Health introduced new guidance on hospital discharge. This guidance replaces the old 1994 guidance. The guidance stresses that it is only possible to provide effective discharges when all organisations (including independent sector care homes, social services departments and housing departments) who are required to provide care for the older person can work together and share information. Figure 9.2 outlines the key messages in this document.

- On admission, identify those individuals who may have additional health, social and/or housing needs to be met before they can leave hospital and target them for extra support.
- At ward level, identify and train individuals who can take on the role of care co-ordination in support of the multidisciplinary team and individual patients and their carers.
- Recognise the important role carers play and their own right for assessment and support.
- Agree, introduce and manage a joint discharge policy on wards that encourages multidisciplinary working at ward level and also with different organisations.
- Ensure that individual patients and their carers are involved in the planning and delivery of care.
- Ensure that community staff, hospital-based staff and social workers work together to provide effective treatment.
- Ensure that funding decisions do not delay hospital discharge or care home placement.

Figure 9.2 Department of Health guidance on effective discharge

9.8 Working together for effective transfer of care

Older people's care needs change as they progress through the care system. The aim of effective care is to give the right patient the right level of care at the right time in the right place using the right resources. There is a time for acute hospital care and a time for rehabilitation in a residential bed or at home. There is a time for care within the community and a time when care needs are too great or too acute to be delivered in community settings. Those who work in a particular care setting can have a distorted view of what level of care can be provided in other care settings and when it is appropriate to transfer patients to other settings. If you do not understand how other parts of the system work, it is difficult for you to give patients and relatives accurate information and to communicate effectively with colleagues working in other settings. The case study below illustrates how misunderstandings can cause problems.

CASE STUDY — Misunderstandings

Mrs Dorothy Jones has been admitted to Lawton War Memorial Hospital. Staff have begun the rehabilitation process and Mrs Jones is making good progress. Sherry Pearce met Mrs Jones's daughter, who said: 'I don't understand why my mother is having all this rehabilitation. At the general hospital they said that my mother had made poor progress and would probably be going to a nursing home.' Mrs Jones had suffered a major stroke and requires extensive rehabilitation but the aim is to enable her to return home.

This is the third time in the last six months that Sherry has come across this problem. It's clear that staff at the general hospital have little idea how much progress some older people can make with extensive rehabilitation. Sherry decided it was time she tackled this problem.

Reflect on practice

Why do you think staff at the general hospital were unaware of Mrs Jones's potential recovery? How do you think the suggestion that she would require permanent nursing home care might affect her recovery? If you were Sherry Pearce, how would you improve communication with the general hospital?

In the case study above, staff working in a busy acute unit found it difficult to assess the potential of an older person who had suffered an extensive stroke and was slow to regain ability. Staff from the general hospital have never visited Lawton War Memorial Hospital and are unaware what care can be provided. This is a common problem. Staff in acute wards might be unaware of the difference between care homes and care homes that employ registered nurses to provide nursing care.

The introduction of the Care Standards Act has increased confusion. In the past, there were residential and nursing homes. Residential homes offered that level of care a relative could offer; nursing homes, on the other hand, offered skilled nursing care. Now all homes are officially known as care homes. Those that offer nursing care are officially called care homes with nursing. Some homes continue to call themselves residential or nursing homes. Nursing and residential homes also differ. Some nursing homes are willing and able to look after people with complex care needs and to provide high-level palliative care; others are not.

So how can you gain an insight into how other parts of the system work and the problems your colleagues face? There are a number of strategies that you can use. You could arrange to visit another care setting, where you frequently send patients, and meet the staff there. If you work in a nursing home, you might want to visit acute wards in the local hospital. If you work in a hospital, you might want to visit the local community hospital or intermediate care centre where you send patients. A visit to another care setting will enable you to gain some insight into how other parts of the system work.

You might like to invite someone from another care setting to your workplace to give a presentation on how his or her service works and to discuss how you can work together more effectively. You could also offer to visit that service and give a similar presentation. Sometimes working with staff and shadowing them for a shift gives you an insight into how other parts of the system work.

Joint education can also help you to get to know people who work in related settings and to understand how their system works and what difficulties they face. Some primary care trusts have developed educational programmes and invite staff working in community hospitals, GP practices, nursing homes and district nurses to study days and courses. These can help improve your knowledge of practice and help you to see the whole care picture and how different services help the older person at different times.

You can use all this knowledge to help you communicate more effectively with older people, with their relatives and with colleagues working in different services.

9.9 Conclusion

Older people who are unwell need the support of family and friends more than ever but, sometimes, in your efforts to provide effective care, you can put up barriers that make it difficult for relatives to provide support and care. Effective care is dependent on teamwork, and relatives and carers are often an important but sometimes unrecognised part of the care team. If you are to involve relatives and carers in the care process, you need to do things differently and to identify and dismantle the barriers that prevent them becoming involved in care and support.

Older people's care needs change and, during the care journey, they will require care from different professionals who work in different places and provide different services. If you provide care that appears to be seamless at the point of delivery, you need to understand the whole care picture and the place of your services within that picture. You need to be able to understand where other services fit in and be able to explain this to patients, carers and junior staff. You also need to be able to communicate effectively with others and to have the ability to solve problems when they occur. Understanding how other services work and developing good relationships with colleagues in these services will enable you to help patients and relatives through the care process.

Key Points

○ The majority of care provided to older people in the UK is given informally by carers.

○ There are seven million carers in the UK. The carer's role is often unrecognised. This lack of recognition means that carers are not always consulted about inpatient care and discharge planning.

○ Relatives and carers find staff are not proactive in seeking their views.

○ Government policy now requires NHS staff to work with patients, carers and other staff (including those in the independent sector and social services) to provide high-quality discharge and transfer of care.

○ If you are to offer the right care at the right time to the right patient in the right care setting, you need to understand what others do to communicate effectively with them.

○ An understanding of how the whole healthcare system works enables you to provide patients and relatives with accurate information.

References and further reading

WEBSITES

10 Downing Street Facts – the government site that contains a 'Life Stages' section which tells you about the public services available at certain life stages – for example, for families with young children, for retired people and in bereavement (**www.number-10.gov.uk**).

Age Concern England – the national campaigning and information office of the Age Concern charity. For anyone aged 55+. Good factsheets and other publications and services; links to local Age Concern branches (**www.ageconcern.org.uk**).

Birmingham Carers Association – a local voluntary organisation for carers in the Birmingham area, but interesting to any carer ((**www.birminghamcarers.org.uk**).

British Epilepsy Association (**www.epilepsy.org.uk**).

British Heart Foundation (**www.bhf.org.uk**).

British Lung Foundation ((**www.lunguk.org**).

CancerBacup (**www.cancerbacup.org.uk**).

Carers – the government information site for carers, describing policy and legislation (**www.carers.gov.uk**).

Carers UK – a national organisation for carers; very involved in campaigning, with a good success rate in influencing government policy. Membership, newsletter, helpline, good information booklets (**www.carersonline.org.uk**).

Department for Work and Pensions – the government site giving details of all benefits and pension rights ((**www.dwp.gov.uk**).

Depression Alliance (**www.depressionalliance.org**).

Headway (Head Injuries Association) (**www.headway.org.uk**).

Inland Revenue – the government site giving information on tax and national insurance. Also tells you about Child Tax Credit and Working Tax Credit, with an online claim form (**www.inlandrevenue.gov.uk**).

Mental health: MIND (**www.mind.org.uk**); Mental Health Foundation (**www.mhf.org.uk**); Mental Aftercare Association (**www.maca.org.uk**); Motor Neurone Disease Association (**www.mndassociation.org**).

Multiple Sclerosis Society (**www.mssociety.org.uk**).

Parkinson's Disease Society (**www.parkinsons.org.uk**).

Princess Royal Trust for Carers – a national organisation for carers with information, news, surveys, discussion boards, benefits check and more (**www.carers.org**).

Residential care home fees: Help the Aged (**www.helptheaged.org.uk/carefees**); Nursing Home Fees Association (**www.nhfa.co.uk**); Stroke Association (**www.stroke.org.uk**).

Royal National Institute for the Blind (**www.rnib.org.uk**).

Royal National Institute for the Deaf (**www.rnid.org.uk**).

References

SECTION 9.1

Department of Health (2001) *National Service Framework for Older People*. Stationery office, London.

Department of Health (2002) *Delivering the NHS Plan*. Department of Health, London (available at **http://www.doh.gov.uk/deliveringthenhsplan/ deliveringthenhsplan.pdf**).

Health and Social Care Act (2001) Stationery Office, London (further details available at **www.doh.gov.uk/jointunit/freenursingcare**).

Iles, A. (2003) 'Forty per cent of carers have illness or disability', *British Medical Journal*, 327: 832.

National Audit Office (2003) *Ensuring the Effective Discharge of Older Patients from NHS Acute Hospitals. Report by the Comptroller and Auditor General*. Stationery Office, London.

Rowlands, O. (1998) *Informal Carers: 1995 General Household Survey No. 25, Supplement A*. Stationery Office, London.

Wenger, G. (1990) 'Elderly carers: the need for appropriate intervention', *Ageing and Society*, 10: 197–219.

SECTION 9.2

Holzhausen, E. (2001) *You Can Take Him Home Now*. Carers National Association, London (available at **http://www.carersonline.org.uk**).

SECTION 9.3

Henwood, M. (1998) *Ignored and Invisible? Carers' Experience of the NHS*. Carers National Association, London.

SECTION 9.4

Collier, J.A.H. and Schirm, V. (1992) 'Family-focused nursing care of hospitalized elderly', *International Journal of Nursing Studies*, 29: 49–58.

Duncan, M.T. and Morgan, D.L. (1994) 'Sharing the caring: family caregivers' views of their relationships with nursing home staff', *The Gerontologist*, 34: 235–44.

Jewel, S.E. (1994) 'Patient participation: what does it mean to nurses?', *Journal of Advanced Nursing*, 19: 433–8.

National Audit Office (2003) *Ensuring the Effective Discharge of Older Patients from NHS Acute Hospitals. Report by the Comptroller and Auditor General*. Stationery Office, London.

Royal College of Nursing (2004) *Stepping Stones. Careers of Nurses in 2003*. RCN, London (available at **www.rcn.org.uk**).

Walker, E. and Dewar, B. (2001) 'How do we facilitate carers' involvement in decision making?', *Journal of Advanced Nursing*, 34: 329–37.

SECTION 9.6

Bowers, L. (1989) 'The significance of primary nursing', *Journal of Advanced Nursing*, 14: 13–19.

Department of Health (2000) *Shaping the Future NHS: Long Term Planning for Hospitals and Related Services. Consultation Document on the Findings of the National Beds Inquiry*.

Department of Health, London (available at **http://www.doh.gov.uk/pub/docs/ doh/nationalbeds.pdf**).

Rafferty, A.M., Ball, J. and Aitken, L.H. (2001) 'Are teamwork and professional autonomy compatible, and do they result in improved hospital care?', *Quality in Health Care,* 10(supple 2(ii)): 32–7.

Section 9.7

Department of Health (2003) *Discharge from Hospital: Pathway, Process and Practice.* Department of Health, London (available at **http://www.publications.doh.gov.uk/ jointunit/delayeddischarge/discharge_get_ri.pdf**).

CHAPTER 10

Managing expectations

Introduction

Healthcare has changed enormously in recent times. Once you cared for people who were in their seventies and perhaps their early eighties. Now as life expectancy has grown, you care for increasing numbers of people in their eighties and nineties. Once you offered older people care rather than any prospect of cure, and there were limits to the level of active treatment you could offer to older people. Advances in medical care have pushed back those frontiers. Now an older person who falls and fractures a femur can expect to have surgical repair and rehabilitation to enable him or her to return home. Older people, however, have special needs as they are more likely to develop complications after surgery or illness. They are also more likely to have other chronic illnesses. Similarly, older people take longer to recover, and not all older people recover fully after illness or injury.

Older people and their families are not always aware of the complexities of surgery and treatment and might expect a swift and uncomplicated recovery. Recovering after major surgery or illness requires hard work from staff and from the patient. This chapter explores older people's expectations of healthcare and some of the barriers to effective communication. It uses real worked examples to enable you to reflect on how to improve communication.

Sometimes older people and their families expect nurses to do everything for the older person but still wish the person to recover fully. This is seldom possible – recovery is hard work for the older person and staff who provide care and support. If we have good communication strategies in place we can work with relatives and carers to support the older person in recovering. This chapter explores the ways in which you can work with the older person and his or her relatives to develop a true partnership in caring.

Sometimes the ability to recover following accident or illness is extremely limited and the older person will require ongoing support. This chapter explains how effective communication helps in such circumstances.

Expectations of healthcare services are higher than ever, and sometimes we fail to meet those expectations. This might be because expectations were unrealistic or it might be because our standards are not high enough. This chapter explores how to manage expectations and how to deal with angry people to resolve problems at the lowest possible level.

Management can at times feel like being the meat in a sandwich – everyone wants a piece of you. The older person and his or her family have expectations, staff have expectations and so does your manager. This chapter explores what staff really want of their manager and how you can manage fairly and ethically. There are also tips on what your manager requires of you and how to build a relationship with your boss.

Aims

10.1	Patient expectations	10.5	Non-verbal communication
10.2	Relatives' expectations	10.6	Setting limits
10.3	Effective communication in care homes	10.7	Making allowances
		10.8	Staff expectations
10.4	Dealing with difficult situations	10.9	Managers' expectations
		10.10	Conclusion

10.1 Patient expectations

Many nurses believe that older people are undemanding and do not have high expectations of staff. In Chapter 1 research was examined that shows this is not true. Older people do expect high-quality care and do notice when they do not receive it. Older people, however, might hesitate to bother nurses when they feel that care is not meeting their needs. They might consider that nurses are too busy or will not take their concerns seriously and often find it easier to tell relatives. It is important, therefore, that nurses are sensitive to the older person's concerns and do not appear so busy that the person cannot raise his or her problems.

Sometimes nurses who are familiar with a care environment take things for granted and are not fully aware of how disorientating it is for the older person to come into a hospital or a care home. Older people might not be aware of the routine in a care environment, of what is expected and how to raise any concerns.

Communicating effectively with the older person

In Chapter 8, the importance of communicating effectively with older people and how you might overcome some of the barriers to communication were examined. It's important, though, to network with other organisations that do similar work. You can share ideas and good practice to enable you to improve quality, as the following case study shows.

CASE STUDY — Sharing ideas to improve quality

Gloria Lennox was pleased with the improvements at Lawton War Memorial Hospital and felt that they had made real progress in rehabilitating patients more quickly. She proudly told a colleague whom she met at a conference that average length of stay was now 33 days. She was surprised to hear that the average length of stay in a similar hospital was 21 days.

Gloria went to visit the community hospital and found that they had solved many problems her hospital was still grappling with. Gloria returned to Lawton Memorial full of new ideas and found that Dora Evans and her team were enthusiastic. However, Andrew Blackstock, the charge nurse on Lancaster Ward, was less enthusiastic: 'We're doing as much as we can, and ever since you've come you've pushed and pushed. Everyone is very unhappy. All you're interested in is making a name for yourself, and then you'll be off. I've been here for 20 years and I know that what you are asking is just going to make things worse.'

Reflect on practice ....

Imagine that you are Gloria Lennox. Why do you feel that Andrew is resistant to change? Do you feel that his concerns are justified? How might you deal with his resistance and continue to improve practice?

10.2 Relatives' expectations

Sometimes it can appear that relatives have more challenging expectations than patients. This might be because an older person is asking a relative to raise issues that he or she is reluctant to raise with staff.

In acute settings, relatives suddenly find that the older person who has been in fairly good health is now ill and vulnerable. Perhaps the older person does not recover fully from an accident or illness and has to be moved to sheltered accommodation or a care home. Relatives are often reluctant to place their loved one in a home but are unable to care for the person at home. Relatives can thus be pleasant, kind and supportive or difficult, demanding and, at times, abusive. If healthcare settings are to be happy places to work and stay in, nurses must manage relatives' expectations, develop constructive relationships and set clear limits on what is and what is not acceptable behaviour.

Needs and expectations

Healthcare is the ultimate distress purchase. People do not choose to enter hospitals, rehabilitation centres or care homes – they are forced to enter homes because of accident, illness or increasing frailty.

In hospitals and acute settings relatives might expect the older person to receive high-quality care that enables the person to recover fully and return to the life that he or she left before admission. This may or may not be a realistic expectation. Sometimes older people recover fully but sometimes they do not. It is important to work with relatives so that they have realistic expectations and are aware of what ongoing care is planned and how it will be delivered. It is also important not just to focus on complaints but also on good practice, as the case study below illustrates.

CASE STUDY – Focusing on the good, not just the bad

Veronica Gibbs had had a busy morning. When she opened her post and read 'I am writing to you about the care my mother, Mrs Adele Morris, received following a stroke' her heart sank. Not another complaint. As she read on she was delighted to hear that Cecilia Adejeboye and the staff on Annie Zunz Ward were effectively communicating with patients and relatives at all times. Veronica was pleased because she knew that, on other wards, there were real problems.

Reflect on practice ....

If you were Veronica, how might you spread the good practice developed by Cecilia and the staff on Annie Zunz throughout the trust?

Relatives' expectations of care homes

Many older people and their relatives are unhappy about the prospect of a move to a care home. In some ways, moving to a care home signals the end of one life (living independently at home) and the beginning of dependency and increased frailty. One survey found that 80 per cent of older women would rather die than enter a nursing home after a hip fracture (Salkeld et al., 2002). Older people might blame their family for placing them in a nursing home, and relatives can feel guilty and worry that they have done the right thing and chosen the right home (Morley and Flaherty, 2002).

Relatives also worry about safety (Kapp, 2003). Often they will expect you to ensure that their relative does not fall. Although staff can do a great deal to reduce the risks of falls, it is not possible to guarantee this. Relatives can similarly be concerned that pain and distress are not picked up and treated (Hall-Lord et al., 2003). They also worry about the quality of care but are often frightened about complaining (Hertzberg and Ekman, 2000). They can feel that it is difficult to establish a relationship with the staff in the home, considering themselves to be outsiders who have abandoned the caring role (Hertzberg et al., 2001). Figure 10.1 summarises relatives' expectations of care homes.

- To continue to be involved in the older person's life.
- To be given information about the person's daily life.
- To talk to staff under relaxed conditions.
- To be able to communicate with staff.
- To feel confident about the quality of care.
- To be consulted about major changes in care or treatment.

Figure 10.1 Relatives' expectations of care homes

10.3 Effective communication in care homes

National Minimum Standards 16 and 17 relate to complaints and protection. You are required to have a complaints procedure that states who deals with the complaint. You must also respond to complaints within 28 days. The complaints procedure must give details of how to refer a complaint to the National Care Standards Commission.

Most complaints can be avoided and concerns dealt with effectively if you have good communication. Communication is the key to quality care: relatives want their family member to have high-quality care and that's what everyone wants. If you can develop effective communication systems, you can work together. Chapter 9 gives details of ways to improve communication within care settings.

Bridgetown Primary Care Trust

COMPLAINTS POLICY AND PROCEDURES

Version 2 Date July 2004
Source: Director of Primary Care Development, Clinical Governance, Risk Management
Authorised: Chief Executive

---

1.   COMPLAINTS POLICY

1.1   Introduction

This policy applies to all staff working within Richmond and Twickenham Primary Care Trust ["the PCT"] and refers to complaints made about services provided by the PCT. A detailed complaints procedure is attached [Schedule One]. The PCT also has responsibility for the management of complaints made about services provided by Primary Care Contractors [GPs, Pharmacists, Dentists, Opticians and their staff]. A detailed procedure is attached [Schedule 2].

This policy should be read in conjunction with policy and procedures formulated by the PCT's Patient Advice and Liaison Service [PALS].

1.2   Policy statement

The PCT is committed to the early resolution of complaints and believes that all staff have a duty to recognise an expression of dissatisfaction at the earliest stage and to resolve it personally or refer promptly to the appropriate person.

The PCT also recognises that handling complaints can be stressful for employees and will ensure that appropriate training and support are available. This procedure is drawn up in line with EL(96)19 Implementation of the NHS Complaints Procedure, and subsequent Directions and Guidance [Appendix 3].

1.3   Definition of a complaint

A query or concern becomes a complaint when, having had immediate action taken to resolve concerns, a person remains dissatisfied with any aspect of our services. Complaints will vary in their degree of complexity and seriousness. The PCT's PALS can also provide assistance in resolving concerns raised by service users. PALS can help in many situations, but especially when the problem or concern is about ongoing treatment, where prompt intervention to resolve the problem can avoid the need for the service user to seek redress under the NHS complaints procedure.

1.4   Aims

We aim to:
- Develop an organisational culture which treats complaints honestly and thoroughly with a primary aim of resolving problems and satisfying the concerns of the complainant
- Empower and support front line staff to recognise and deal with complaints
- Give service managers the responsibility for resolving and closing most complaints
- Implement appropriate change in response to complaints
- Improve the system of recording and managing complaints locally
- Ensure complaints management is integral to clinical governance.

Complaints policy

10.4 Dealing with difficult situations

Sometimes, despite your best efforts, you're confronted with highly emotional people making difficult demands on you. Difficult situations rarely occur at convenient times – they usually arise when you have least time to deal with them and when you're tired or stressed. This section goes on to look at some of the difficult situations that you might face in day-to-day practice.

Exercise 1

Use the table below to list the names and roles of the people who complain about you or who make unreasonable demands on you. Also use this to list the types of complaints you have to deal with.

NAME	ROLE	TYPE OF COMPLAINT

The people you have identified will probably include relatives, co-workers, staff and your boss. Now you need to look at why these people are so difficult to deal with.

Exercise 2

Spend a few minutes thinking about these difficult people. List the complaints they make in the table below.

PERSON	COMPLAINT

These difficult, demanding, complaining people are angry. They are angry because their expectations have not been met. Their expectations might or might not be reasonable but these people have expectations and you have to deal with them. It might be helpful to think of this situation not as a problem but an opportunity. The person confronting you has given you the opportunity to deal with the problem. This person might be angry or difficult, but he or she believes in you enough to give you the opportunity to resolve the problem.

Exercise 3

Now make a list of the words you would use to describe this angry person. You might use words like angry, aggressive, emotional and out of control.

Difficult people often come at you when you least expect it. You might be busy, you might have just about had as much as you can take, you might be about to go home. You can do without this – but you've got to deal with it. How do you feel?

Exercise 4

Suddenly, you're confronted by this angry, aggressive, demanding, unreasonable, emotional, out-of-control person. How do you *really* feel? Make a list of the words that describe your feelings.

The natural response in such situations depends on your dominant management style. You will respond to attack either by retaliating or retreating. These natural emotional reactions are unhelpful. You need to take control of the situation, not send it spinning further out of control.

Dealing with anger

People respond to other people on three levels: physical, mental and emotional (Gretz and Drozdeck, 1992). Psychologists estimate that 90 per cent of our communication takes place on an unconscious level; it has little or nothing to do with what is said. This section aims to show you how to communicate effectively on a conscious and unconscious level.

First, you need to establish rapport with people before you can achieve anything. Use **CLAP** techniques to establish rapport and to enable you to deal with the situation: **C**larify, **L**egitimise, **A**cknowledge, **P**robe.

CLARIFY

It's vital to be sure you are dealing with the real problem before attempting to solve it. Sometimes a person will be angry and aggressive because he or she doesn't understand what is going on. The real problem is a breakdown in communication. You might have to help this person explore, identify and discuss the problem. The complaint is often only a symptom. Persist with clarification until you have identified all the symptoms. Try asking: 'Is there anything else that's bothering you?'

LEGITIMISE AND ACKNOWLEDGE

When someone is angry with you, it's often because he or she has anxieties you haven't relieved. Before you can respond to those feelings, you need to get the message across that it's okay to be angry and that you are not threatened by this person's feelings: 'I can understand why you feel angry if you really feel that the staff don't care for your mother properly. Anyone would be upset if they felt like that...' Continue to clarify. At no time have you given the message that you agree with the relative – only that you understand the concern.

PROBE

When you've demonstrated that you understand and accept the person's concerns, you must probe to find out if you've made an accurate assessment. Even if your initial assessment is wrong you've gained the person's goodwill. You've demonstrated your interest and concern. The person will appreciate your efforts and will make every effort to help you understand the situation. Continue to clarify: 'So you feel that the staff have *never* cared for your mother properly. None of the staff have ever shown your mother any kindness?'

PARAPHRASE

Paraphrasing enables you to clarify, acknowledge, legitimise and demonstrate your understanding or your desire to understand:

'My mother looked a state yesterday. Her clothes were covered in food stains and she was wearing someone else's cardigan. I am disgusted when I think of all the money I pay.'

'Let me get this straight. You came in and found your mother's blouse had food stains on it and she was wearing someone else's cardigan. Is that right?'

RESPONDING

Now that you've discovered the cause and nature of the problem, you need to respond. Use the **KISS** technique – **K**eep **I**t **S**hort and **S**weet. Decide how you intend to respond to the situation. Once you have dealt with the person's problem, probe again. Check that the person has understood and accepted your response and ask if he or she has any further problems or concerns.

Speaking the same language

I know that you think you understand what you thought I said. I'm not sure that you realise that what you heard is not what I mean.

Close your eyes for a few minutes and think of a pleasant memory. Relive it in detail and then open your eyes. You might have seen the memory vividly or you might have heard it vividly; either way, your feelings more than likely predominated your memory.

Although people have five senses, they tend to rely most of the time on just one or two. Speech and language reflect how people think, so you can use language to work out a person's sensory orientation. Look at the words given in Figure 10.2.

VISUAL	Aim, Angle, Clear, Examine, Glance, Horizon, Illustrate, Observe, Picture, Regard, View, Watch
AUDITORY	Announce, Articulate, Converse, Divulge, Enunciate, Interview, Listen, Remark, Rumour, Scream, Tone, Volume
KINAESTHETIC	Active, Affect, Concrete, Feel, Foundation, Grip, Feel, Intuition, Numb, Pressure, Stress, Warm

Figure 10.2 How words reflect a person's sensory orientation

If you are to build rapport with people you need to speak the same language. The first example below shows how the manager fails to pick up on the clues in the nurse's language. The manager and the nurse are speaking a different language, and that makes it more difficult for the manager to communicate effectively:

'I heard you wanted to see me.'
'Yes, I'd like to show you these new care plans.'
'Listen, I heard Angie talking about these. She said...'
'If you'll just take a look.'

In the next example, the nurse and her manager are in tune. They are speaking the same language and are communicating effectively. The nurse feels at ease with the manager and is able to listen and communicate more effectively:

'I heard you wanted to see me.'
'Yes, I'd like to discuss the new care plans with you.'
'I've heard about them.'
'Did what you've heard ring a bell?'
'Yes it did...'

10.5 Non-verbal communication

People usually make up their minds about whether or not they like someone in the first seven seconds of meeting him or her (Maslow, 1971). People also make 90 per cent of their decisions at a subconscious level, although they will rationalise these decisions if challenged (Perkins, 1981).

Pacing

When you are physically, mentally and emotionally aligned to another person, you pace each other. Unconsciously, you both become similar and you use similar body language. You can use pacing to build an unconscious rapport with another person.

Mirroring

Matching and mirroring a person's gestures a moment or two later will not be noticed consciously by the person, but you will begin to establish rapport on a subconscious level. Be casual, be subtle; try it and master it.

Cross-matching

If someone is very agitated, upset or anxious, it can be impossible to mirror him or her, and the person will almost certainly become aware of your attempts so to do. In such situations, employ cross-matching techniques. This involves using one part of your body to match one part of the other person's body. If he or she crosses his or her legs, cross your wrists or ankles. If the other person leans back in his or her chair, lean slightly to the side and back. If the person puts his or her hand on his or her chin, put your hand near your head.

How do you know it's working?

After several minutes of pacing, check for rapport. Change your position slightly and wait. If you have established rapport, the person will change his or her movements to match yours. It will take between 2 and 45 seconds for the person to follow. If he or she does not follow, go back to pacing.

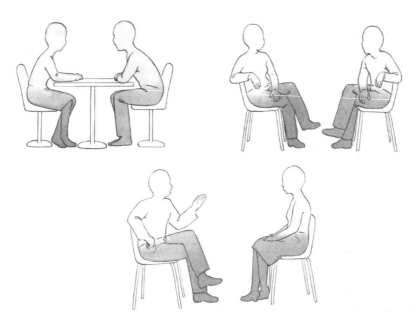

Non-verbal communication: a) pacing, b) mirroring and c) cross-matching

Leading

Now that you've established rapport you can lead. This enables you to lead the anxious person into more relaxed body postures and a more relaxed psychological state.

10.6 Setting limits

There are limits to the level of care that can be provided in any care setting. You cannot provide one-to-one care on an ongoing basis and meet every want and need instantaneously. There are times when you have to prioritise. There are also times when you have to explain to relatives that you cannot meet a particular set of expectations because you do not have the staff or the resources. This occurs in all healthcare settings. Most people acknowledge this and, if you explain when there are problems, most people are reasonable.

Communication is important in such circumstances. If staff are busy with someone who is acutely ill and medications are delayed, informing patients or residents of this allays anxieties and makes everyone aware of the situation.

Sometimes relatives and friends do not want to acknowledge that there are limits to what can be provided. Relatives and friends can have unrealistic expectations and can bully staff or be abusive if these expectations are not met. A great many people know their rights but some fail to acknowledge the responsibilities that accompany these rights. Staff have the right to work in an environment where they are free of abuse. However, a minority of relatives can abuse staff, and so staff can be subject to verbal abuse, threats, racial abuse and even physical intimidation.

It is important to provide relatives and friends with clear guidance on what is and is not acceptable behaviour and to train staff in how to deal with such situations. You could have a paragraph on this in the relatives' and friends' information leaflet. Find out what training and support are available in your organisation on dealing with abuse. Are you aware of what you should do if relatives abuse you or any member of staff? If staff are subject to abuse, it is important for them to document this and to report it at the earliest possible opportunity.

If you are in a senior position and receive such reports, it is important to tell staff how you are dealing with the situation. If staff do not feel that their concerns are being taken seriously, they will hesitate to report incidents in the future. If you are working at ward level and report an incident, find out from your manager what action he or she is taking so that you can inform other staff.

10.7 Making allowances

Relatives are often anxious and upset when their loved one enters a healthcare setting. Good communication strategies will enable you to work with relatives to ensure that everyone is working together so that the older person is happy and well cared for.

10.8 Staff expectations

Adults expect the senior staff who manage them to behave fairly and consistently. They expect them to behave professionally and to act ethically. Staff want to be led by people who are accessible and who understand the difficulties they face in practice. Staff who work in hospital settings want leaders who listen, who respond to their concerns and who help them to resolve difficulties (Upenieks, 2002). Staff who work in nursing homes, on the other hand, want managers who work with them and who are not remote from day-to-day practice. They want to work in a co-operative rather than a hierarchical environment (Wicke et al., 2004).

Getting the best from staff

If you are to manage staff well, you need to be clear and consistent, and you need to respond appropriately to problems and to document your actions clearly.

It is important that staff know what the rules are. The rules of an organisation are much more complex and subtle than what's written in the policy and procedure book. It may say in the regulations that lateness will not be tolerated. Some organisations will take that very literally and penalise staff who are a few minutes late; others will give people leeway. Sometimes different people in the organisation apply different rules – one sister might be laid back about lateness whilst another might be very hot on it.

Generally, staff can cope with the fact that different senior staff have different attitudes. Staff do become confused and upset, however, when a senior member of staff is inconsistent in approach: staff don't know where they stand. Sometimes the inconsistent person is moody, and staff say privately: 'You never know where you are with her.' The inconsistent member of staff might also have favourites who get away with murder, but he or she might come down heavily on other staff for minor issues. Treating staff differently is disastrous and can lead to poor morale and cliques.

A manager's response should be timely and appropriate. It's always tempting to ignore problems in the hope that they will go away – they seldom do. Sometimes, if you ignore small problems, they become big problems, and if you ignore inappropriate attitudes and approaches you inadvertently send out the message that it is acceptable for staff to provide poor-quality care.

Staff are observant and will quickly pick up on any inconsistencies in your behaviour. If you say one thing but your actions do not back up your words, staff will notice this. You might send the message that you talk about quality care but your actions do not bear this out. The effective leader says what he or she means and means what he or she says. You must, therefore, act as a role model for staff and never behave in ways that you would not find acceptable in colleagues.

10.9 Managers' expectations

The manager's role is changing, and managers at all levels have to reconcile different elements of their role. There are the traditional management elements, such as managing budgets, managing sickness absence and dealing with complaints. There are also new elements, such as enabling staff to change and to provide services that meet the needs and aspirations of older people and their families. The manager, like everyone else, has pressures from above and targets to meet.

Reflect on practice

Imagine that you are one of the staff whom you manage. What would this member of staff say about you as a manager? What are the things you do best? What would this person think are your weakest points? How do you feel you could build on your strengths and address your weak points?

What do you expect of your staff? Are your expectations reasonable? Do all the staff you manage meet your expectations? If they do not, are they aware of this?

Does your manager have reasonable expectations of you? Are you aware of any areas where you do not meet your manager's expectations? If so, do you have a development plan?

Working effectively with your manager

Management at all levels is about trust and communication

Management at all levels is about trust and communication. You have to be sure that you can trust the junior staff whom you work with because they are caring for very vulnerable people. You need to be sure that junior staff will always put the patient or resident first and be caring, kind and efficient. Your manager needs to be able to trust you to do your job, to get in touch if you need advice and to warn him or her of any potential problems. Your manager needs to feel that you can be counted upon to meet deadlines and to complete any work that you have been asked to complete. Sometimes you may find that you are unable to meet deadlines because of other pressures. If you are proactive and contact your manager when these problems occur rather than waiting for the manager to chase you, you will develop a more effective working relationship.

If your manager asks you to do something and you do not feel that you have the time or the skills to do this, be honest and explain. If you develop an honest and open relationship, your manager might be able to help you to develop your skills further or to give you some protected time to carry out the work.

What can you expect from your manager?

Your manager can offer you a different perspective on a situation. This may be because your manager is more experienced than you and has worked through similar problems in the past. It may because you are new to a post but your manager has been in post for some time and knows the people you are working with well. Your manager will almost certainly have a wider view than you. He or she might also be able to help you understand where certain requirements, actions or plans fit into the organisation's wider strategy.

Your manager can offer you advice on guidance. If you wish to introduce change, he or she can help you to understand the politics of some actions and how to present them so that they fit into the organisation's overall strategy.

Your manager can be a critical friend who helps you to understand some of the pitfalls in your plans and how to avoid some of these. Your manager can help you to formulate a strategy to help you change practice.

Your manager should be open and honest with you. You should be aware of his or her expectations and how you need to build on your strengths and tackle your weaker points.

What can your manager expect from you?

Your manager will expect that you keep him or her informed of important changes or potential problems within the workplace. He or she will expect you to be loyal, to behave professionally and to support him or her. These are the same expectations you have of the staff you manage (Pearce, 2004).

Figure 10.3 on page 258 lists some top tips to enable you to work well with your manager.

- Get to know your manager: be aware of his or her priorities and his or her red flags (things that upset your manager if they are or are not done). If, for example, your manager is always punctual, do not risk alienating him or her and appearing uncommitted by being consistently late for work or for meetings.

- Build rapport with your manager by communicating well, both formally and informally.

- Be aware of what your role involves and what your manager's expectations are, and do your best to fulfil your role and meet those expectations.

- Be reliable. If you agree to do something or complete a report by a certain time, meet that deadline. If you are unable to do so, contact your manager, explain your reasons and set another date.

- Be professional and loyal. Do not criticise your manager to junior staff – this will often get back to him or her and can seriously damage your working relationship. Do not go over your manager's head and report him or her to his or her manager other than in the most exceptional circumstances. Exceptional circumstances might be if your manager is abusing patients or bullying staff. In such circumstances you must act carefully and take advice from your professional organisation before taking any action.

Figure 10.3 Top tips for working well with your manager

10.10 Conclusion

Most people are reasonable most of the time but everyone can be unreasonable at some time. People might be unreasonable because they've been trying to solve a problem for some time but without success. They might be unreasonable because they expect others to understand what they mean when they haven't properly explained themselves. In a work situation, you might be unreasonable because you expect the people you manage to behave better than you do when you are being managed. And everyone can be unreasonable when tired or stressed.

Being unreasonable and emotional can damage relationships and reputations. If you are to manage staff effectively, you must first learn to manage yourself before you can teach others to do as you do.

If you communicate effectively and help junior staff to develop their communication skills, you will find that the culture in your workplace is one where patient, relative and nurse work together as partners in care. In such settings people feel free to express concerns early on before they become major concerns that might lead to people losing control.

References and further reading

SECTION 10.2

Hall-Lord, M.L., Johansson, I., Schmidt, I. and Larsson, B.W. (2003) 'Family members' perceptions of pain and distress related to analgesics and psychotropic drugs, and quality of care of elderly nursing home residents', *Health and Social Care in the Community*, 11: 262–74.

Hertzberg, A. and Ekman, S.-E. (2000) '"We, not them and us?" Views on the relationships and interactions between staff and relatives of older people permanently living in nursing homes', *Journal of Advanced Nursing*, 31: 614–22.

Hertzberg, A., Ekman, S.-L. and Axelsson, K. (2001) 'Staff activities and behaviour are the source of many feelings: relatives' interactions and relationships with staff in nursing homes', *Journal of Clinical Nursing*, 10: 380–8.

Kapp, M.B. (2003) '"At least Mom will be safe there": the role of resident safety in nursing home quality', *Quality and Safety in Health Care*, 12: 201–4.

Morley, J.E. and Flaherty, J.H. (2002) 'Putting the "home" back in nursing home', *Journal of Gerontology: Medical Sciences*, 7A: M419–21.

Salkeld, G., Cameron, I.D., Cumming, R.G. et al. (2002) 'Quality of life related to fear of falling and hip fracture in older women: a time trade off study', *British Medical Journal*, 320: 341–6.

SECTION 10.4

Gretz, K.F. and Drozdeck, M. (1992) *Empowering Innovative People*. Probus, Chicago, IL.

SECTION 10.5

Maslow, A. (1971) *The Farther Reaches of Human Nature*. Viking Press, New York.

Perkins, D.N. (1981) *The Mind's Best Work*. Harvard University Press, Cambridge, MA.

SECTION 10.8

Upenieks, V. (2002) 'Assessing differences in job satisfaction of nurses in magnet and nonmagnet hospitals', *Journal of Nursing Administration*, 32: 564–76.

Wicke, D., Coppin, R. and Payne, S. (2004) 'Teamworking in nursing homes. Issues and innovations in nursing practice', *Journal of Advanced Nursing*, 45: 197–204.

SECTION 10.9

Pearce, C. (2004) 'How to manage your boss', *Nursing Times*, 100: 72–3.

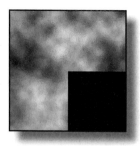

Index